T0334123

Conversations with
Diane di Prima

Literary Conversations Series
Monika Gehlawat
General Editor

Conversations with Diane di Prima

Edited by David Stephen Calonne

University Press of Mississippi / Jackson

The University Press of Mississippi is the scholarly publishing agency of
the Mississippi Institutions of Higher Learning: Alcorn State University,
Delta State University, Jackson State University, Mississippi State University,
Mississippi University for Women, Mississippi Valley State University,
University of Mississippi, and University of Southern Mississippi.

www.upress.state.ms.us

The University Press of Mississippi is a member
of the Association of University Presses.

First printing 2022
∞

Library of Congress Cataloging-in-Publication Data

Names: Calonne, David Stephen, 1953– editor.
Title: Conversations with Diane di Prima / David Stephen Calonne.
Other titles: Literary conversations series.
Description: Jackson : University Press of Mississippi, 2022. |
    Series: Literary conversations series | Includes index.
Identifiers: LCCN 2021062295 (print) | LCCN 2021062296 (ebook) |
    ISBN 9781496839664 (hardback) | ISBN 9781496839671 (trade paperback) |
    ISBN 9781496839688 (epub) | ISBN 9781496839695 (epub) |
    ISBN 9781496839701 (pdf) | ISBN 9781496839718 (pdf)
Subjects: LCSH: Di Prima, Diane—Interviews. | Poets, American—
    20th century—Interviews. | Poets, American—21st century—Interviews. |
    Beats (Persons)—Interviews.
Classification: LCC PS3507.I68 Z46 2022 (print) | LCC PS3507.I68 (ebook) |
    DDC 811/.54 [B]—dc23/eng/20220208
LC record available at https://lccn.loc.gov/2021062295
LC ebook record available at https://lccn.loc.gov/2021062296

British Library Cataloging-in-Publication Data available

Books by Diane di Prima

This Bird Flies Backward. New York: Totem Press, 1958.

Various Fables from Various Places. New York: G. P. Putnam's Sons, 1960.

Dinners and Nightmares. New York: Corinth Books, 1961.

The New Handbook of Heaven. San Francisco: Auerhahn Press, 1963.

Poet's Vaudeville. New York; Feed Folly Press, 1964.

Combination Theatre Poem and Birthday Poem for Ten People. New York: Brownstone Press, 1965.

Seven Love Poems from the Middle Latin [translation]. New York: Poets Press, 1965.

The Man Condemned to Death [translation with Alan Marlowe, Harriet and Bret Rohmer of Jean Genet]. New York: Privately published, 1965.

Haiku. Topanga, CA: Love Press, 1966.

Hymn. Pleasant Valley, NY: Kriya Press, 1967.

New Mexico Poem. New York: Poets Press, 1968.

Hotel Albert. New York: Poets Press, 1968.

Earthsong: Poems, 1957–1959. New York: Poets Press, 1968.

War Poems. New York: Poets Press, 1968.

Revolutionary Letters. New York: Privately published, 1968.

L.A. Odyssey. New York: Poets Press, 1969.

Memoirs of a Beatnik. New York: Olympia Press, Traveler's Companion Series, 1969.

Revolutionary Letters. London: Long Hair Books, 1969.

Kerhonkson Journal. Berkeley, CA: Oyez, 1971.

Revolutionary Letters. San Francisco: City Lights, 1971.

Discovery of America. New York: Theatre for the New City, 1972.

The Calculus of Variation. San Francisco: Eidolon Editions, 1972.

Loba: Part 1. Santa Barbara, CA: Capra Books, 1973.

Freddie Poems. Point Reyes, CA: Eidolon Editions, 1974.

Selected Poems: 1956–1975. Berkeley, CA: North Atlantic Books, 1975.

Loba as Eve. New York: Phoenix Book Shop, 1975.

Whale Honey. San Francisco: Poets Institute, 1975.

Loba Part II/Starstream. Drawings by Josie Grant. Kathmandu, Nepal: Eidolon Editions and Dreamweapon, 1976.

Loba: Parts I–VIII. Berkeley, CA: Wingbow Press, 1978.

Wyoming Series. San Francisco: Eidolon Editions, 1988.

The Mysteries of Vision: Some Notes on H.D. Santa Barbara: Am Here Books, 1988.

Pieces of a Song: Selected Poems. San Francisco: City Lights, 1990.

Seminary Poems. Point Reyes, CA: Floating Island Publications, 1991.

Zipcode. Minneapolis: Coffee House Press, 1992.

Loba. New York: Penguin, 1998.

Towers Down. San Francisco: Eidolon Editions, 2002.

The Ones I Used to Laugh With: A Haibun Journal. San Francisco: Habenicht Press, 2003.

TimeBomb. San Francisco: Eidolon Editions, 2006.

Revolutionary Letters. San Francisco: Last Gasp, 2007.

Poems are Angels. San Francisco: Omerta Publications, 2013.

The Poetry Deal: San Francisco Poet Laureate Series No. 5. San Francisco: City Lights Foundation, 2014.

Out-Takes. San Francisco: Omerta Publications, 2016.

Spring and Autumn Annals. San Francisco: City Lights, 2021.

Revolutionary Letters: Expanded 50th Anniversary Edition. San Francisco: City Lights, 2021.

Contents

Introduction

Diane di Prima (1934–2020)—although for over six decades an indomitable force in American cultural life—remains unfamiliar to many readers. Because she was the major female identified with the Beat movement and author of hip-language-inflected *This Bird Flies Backward* (1958) who lounged in slacks sitting atop a piano—as a famous photograph from the Fifties depicted her during a poetry reading—and due to the appearance a decade later of *Memoirs of a Beatnik* (1968), she has been misperceived as a "Beat chick." In the twenty interviews assembled here we may witness just how mistaken is this interpretation of Diane di Prima's life and work. One purpose of *Conversations with Diane di Prima* is to reveal a portrait of the artist far from the drug-addled, lazy, unfocused, and laughable countercultural stereotype fabricated by the American mass media; rather, di Prima emerges here as a fiercely curious, energetic intellectual of genius. Virginia Woolf speculated concerning the life of a literary young woman during Shakespeare's time in *A Room of One's Own*: ". . . any woman born with a great gift in the sixteenth century would certainly have gone crazed, shot herself, or ended her days in some lonely cottage outside the village, half witch, half wizard, feared and mocked at. For it needs little skill in psychology to be sure that a highly gifted girl who had tried to use her gift for poetry would have been so thwarted and hindered by other people, so tortured and pulled asunder by her own contrary instincts, that she must have lost her health and sanity to a certainty."[1] Di Prima voiced a similar opinion as Woolf regarding female authors of her own generation, confiding to Anne Waldman in 1978 that "a lot of potentially great women writers wound up dead or crazy." However, di Prima would struggle, survive, and ultimately triumph as mother of five children, political activist, publisher, and prolific author.

These interviews provide not only singular details concerning di Prima's biography and clues to the complex interweaving of allusions in her work; they also sketch out an informative documentary chronicling the entire range and scope of the turbulent, Dionysian history of the American counterculture from the 1950s to the present. As a child, di Prima was exposed to Dante Alighieri and the great philosopher Giordano Bruno—much beloved by James Joyce—by her maternal grandfather Domenico Mallozzi, who also schooled her in communitarian, idealistic thought. Di Prima recalls in her interview with Raul Sebazco her grandfather's profound influence upon her. He once took Diane to an anarchist rally where "he was talking about love— how if we don't all love each other we are all going to die. Everyone will die if we don't learn to love." It is a moving, tender memory that shaped di Prima's entire life trajectory in her deep commitment to justice and freedom for the disenfranchised of America. Her interests in literature and philosophy now awakened by Domenico, by age fourteen the precocious adolescent was already reading John Keats, Plato, Arthur Schopenhauer, and Friedrich Nietzsche. And like many others of her generation, di Prima was profoundly dissatisfied with the world bequeathed to her by her elders. The dropping of the atom bomb on Hiroshima in 1945 on her eleventh birthday; the murder of Julius and Ethel Rosenberg in 1953; the death of the "heretic" Wilhelm Reich in prison at age sixty in 1957; the Korean and Vietnam Wars; the assassinations of Martin Luther King Jr. and Robert Kennedy: all led to a deep sense of alienation and a quest for new values. Experimenting with entheogens, the fight for justice for Native Americans, African Americans, homosexuals; the search for alternative living arrangements as exemplified by the commune; challenges to conventional ideas concerning marriage and family; the antiwar movement; the turn toward Buddhism, Hinduism, and Gnosticism; the fascination with astrology, tarot, esotericism, the occult and magic: di Prima was at the vanguard from the beginning. Admitted to the elite Hunter High School in New York, di Prima became friends with a circle of women artists including poet Audre Lorde and began her lifelong fascination with what she would later call "the hidden religions." She spent a year and a half at Swarthmore College, which she found stifling, and moved back to New York City, renting her own apartment. Di Prima corresponded with Ezra Pound in 1955, spent approximately two weeks visiting him in March 1956 at St. Elizabeth's in Washington, DC, and proceeded to follow the recommendations in Pound's *ABC of Reading, Guide to Kulchur*, and *The Spirit of Romance* by perusing the troubadours, Guido Cavalcanti, and sounding out passages from Homer in ancient Greek as well as studying medieval philosophers such as Robert Grosseteste.[2] In 1968, di Prima's life and work shifted in new directions. She moved to California, as she recalled, to work with the Diggers in their efforts to help the poor and to continue her study of Zen Buddhism with Shunryu Suzuki.

The conversations in this volume appeared over four decades—from 1972 to 2010—in diverse places ranging from the underground newspaper *Grape*, published in Vancouver, Canada; to Jerry Paulsen's *Psyclone*, one of the first-wave punk magazines from San Francisco; to *Gnosis*, edited by Jay Kinney and devoted to theosophical and esoteric topics. Di Prima's thoughtful dialogues with a variety of journalists and fellow writers such as Anne Waldman provide valuable source material concerning the genesis, themes, and sources of some of her most significant poetry and prose: *Calculus of Variation*, "The Canticle of St. Joan," *Memoirs of a Beatnik*, *Revolutionary Letters*, *Loba*, and *Recollections of My Life as a Woman*. Because di Prima was so astonishingly learned, her works are often virtuosic displays of allusions that may be unfamiliar to the general reader. References to Martin Nilsson's *Primitive Time-Reckoning*, Sir George Frazier's *The Golden Bough*, Robert Graves's *King Jesus* and *The White Goddess*, the I Ching, John Dee's *Monas Hieroglyphica*, Heinrich Cornelius Agrippa, Paracelsus, the Tibetan yogi Milarepa, and alchemical and Gnostic texts proliferate throughout di Prima's writings, and these interviews help us place her work within the wider context of her lifetime of intense reading and contemplation. In her discussion with the *Colorado State Review*, di Prima reveals her interest in the great English physician, occultist, and alchemist Robert Fludd (1574–1637)—she had worked on a translation of Fludd's works written in Latin—whose ideas concerning the relationship between the microcosm of the world to the macrocosm of the universe greatly influenced the German artist Anselm Kiefer. However, di Prima never appears overly serious or dour and one notices how often she laughs; she is humorous as well as wise.

In a 1972 interview conducted in Vancouver, British Columbia—Vancouver was the locus of the celebrated poetry conference organized by Warren Tallman in 1963 where Charles Olson, Denise Levertov, Allen Ginsberg, Robert Duncan, and Philip Whalen gave readings—di Prima discusses her impatience with the progress of revolutionary politics.[3] She also recalls her time in communes during the Sixties: ". . . I've been in two religious, and one quasi-religious commune. Tassajara, a Zen place, that has a very set practice and schedule, and an ashram in New York. And Millbrook, where Timothy Leary ran his madness for a while. That was like mostly all super-money. Super-money and weird models. It was weird because you had the sense that you had completely lost touch with reality. You just didn't know what was happening anywhere. I mean, I used to play Bob Dylan because he was the nearest thing to reality that I could get there. I always meant to write him a postcard and tell him that. But it was like, it was interesting. . . . I have never before, or since, been in a situation where I had absolutely no worries. I had absolutely nothing to concern myself with. It's interesting to find out what your head does if you don't have to worry about food, clothing, shelter, the police, anything." As di Prima reveals, Timothy Leary's Millbrook, the Zen Center at Tassajara, and Rammurti Mishra's ashram in Monroe, New York, would be significant places in her unfolding spiritual life. Di Prima dedicated her *Revolutionary Letters*—the first edition of which was published in 1968, two years after she entered Millbrook, where Bob Dylan's music had kept her company—to Dylan.[4]

Di Prima shares with Anne Waldman her methods of composition as she explains the background of sections of her masterwork *Loba*. The section on Helen was composed on an airplane on the back pages of Robert Duncan's autobiographical *The Truth and Life of Myth*, while "the Lilith section of the poem was written in one afternoon and evening, started at 2:00 in the afternoon and went until 10:00 that night under the most ordinary household circumstances of phonograph on, the kids around, everything going on and *it* just kept going on. The sensation isn't different from tripping, from being on a trip of your own so that the life of the family or the body of people continues and you just stay with one thing." Di Prima also discusses the origin of other sections of *Loba*, including the "Annunciation" as well as "Nativity" and "Iseult on the Ship," clarifying their connections to Robert Graves and artist William Morris. Di Prima describes the experience of poetic inspiration in which she receives a kind of "dictation" as the Muse reveals to her lines of poetry. Verses began—she tells us in several interviews—to speak to her while she was talking to the driver of an automobile or while her body was being climbed over by children seeking her attention. Di Prima explores the visioning techniques she has taught to students in order to access material for poetic composition, and her conversation with Waldman is also noteworthy for the light it sheds on her relationship with the life and work of poet H.D., which she defines as "definitely a gut connection, almost like a mother figure for me." We learn about di Prima's founding of the New York Poets Theatre in spring 1961, where one-act plays by Frank O'Hara, Wallace Stevens, Robert Duncan, and di Prima's own plays were performed. Indeed, di Prima composed several plays, including *Whale Honey, The Discontent of the Russian Prince, Orange Ice, Hanker, Paideuma, Poets' Vaudeville, Monuments, The Discovery of America, Rain Fur,* and *Zipcode,* in which she employed aleatoric techniques inspired by John Cage and James Waring. Her plays are often wildly absurdist, lyrical, and comic and give free rein to a zany inventiveness.[5]

Our interviews reveal di Prima's transition during the eighties toward a more intense involvement in the history of spiritual traditions. Di Prima conversed with Mary Zeppa in 1985 regarding the class she taught at the New College of California, "The Hidden Religions in the Literature of Europe": "And I teach Hidden Religions every other year and in between things like a course in John Dee, Paracelsus, and Giordano Bruno, three Magicians from the Early Renaissance. . . . It's a very, very rich program at New College. You can really make great strides in your own work while you're teaching. I don't know how I would do in a regular university." Indeed, di Prima's deep studies in the "Hidden Religions"—that is, the tradition of heterodox esoteric thought that has existed through the millennia outside the framework of the monotheistic, orthodox religions of Christianity, Judaism, and Islam—began to become increasingly prominent in her work, as we see in her frequent allusions to Gnosticism, Kabbalah, magic, theosophy, alchemy, tarot, paganism/"witchcraft" and astrology. This theme is also explored in one of the most extensive and rich interviews conducted by Jay Kinney of *Gnosis* magazine. Kinney had been one of the colleagues of artist Robert Crumb during the "comix" revolution in San Francisco, publishing *Bijou* magazine, and has also written extensively on the "hidden religions." One notes di Prima's conscientious discipline, as we see in her comments regarding the center she founded, SIMHA, San Francisco Institute of Magical & Healing Arts: "Our first idea was to investigate Alchemy, but we decided that we were not very prepared, so we would just start with the four elements. We made tattvas of the elements and the subelements, and we spent something like three and a half years meeting once a week at first and then every two weeks, and going deep and using the old Golden Dawn technique of parting the curtain, entering the tattva, and recording the material. . . . So we did that—we completed that work, and then we began working with the Major Arcana." The *Gnosis* interview also sheds light on di Prima's LSD experiences: "Most of my early acid was taken at Millbrook, with Timothy Leary and the community there, and I learned that if I set my course before I got high, I could learn those irregular Sanskrit verbs in fifteen minutes when I was on the re-entry part of the trip, or I could use the peaking time to investigate this or that about the space between the worlds, or wherever I wanted to go." Di Prima has always been careful not to waste precious time, here putting her "re-entry" period from her mind-expanding trips to good use in pursuit of the practical and challenging task of learning Sanskrit.

In a revealing 1992 interview with di Prima and her then twenty-seven-year-old daughter Dominique, Alice Kahn creates a tender portrait of the ways di Prima has passed on poetic traditions to her family and documents the rising popularity of rap music. Dominique was host of the award-winning television show *Home Turf*, which aired on KRON-TV in San Francisco from 1984 to 1992 featuring hip-hop, break-dancing, skateboarding, graffiti art, and politics. Like her mother, Dominique sought to restore written poetry to its oral beginnings, telling Kahn: "People think of poetry as something on paper, a dead form. All rap is a form of poetry." We may compare her daughter's observation to di Prima's astute comments in her 1996 interview concerning Homer's *Iliad*. Stephen Schwarz asked her: "If I had a fifteen-year-old and said, 'I'm going to send you to Diane di Prima and she's going to give you a reading list,' what would be on your list?" Di Prima responded: "I had a wonderful dream recently in which the *Iliad* was cast, in the dream, as gangster rap, which is precisely what it is. These guys and those guys you dissed my chick and blah blah blah." This hip counterpointing of the archaic Greek world—Achilles's wrath at Agamemnon for taking his war-prize Briseis as an analogue to modern gang fights over women—with contemporary experience is typical of di Prima's literary imagination. Her granddaughter Chani is also a poet influenced by hip-hop who has published a book entitled *lookinside* (2014). Di Prima participated with Jack Hirschman and Kathy Acker in readings at a poetry series titled "Wordland" at the Women's Building in San Francisco that featured poetry alongside hip-hop performances.[6] Dominique also zeroes in on her mother's unique qualities, revealing she has inherited her quick wit and razor-sharp perceptiveness: "My mom broke the mold. I think people don't give mom enough credit 'cause she's got kids—she's fine and we're fine. There's no *People* cover story here—no junkie, no Betty Ford clinic."

With Ron Whitehead, di Prima discusses aspects of her upbringing she would begin to explore more fully in her autobiography *Recollections of My Life as a Woman* (2001). Di Prima speaks of her "rage" at her home life and the desire to get away from its turbulent emotional violence. She was changing diapers of her family members at age four and realized that "something about the dysfunction of the situation made me who I was . . . and rather than going crazy I became a writer." She points out that "there was within my immediate family my father who was very repressive. He was born in America but raised in Sicily. And he was a batterer, he was a rage-aholic." It is evident that as di Prima set to work on her autobiography, it was necessary to revisit the often painful scenes of her childhood in the attempt to piece together the complex narrative of an Italian American upbringing during the Depression, the buildup to World War II, and her young adulthood as an aspiring author.

With the new millennium in 2001, in an interview with David Hadbawnik, di Prima recalls her relationships with LeRoi Jones and Frank O'Hara in the fifties as well as her move to California in 1968. In California she would continue her friendship with Michael McClure and artist George Herms and also form an important relationship with Robert Duncan. She discusses Duncan's attitude toward magic, telling Hadbawnik: "He would never practice magic, though, and when in one summer course that we did there I brought in devices for visualization from the Golden Dawn, showed them to people and talked about actually practicing trance work with these symbols of the elements and sub-elements—he was quite upset. He would never practice it, and [said] that he needed neither religion nor magic, because poetry was a complete path in itself. And I think for him it was, but also he was a little afraid, because of his upbringing, of actually getting his feet wet. So we had lots of interesting tugs of war like that." In her interview with V. Vale, di Prima returns to her fascination with magic and the desire to combine her interests in Tibetan Buddhism as espoused by guru Chögyam Trungpa with Western esoteric traditions: "I decided to ask Trungpa to be my teacher, because I knew that Tibetan Buddhism openly embraces the whole Western magical view. So I had an interview with Trungpa in '83. I wasn't teaching that year, but I flew out to Naropa in Boulder and stayed at Allen's house. Both Sheppard and I had interviews, and we asked Trungpa to be our teacher. I told him I was doing all this Western magic, and that sometimes I needed *backup*. I said, 'I'm not prepared to give up Western practices and Western philosophy for the East.' In my mind we're involved in a process that is going to take five hundred years to amalgamate all these things. We're bridge-makers, but we're barely at the beginning of the bridge!" Trungpa responded positively, declaring that it was perfectly acceptable to combine Eastern and Western spiritual traditions.

However, di Prima has never turned away from the world and taken refuge in escapism. She has pursued a rigorous and disciplined spiritual life, but has not attempted to hide from the terrors and injustices of "the real world." Her poetry continued to reflect the social and political upheavals of our time, and we note she composed poems on 9/11, the US involvement in Iraq, and the Hurricane Katrina crisis. As she told Melkina in the *Ars Interpres* interview, di Prima responded to the events of 9/11 when her daughter called to tell her about the World Trade Center: "We finished talking, and I turned on the TV. And it was the second tower coming down . . . Between you and me, what did we expect? How can that be so stupid not to expect it if it is happening everywhere else . . ." Di Prima saw America as overstepping boundaries in its imperial ambitions and thus reaping karmic recompense for many transgressions.

In a fascinating discussion with Jackson Ellis, editor of *Verbicide*, we can see how at age seventy-five, di Prima's lifelong interest in the various modes of publishing continued apace. She had learned the art of operating a printing press and intrepidly founded her own publishing enterprises such as Poets Press, which between 1965 and 1969 created twenty-seven books including *Huncke's Journal* (1965) by Herbert Huncke; Gregory Corso's *10 Times a Poem* (1967); Allen Ginsberg's *Scrap Leaves* (1968); Audre Lorde's *The First Cities* (1968); John Ashbery's *Three Madrigals* (1968); Robert Creeley's *5 Numbers* (1968) and *Mazatlan: Sea* (1969); Frank O'Hara's *Odes* (1969); and Robert Duncan's *Play Time Pseudo Stein* (1969). On the back cover of these books, di Prima often featured an *ouroboros*—a serpent eating its own tail with a sun at the upper left and the moon at the upper right, a symbolic image she reproduced from Horapollo's *Hieroglyphica,* printed in Rome in 1597—thus silently signaling to the attentive reader her ongoing interest in alchemy and Gnosticism. Later, di Prima would create Eidolon Editions which published titles by Audre Lorde as well as several books of her own. Di Prima discusses with Jackson Ellis the shift to computers—Ellis had created his own magazine *Verbicide* on the Web—as she explores the ways the internet has transformed the ways literature is disseminated.[7] Di Prima also shares with Ellis her fond memories of William S. Burroughs, with whom she conducted long conversations concerning magic; she required Burroughs's book *The Third Mind* (1978) in her classes studying random techniques of composition.

We can also trace in the later interviews di Prima's election to Poet Laureate of San Francisco and her concerns over the mass of unpublished work she had gathered. She tells Ellis that now at age seventy-three, "I have more books unpublished than I have out in the world, by far. I'd like to get my work in some kind of order, my papers in some kind of order, so that people can make some sense of things. I tend to have a habit of writing a poem wherever I am on whatever I've got, like in the back of whatever book I'm reading. I'd like to be able to help people *find* those later. I'd like to get my work in order, and aside from that, make sure that whatever—if anything—arrives from it in the way of [money] goes to my sweetie and my kids. I love to paint—but I have no ambitions for it. If I had my druthers in this world right now, I would be doing nothing except writing, typing up the writing I've got, painting, and meditating."[8] Di Prima continued to be prolific, as she told Ron Whitehead in 1992: "I've got two four foot shelves of spring binders and I've got 70 bound journals with collages and writings that I want to place somewhere." Indeed, di Prima has remained consistently productive throughout her career, and even during the last years, when she has battled serious health issues, her creative energy has been unflagging.

Thus, these interviews depict a vibrant, creative, and indefatigable force in American letters whose example is inspiring to all those who seek a better world. As Allen Ginsberg described her: "Diane di Prima, revolutionary activist of the 1960s' Beat literary renaissance, heroic in life and poetics; a learned humorous bohemian, classically educated, and twentieth-century radical, her writing, informed by Buddhist equanimity, is exemplary in imagist, political and mystical modes. A great world poet in the second half of American century, she broke barriers of race-class identity, delivered a major body of verse brilliant in its particularity." Di Prima's ability to sustain a long and productive career in the face of poverty and neglect by the critical establishment is indeed nothing short of heroic. These interviews reveal di Prima as a true American national treasure and it is hoped they will demonstrate the power and integrity of her life and work to a new generation of readers.

DSC

Notes

1. Virginia Woolf, *A Room of One's Own* (New York: Houghton Mifflin, 1989), 49.

2. Ezra Pound's biographer asserts that di Prima's visit to Pound took place in December 1955, citing a letter in the files of St. Elizabeth Hospital. See A. David Moody, *Ezra Pound: Poet, A Portrait of the Man and His Work; Volume III: The Tragic Years 1939–1972* (Oxford: Oxford University Press, 2015), 311, 588; Ezra Pound, *ABC of Reading* (New York: New Directions, 1960), *Guide to Kulchur* (New York: New Directions, 1970), and *The Spirit of Romance* (New Directions: New York, 1968). On di Prima's relationship with Pound, see David Stephen Calonne, *Diane di Prima: Visionary Poetics and the Hidden Religions* (New York: Bloomsbury, 2019), 31–34.

3. Daniel Arasse, *Anselm Kiefer* (London: Thames and Hudson, 2019), 262–71; Steven Clay and Rodney Phillips, *A Secret Location on The Lower East Side: Adventures in Writing, 1960–1980* (New York: New York Public Library, 1998), 26.

4. On Tassajara, see Marilyn McDonald, *A Brief History of Tassajara: From Native American Sweat Lodges to Pioneering Zen Monastery* (San Rafael, CA: Cuke Press, 2018).

5. On di Prima's playwriting, see Brenda Knight, *Women of the Beat Generation: The Writers, Artists, and Muses at the Heart of a Revolution* (New York: MJF Books, 2000), 126; and Nancy M. Grace, "Diane di Prima as Playwright: The Early Years 1959–1964," in Deborah R. Geis, ed., *Beat Drama: Playwrights and Performances of the "Howl" Generation* (New York: Bloomsbury, 2016), 155–75.

6. Jack Foley, *Visions and Affiliations, A California Literary Time Line: Poets and Poetry 1940–2009* (Oakland, CA: Pantograph Press, 2011), 268. On December 13, 1997, Sheppard Powell recited di Prima's "Litany (for Kathy Acker)" at a memorial wake for Acker, who had died on November 30, 1997. See Chris Kraus, *After Kathy Acker: A Literary Biography* (South Pasadena, CA: Semiotext[e], 2018), 21–23.

7. On Poets Press, see Jolie Braun, "A History of Diane di Prima's Poets Press," *Journal of Beat Studies* 6 (2018): 3–22.

8. For a recent dissertation exploring di Prima's massive personal library and the annotations and original poetry she composed in many of her books, see Mary Catherine Kinniburgh, *The Shape of Knowledge: The Postwar American Poet's Library, With Diane di Prima and Charles Olson*, City University of New York, 2019. And for one example of the fascinating work in her archives, see Diane di Prima, "*Prometheus Unbound* as a Magickal Working," ed. Iris Cushing, *Lost and Found, The CUNY Poetics Document Initiative*, Series 8, no. 2, fall 2019.

Chronology

1934   Diane di Prima born August 6, in Red Hook, Brooklyn, New York, daughter of Francis and Emma di Prima. Di Prima's ancestors came from Sicily, and Italian culture became an important aspect of her identity as an artist.

1935   Di Prima spends a great deal of time from the ages of one to six with her anarchist grandfather on her mother's side, Domenico Mallozzi—an "anti-authority authority figure"—and friend of Carlo Tresca and Emma Goldman. They listen to opera together and he takes her to anarchist rallies: this will profoundly influence di Prima's later politically egalitarian commitments. At age four, Domenico reads to her Dante Alighieri and also introduces her to the great "heretical" philosophical genius Giordano Bruno.

1940   Di Prima composes her first poems, one of which records a desire to "remember forever" stars in the sky above her grandparents' apartment. Diane's parents separate her from seeing her grandfather Domenico because they think he is having too much influence upon her. Skips a grade, "which made life miserable in grammar school—all the kids hated me."

1944   At age ten—she reports elsewhere this occurred when she was seven years old—di Prima's father has her read Machiavelli's *The Prince* in order to understand history, telling her "you're never going to understanding what's going on in the world because no one is telling you, what they're writing is all propaganda."

1945   On August 6, di Prima's eleventh birthday, the United States drops an atomic bomb on Hiroshima, which she recalled in *Recollections of My Life as a Woman* as a decisive event in her young life. Over the next few years, she begins her readings of philosophy—including Plato in the Jowett translations, marking her comments in the margins; Spinoza; Schopenhauer's *Die Welt als Wille und Vorstellung* (The World as Will and Idea), which she read in its entirety and which she loved; and Immanuel Kant, which she found a bit more difficult—in the Carroll Street Branch of the Brooklyn Public Library. When she discovers Friedrich Nietzsche's *Also Sprach Zarathustra* with her friend Pia, her mother weeps and sends di Prima and her friend to consult the parish priest who shouts at them: "Don't think! Don't think! It will spoil your faith."

1948   Enters Hunter High School, where she studies Latin. Tries to dye all of her clothes black in the family washing machine, with mixed results. Typical wardrobe during this time includes jeans, a peacoat, and berets. Discovering the pirate novels of Rafael Sabatini, she adds a red sash to her fashion accessories. Reading the letters of John Keats and Percy Bysshe Shelley, she realizes she must dedicate her life to being a writer and writes every day—*Nulla dies sine linea*—for the next four years. The school admitted only women and di Prima belongs to a group called "The Branded," sharing her writings with fellow students, among whom is Audre Lorde. They experiment with the paranormal: trance, séances, and telepathy.

1949   Becomes increasingly interested in dance, now sporting black leotards and pink slippers to school. To pursue her interest in dancing, di Prima attends New Dance Group on East 59th Street near Central Park. Sees Jean Cocteau's *Blood of the Poet* at the theatre on Irving Place and later all of Cocteau's films, which make a deep impression upon her. Frequents the bookstores on Fourth Avenue in Manhattan.

1950   On June 25, the Korean War begins, an event di Prima considered a key moment in creating cynicism and skepticism among her generation regarding the supposed "peace" that had been promised following World War II.

1951   Goes to summer school and graduates from Hunter High. Di Prima receives a prize for Latin translation and intends to major in Greek at Latin at Swarthmore College. However, she was in the top two percentile in mathematics and physics and was encouraged to major in physics. Receives $300 scholarship to attend Swarthmore, which she finds unappealing because it is a place "where everyone is mostly from the upper class, all dressed in their little cashmere sweaters and a strand of pearls. There was this whole 'everything-is-all right' veneer about their world." She recalls one positive aspect of her time there was that she bought books by Ezra

Pound, e. e. cummings, and W. H. Auden from the college bookstore—volumes she didn't have access to in the Brooklyn Public Library.

1952   Di Prima's early poetic style is influenced by Ernest Hemingway and the spare line drawings of Henri Matisse, which she studies during this period: "I was very interested in how little you could use to imply how much."

1953   February 2, 1953, was di Prima's last day in attendance at Swarthmore. She now rents an apartment with a comfortable room, bathroom, and kitchen for forty-five dollars a month in New York City at 521 East Fifth Street, Apartment 4C on the Lower East Side between Avenue B and Avenue C. Spends time at the Rienzi Café and Washington Square Park, becomes acquainted with painters, and takes dance classes. Designs her own sandals made with rawhide laces that crisscross at the ankle and up the leg. Listens to Miles Davis and Charles Mingus at the Café Bohemia and Charlie "Bird" Parker at the Open Door in the Village. Takes classes in integral calculus at Brooklyn College and theory of equations at Columbia, ancient Greek at Hunter College, and also studies at the New School for Social Research. Works in an office on Wall Street and in the electronics lab at Columbia. Julius and Ethel Rosenberg are executed for spying on behalf of the Soviet Union on June 19, adding to the atmosphere of "repression and fear" that troubles the young di Prima.

1954   Meets dancer Freddie Herko in Washington Square Park. Models for painters Nikolai Cikovsky, Raphael and Moses Soyer, and Joseph Floch, who worked at the Lincoln Arcade on the West Side, for which she is paid $3 or $3.50 an hour at a time when the minimum wage was seventy-five cents. Frequently goes to the movies at the Museum of Modern Art and the Thalia. Follows the suggestions of Pound in *The ABC of Reading* and begins writing the material she will later include in *Dinners and Nightmares*.

1955   Begins to correspond with Ezra Pound, sending him her poems. Di Prima's essay "Movement and Tableau in the Dance" is published in the *Carolina Quarterly*.

1956   On January 28, writes to poet Kenneth Patchen. Visits Pound at St. Elizabeth's in Washington, DC, daily for about two weeks in March, staying with Pound's "Muse" Sheri Martinelli. On November 10, hears Billie Holiday's concert at Carnegie

Hall, declaring that Holiday "was already for many of us the su-
preme artist, the one with no equal." Meets choreographer James
Waring, with whom she studies Zen and meditative composi-
tion. Corresponds with Allen Ginsberg and sends Lawrence
Ferlinghetti her "Thirteen Nightmares," composed the pre-
vious year.

1957   In winter, meets Jack Kerouac, Allen Ginsberg, and Gregory Corso,
who are on their way to meet William S. Burroughs in Morocco.
Begins work on *Poems for Freddie*. Gives birth to first child,
Jeanne. Meets LeRoi Jones (later Amiri Baraka), who visits her
with photographer James Oliver Mitchell.

1958   *This Kind of Bird Flies Backward* published by Totem Press.
Smokes Jamaican marijuana with James Waring and Freddie
Herko and experiences first "past life" memories.

1959   Works at the Phoenix Book Store for Larry Wallrich at 18 Cornelia
Street, which becomes for the next few years the hangout where
di Prima would write and see her friends. Becomes stage manager
for James Waring at the Living Theatre, where she will have the
first staged reading of her play *Murder Cake*, the composition of
which was "part random exercise, part free association." Spends
time with friends A. B. Spellman and Hubert Selby Jr. and helps
Alexander Trocchi, who was in flight from drug charges, hide
in the Phoenix Bookstore. Takes peyote, which influenced her
poetic style, resulting in the "long lines like those in *The New
Handbook of Heaven*." Studies medieval philosophy, especially
Robert Grosseteste. Composes plays *The Discontent of the Russian
Prince* and *Rain Fur*.

1960   Always a voracious reader, during this period di Prima, influenced
by John Cage's "Music of Changes," purchases the two-volume
boxed set of the *I Ching: The Book of Changes*, which becomes
a central text for her in the coming decades. Also reads C. C.
Chang's *The Six Yogas of Naropa*. *Dinners and Nightmares* published
by Corinth Press. Edits *Various Fables from Various Places*,
published by G. P. Putnam. Michael McClure visits from California.
Composes plays *Paideuma, Like, Murder Cake*, and *The Discovery of
America* (revised in August 1972).

1961   Coeditor with LeRoi Jones, then sole editor after 1963 until 1969,
of *The Floating Bear*, a literary journal. During trip to California
stays with Michael McClure and meets Robert Duncan, Philip

Lamantia, and Philip Whalen as well as Kirby Doyle, Wallace Berman, and artists George Herms and Jay DeFeo. In spring, cofounder of New York Poets Theater with LeRoi Jones, James Waring, John Herbert McDowell, Freddie Herko, and Alan Marlowe. Produces one-act plays by poets including Michael McClure, Wallace Stevens and Frank O'Hara, with sets designed by painters. On October 18, FBI agents arrest di Prima and Jones for "obscenity" but the grand jury throws out the case. Contributing editor to *Kulchur*, 1961–62. As a birthday gift to herself, purchases and reads fourteen-volume edition of Sir James George Frazer's *The Golden Bough*; also studies Heinrich Zimmer's *Philosophies of India*. Begins the experimental prose work *The Calculus of Variation*, which she completes in 1964 and publishes in 1972. In October, performs her play *The Discontent of the Russian Prince* with Freddie Herko.

1962   Composes play *Poet's Vaudeville* and the first three acts of *Whale Honey*. Larry Wallrich's Phoenix Bookstore is bought by Robert Wilson, who becomes a close friend and helps with the sale of di Prima's manuscripts and letters. Second daughter Dominique is born. In September, meets with Wallace Berman in Beverly Glen, Los Angeles, as well as artist Marjorie Cameron. Travels to San Francisco and while living at Stinson Beach, works on play *Whale Honey*. Meets Shunryu Suzuki, with whom she will undertake a serious study of Zen Buddhism. On November 30, Suzuki marries di Prima and Alan Marlowe at Sokoji, a Buddhist temple on Bush Street. The *Heart Sutra* is chanted during the ceremony. In December, moves to Topanga Canyon in Southern California.

1963   In Topanga, artist George Herms and Wallace and Shirley Berman are neighbors. Billy Name (Linich), a member of Andy Warhol's entourage, visits from New York. Di Prima moves back to Manhattan. Performs in Jack Smith's film *Normal Love*. Play *Murder Cake* published in spring issue of *Kulchur*. In March, her friend Paul Blackburn organizes poetry readings at Le Metro, a coffeehouse on Second Avenue. Purchases a Davidson 214 letterpress machine to learn how to publish books. Celebrates Winter Solstice for the first time. First son, Alexander, is born. New Year's Eve, takes first acid trip, which elucidates what di Prima had been studying regarding "time and emptiness—I could just see it."

1964   Andy Warhol creates a brief film of di Prima and Alan Marlowe. She described it as "a three or five minute movie of me and Alan. Alan is in bed, and he's covered by a tiger skin, which he's stroking the tail of in a very obviously suggestive manner. I get on the bed in a black leotard and tights and kind of trample him. It was a tiny room." Also meets experimental filmmaker Stan Brakhage. George Herms visits di Prima in New York to create sets for Michael McClure's *The Blossom or Billy the Kid*, which was performed at the Poets Theatre. Herms also works on the woodblock prints to illustrate di Prima's *Haiku*, published in 1967. At her house on Cooper Square, di Prima begins hosting Wednesday Night Readings to which her friends were invited. After the first initial meetings, she would begin with a throw of the I Ching and a reading from *The Hundred Thousand Songs of Milarepa*. Near the end of the readings—which continued until fall of 1965—she read all of Rilke's *Duino Elegies*. Discovers *The Tibetan Book of the Dead* at Samuel Weiser's bookstore on Broadway. Di Prima establishes the Poets Press in New York City, which will publish Gregory Corso, Allen Ginsberg, Audre Lorde, Robert Creeley, Robert Duncan, and John Ashbery. On October 27, Freddie Herko commits suicide; a week later, di Prima begins composing *Spring and Autumn Annals* in his memory, not published until 2021.

1965   Becomes associate editor of *Signal* magazine. Moves to Monroe, New York, where she lives in the Ananda Ashram of Rammurti Mishra and writes the introduction to a two-volume edition of the alchemical writings of Paracelsus. Di Prima's Poets Press publishes *Huncke's Journal* as well as her translations, *Seven Love Poems from the Middle Latin*. As will several other Poets Press titles, the back cover features an *ouroboros*—a serpent eating its own tail—with the moon and sun above. The ouroboros originates in ancient Egypt and became a prominent symbol in the history of Gnosticism, hermeticism, and alchemy.

1966   In January, moves to an old farmhouse in Kerhonkson, New York, with Alan Marlowe and her three children, where they remain until September and composes *Kerhonkson Journal: 1966*. During the summer, drives to Gloucester where she meets Charles Olson for the first time: they trip together on LSD for forty-eight hours. Poets Press publishes Timothy Leary's *Psychedelic Prayers after the Tao Te Ching*. Receives National Endowment on the Arts grant for Poets Press. Begins studying Tarot seriously, employing the A. E. Waite deck of cards while living for two months in Ranchos de Taos, New Mexico, and experiences lucid dreams. Visits Timothy Leary's Millbrook community, where she stays for six months experimenting with LSD and studying hatha yoga until 1967. During this period she continues her studies of Sanskrit. *Poems for Freddie* published by Poets Press.

1967   Travels across America in VW bus, reading her poetry at universities, discotheques, galleries, and other locales. During trip to San Francisco, stays with poet Lenore Kandel on Chestnut Street in North Beach. Tara, third daughter, is born. On April 19, gives reading at the Topanga Corral in Topanga Canyon, Southern California.

1968   Di Prima's play *Monuments*, directed by James Waring, is performed on March 10 at the Caffe Cino in New York. Poets Press publishes John Ashbery's *Three Madrigals*. In June, moves to San Francisco to work with the Diggers, an anarchist community. Lives with many other people in a fourteen-room house built around 1915 on Oak Street between Cole and Schrader for $300 a month. Di Prima had a VW van and at the party before leaving New York for California, her friends gave her "rifles and electric typewriters. People decided that's what I needed, so at my going-away party they gave me rifles and electric typewriters." The van is used by the Diggers to deliver and pick up food for the needy in twenty-five communes. Another primary reason for the move to California was di Prima's desire to continue her study of Zen Buddhism with Shunryu Suzuki. Di Prima works on the *Revolutionary Letters* and edits *War Poems*, an anthology containing poetry opposing the war in Vietnam. Serves as contributing editor for *Guerrilla: A Monthly Newspaper of Contemporary Kulchur* until 1970. Poets Press publishes Audre Lorde's *The First Cities* as well as *War Poems*, an anthology of antiwar poems by, among others, Gregory Corso, Robert Duncan, Allen Ginsberg, Philip Whalen, and herself. During this period, di Prima also composes one of her greatest works, "A Canticle for St. Joan."

1969   Di Prima's father dies. Under surveillance by the FBI for her "radical" activities such as her connection with the Black Panthers, di Prima retreats to Black Bear Ranch, where she stays for a year and a half, invited by Elsa and Richard Marley. Studies at Tassajara Zen Mountain Center. Divorces Alan Marlowe.

1970   Moves to a top-floor flat at 452 Page Street in San Francisco. Teaches writing workshop at Tassajara, where she meets Chögyam Trungpa. Second son Rudi is born. John Giorno's "Dial-A-Poem" display from July 2–September 20 at the Information Exhibition at the Museum of Modern Art in New York features a di Prima poem. Has dream of a female wolf figure which begins the genesis of *Loba*.

1971   Teaches women's writing workshop at San Francisco YMCA. Begins "San Francisco Notebooks," which contain her dreams, collages, photographs, and poetry. Teaches community workshops until 1975 at Intersection for the Arts; also teaches until 1977 in National Endowment for the Arts Poetry in the Schools Program with residencies and workshops in prisons, on reservations, and at reform schools in Wyoming, Arizona, Minnesota, and Montana. On August 19, participates with Allen Ginsberg, Lawrence Ferlinghetti, and Michael McClure in benefit reading at UC Berkeley for defense fund in support of Judith Malina and Julian Beck's the Living Theater. In December, begins work on poem *Loba*, composing the preface poem "Ave." Has her last interview with Shunryu Suzuki, who dies on December 4.

1972   In February, continues work on *Loba*. In April, reads at the City Lights Poets Theater at Fugazi Hall in North Beach in support of Greek resistance to the military junta. Marries Grant Fisher. Creates publishing venture, Eidolon Editions. Leads women's writing groups at Esalen Institute. Gives poetry reading for the Politics and Art Symposium at the University of British Columbia.

1973   Moves to Marshall, California, near Point Reyes and over the next several years forms a close friendship with Robert Duncan. Begins studying Tibetan Buddhism with Chögyam Trungpa. On October 11, reads her work at Bard College. Also reads at St. Lawrence University. Gives seminar "History as Paranoia," which is attended by Kenneth Rexroth. Becomes fond during the seventies of wearing T-shirts emblazoned with pictures that include jazz clubs, baseball players, anarchists, favorite artists such as Matisse and Magritte, or one of her favorites: dinosaurs in the act of swallowing several humans with the caption EAT THE RICH.

1974   Teaches visualization, writing, and dream workshops at Intersection for the Arts. Over the next three years, di Prima teaches courses on William Carlos Williams, Ezra Pound, Robert Duncan, Allen Ginsberg, Charles Olson, Gertrude Stein, and H.D. Joins Trungpa, Allen Ginsberg, Allen Waldman, and others to create the Naropa Institute—later named the Jack Kerouac School of Disembodied Poetics—in Boulder, Colorado, where she teaches in 1974, 1975, 1976, and then every other year until 1997.

1975   Di Prima's mother Emma comes to visit her in Marshall. In the summer, play *Whale Honey* performed at Intersection Theatre, San Francisco. Delivers lecture "Light/and Keats" at Naropa. Writes "Preface" to John Dee's *Monas Hieroglyphica: The Hieroglyphic Monad* (1564). *Selected Poems: 1956–1975* published. Divorces Grant Fisher.

1976   In spring, reads sections of *Loba* at Indian Valley Colleges, Novato, California, with Bay Area writers. California Arts Council awards di Prima Arts-in-Social-Institutions Fellowship to teach collage and writing to psychiatric patients at Napa State Hospital. Participates in a political rally concerning Proposition 15 regarding the construction of nuclear power plants in California. Attends Rotterdam Poetry Festival. On November 25, di Prima reads her poetry with Robert Duncan, Lawrence Ferlinghetti, and Michael McClure at the final concert of the musical group The Band, memorialized by Martin Scorsese in his documentary *The Last Waltz* (1978).

1977   Meets Sheppard Powell, who becomes her life partner. In spring, gives lecture and reading for Diabasis House, a center for the treatment of schizophrenia.

1978   Moves back to San Francisco, where she lives at 263 Laguna Street until 1995. On October 1, reads at Tribal Stomp at Greek Theatre in Berkeley with Allen Ginsberg, Lenore Kandel, Michael McClure, and Wavy Gravy. Studies psychic reading with Helen Palmer. Begins visualizing work and teaching "Structures of Magic and Techniques of Visioning." *Loba, Parts 1–8* published.

1979   Visiting writer at New College of California. In June, reads at the City of Rome's International Poetry Festival in Ostia, Italy, with Yevgeny Yevtushenko, Gregory Corso, Lawrence Ferlinghetti, and Allen Ginsberg. In September, lectures at Minneapolis Jung Society on Angels.

1980   Reads on February 26 at Wisconsin Institute for Intermedia Studies in Madison. Begins teaching hermetic and esoteric traditions in poetry at New College of California with Robert Duncan, David Meltzer, Duncan McNaughton, and Louis Patler until 1987. Develops a course entitled "The Hidden Religions in the Literature of Europe" in which she teaches esoteric, hermetic, and alchemical texts by authors such as John Dee, Heinrich Cornelius Agrippa, Paracelsus, and Robert Fludd.

1981 Begins doing private healing work and trance visualization for clients. On February 12, composes poem "Studies in Light."

1982 On February 18, delivers lecture on "Role of the Hermetic in Poetry" at the Detroit Institute of the Arts. Participates in twenty-fifth anniversary conference for Jack Kerouac's *On the Road* at Naropa.

1983 Commences formal study with Chögyam Trungpa, although informing him that she "wasn't ready to give up Paracelsus for Padmasabhava." Trungpa responded that "there was absolutely no problem" and encouraged di Prima to pursue her interests in both Western and Eastern esoteric traditions. With Janet Carter, Carl Grundberg, and Sheppard Powell, di Prima founds San Francisco Institute of Magical and Healing Arts.

1984 In the Fall, di Prima writes letters to her mother—which she never sends—asking her questions about the di Prima family history. Lama Tharchin Rinpoche (1936–2013), born in Tibet and a Dzogchen master of Vajrayana Buddhism, moves to the United States and di Prima will study with him.

1985 Mother dies. In February, gives reading with Allen Ginsberg and Kathy Acker at the Detroit Institute of the Arts. In spring, teaches "Principles of Homeopathy," "Structures of Magic," and "Psychic Self-Defense" at the San Francisco Institute of Magical and Healing Arts. Participates in "Dharma Art" exhibit at San Francisco Dharmadhatu.

1987 In the spring, delivers lecture on H.D. at the New College of California, published in 2011 as "The Mysteries of Vision: Some Notes on H.D." Serves as columnist until 1993 of *Mama Bear's News and Notes*, where several chapters from *Recollections of My Life as a Woman* appear. Participates in "River City Reunion Week" in Lawrence, Kansas, from September 7 to 13 with William S. Burroughs, Ed Sanders, Anne Waldman, Robert Creeley, Michael McClure, and Allen Ginsberg. In the autumn, has a vivid dream of a church in Sicily that appears to be "like a mosque," revealing to her that "it is very important for me to understand how 'Arabic' my people are (the Sicilian side of the family). It will help me to understand my life."

1988   Robert Duncan dies on February 3 and di Prima reads his eulogy at the San Francisco Dharmadhatu on February 21. Delivers lecture "H.D.'s Angel Magic" at Naropa. *Wyoming Series* is published.

1989   Participates in group art show at Naropa Institute, "Word and Image." Obtains a television set for the first time.

1990   Vacations with Sheppard Powell in Puerto Vallarta, Mexico. *Pieces of A Song: Selected Poems* published. Guest lecturer at the University of California, Santa Cruz. Senior lecturer until 1992 at California College of Arts and Crafts.

1991   *Seminary Poems* published.

1992   Seventeen poets and writers, including di Prima, Kathy Acker, and Jack Hirschman, create "Wordland: The Anti-Fascist Spoken Word Ballroom," at the Women's Building in San Francisco, featuring poetry and hip-hop. On July 17, di Prima performs with her daughter Dominique in a program entitled "Spoken Word Meets Rap—At Last." Visiting faculty, San Francisco Art Institute. Works on book *The Language of Alchemy*, based on four-lecture course. Di Prima becomes a columnist until 1993 for *Harbin Quarterly*. Di Prima begins to reduce her traveling to give readings to earn money by a third, preferring to spend time at home painting and writing.

1993   On August 29, performs with Michael McClure, Robert Hunter, and Ray Manzarek at the Great American Music Hall in San Francisco. Lifetime Achievement in Poetry Award, National Poetry Association.

1994   In October, attends Unsettling America Conference. On November 11, delivers lecture subsequently published as "Don't Solidify the Adversary! A Response to Rudolph Vecoli"—at the American Italian Historical Association. Speaks at the Poetry Project, St. Mark's Church in New York City, where she meets with Ted Joans. Writer in Residence, Atlantic Center for the Arts. Teaches at California Institute of Integral Studies.

1996   In May, reads at the Santa Barbara Poetry Festival. Featured in Whitney Museum and De Young Museum exhibit, "Beat Culture and the New America."

1997   On December 13, Sheppard Powell recites di Prima's "Litany (for Kathy Acker)" at a memorial wake for Acker, who died on November 30.

1998   *Loba* published.

1999   Receives honorary Doctor of Literature degree from St. Lawrence University.

2000   Master Poet in Residence, Columbia College, Chicago. On April 27, delivers lecture "Poetry as a Spiritual Practice."

2001   Exhibits watercolors—"Blue Landscapes"—at Passaic County Community College. *Recollections of My Life as a Woman* published by Viking.

2002   Teaches seminar "Theory and Study of Poetics." Publishes *Towers Down/Notes Toward a Poem of Revolution* on the September 11, 2001, attack on the World Trade Center.

2003   *The Ones I Used to Laugh With: A Haibun Journal* published. Gives reading at City Lights Bookshop.

2004   Exhibits collages—"The Interrupted Sleep"—at North Light Book Shop and Café, Cotati, California; also exhibits collages—"The Moon Will Claim Me"—at Beckett Books and Records.

2005   From September 12–13 between 2:00 and 3:30 a.m., di Prima composes *TimeBomb*, which memorializes the disaster of Hurricane Katrina in New Orleans in August.

2006   On January 23, reads *TimeBomb* at Bird and Beckett Books and Records in San Francisco, later published by Eidolon Editions. On April 5, at the 25th Annual Northern California Book Awards held in Koret Auditorium, San Francisco Public Library, receives Fred Cody Award for community service and lifetime achievement. October 18–December 10, di Prima's work featured in "*Semina* Culture: Wallace Berman and His Circle" at the Santa Monica Museum of Art and at the "Crossing Boundaries: Visual Art by Writers" exhibit at Passaic County Community College.

2008   In December, receives the Reginald Lockett Award at the PEN Club ceremony in Oakland.

2009   Di Prima is named the fifth Poet Laureate of San Francisco in May. In August, a ceremony is held in a studio at Mission and Cesar Chavez Streets, during which a laurel wreath is placed upon di Prima's head, her right hand resting on a book containing the collected works of John Keats. Di Prima accepts the award "in the name of all the poets and all the alchemists of all time."

2010   Officially inaugurated as Poet Laureate of San Francisco in February. On October 15, reads at the Segal Theatre, City University of New York Graduate Center, and on October 16 at the Bowery Poetry Club. Participates in the Charles Olson Conference in Gloucester, Massachusetts. The *Paterson Literary Review* devotes a special section to di Prima's work.

2011   Documentary by Melanie LaRosa, *The Poetry Deal: A Film with Diane di Prima*, released by Women Make Movies.

2013   On November 3 and 17 and December 1, teaches course at the Bay Area Public School entitled "The Dream of Pre-History" which explores "the beginnings of what we call 'human'—the fall of Neanderthal and the rise of Cro-Magnon culture—the beginnings, dominance, and eclipse of matriarchy—the double invasions of patriarchy and oligarchy—and the persistent dream of a non-hierarchical society." On November 6, gives reading and lecture— "How I Write"—at Stanford University. Contributes "Forward" to granddaughter Chani di Prima's *look inside.*

2014   February 1, reads at Bird and Beckett Books, San Francisco. *The Poetry Deal* published.

2016   *Out-Takes* published.

2017   Di Prima hospitalized in October and moved to care center. She battles Parkinson disease, Sjogren's syndrome, as well as arthritis.

2019   On September 9, "Litany (for Kathy Acker)" performed at Bird and Beckett Bookstore.

2020   Di Prima dies, Sunday, October 25, in San Francisco. Series VIII of *Lost and Found*, published by the Center for the Humanities, appears featuring di Prima's "*Prometheus Unbound* as a Magickal Working," di Prima's notes to a series of lectures on Percy Bysshe Shelley.

**Conversations with
Diane di Prima**

Diane di Prima

Jeff Marvin and Mason Dixon / 1972

From *Grape*, Vancouver Community Press, March 22–29, 1972.

Diane di Prima came to Vancouver this week to do a poetry reading for the Politics and Art Symposium at UBC. The *GRAPE* recorded this interview, following the reading, at a home in Kitsilano.

Stan Persky, Maureen Seger, Steve Garrod, and several others participated in the conversation.

The poetry of Diane di Prima is like a mirror of our generation. From marching in the streets to ill-fated communal experiments in Zen meditation, Diane has paralleled our experiences, and our disappointments.

Her best-known book is probably *Revolutionary Letters*, printed in 1970 by City Lights in San Francisco, but she has been publishing since 1958.

Grape: You mentioned earlier that you've stopped reading underground papers. Why is that?

Diane: Because I find that that particular level of information just isn't giving me anything I can work with at this point. It's not interesting to me. All that's happening on that level is kind of a sick "history repeats itself" piece of nonsense, as far as I can see. In the Bay area, anyway. I really don't want to go round and round in that circle. There are ways out of it, but they aren't going to be manifested to me, anyway if I just study the surreal phenomena that are going down. I've gotta know something more about the energy gestalts behind them and how they work. I mean, it's really hard to verbalize those things.

Grape: So where do you go for information?

Diane: I go for information to things like astrology, things like . . . whatever . . . like the I Ching.

Grape: What does astrology give you?

Diane: It gives me concepts of form, a feel of energy nodes, of vortexes and how they might interact. I go for information to the I Ching. This particular shift of emphasis for me, I think it showed up in the reading, happened a couple of years ago, really. I really reached a point, an impasse in my head from where I stood and realized that in the States there was not enough coherent, cohesive grouping of people that you could count on for anything, that you could trust in any way. For it to make any sense for me to carry on so-called revolutionary activity. I didn't want to be depending on many of the folks I was seeing. I was seeing their motivation and their scaredness. So, I decided the thing to do was a kind of retreat to find out about more of the things that were going down—on some other levels.

Like, my own feeling and suspicion is there is a lot more to things like the money game than the simple, relatively simple, explanation of Marx. I think there's a lot more black magic involved in the manipulation of the planet that's been going on. And so I decided to get stronger and try to learn more things like that. (My trip of getting stronger was a lot more sitting and zazen). I disentangled my head from anger, 'cause if I was angry I was gonna get myself in a bad fix. So trying to find that all out led me into a lot of other places.

Grape: It seemed to me, reading *Revolutionary Letters*, that you had faith then in what I guess for lack of a better word we can call "counterculture."

Diane: I still do have faith in the streets and the people. But I don't have any faith at all in the movement.

Grape: In the political movement . . .

Diane: In the movement per se. From where I stood in San Francisco, they moved in and preempted a kind of a beginning, a very vulnerable opening up of people's heads. The whole trip down there is so rigid, and so boring, that I could no more care about whether a radical was mayor of Berkeley—it's like, predictably dull, and predictably closed to anything new.

Grape: Do you think other people care about those things? Are you talking just from a personalistic stance or . . .

Diane: I don't talk to too many people, so I can't tell you. I think there's a lot of apathy in the States. But a lot of that may be that people care, but people are scared. But a revolution that doesn't have room for a lot of surprises is not anything I care about. I want to be surprised sometimes.

Grape: Where's the solution, then, to getting people you can count on? My thoughts would flow in the direction of organization.

Diane: No, my thoughts don't, because I've seen that we've been at this point in America a dozen times, well, half-a-dozen times, if you want. My feeling is that we got to, there's something wrong . . . what's wrong it seems to me, is the eternal problem of—you can say "anarchism against Marxism," but that doesn't explain. What's wrong finally is that every free expression that occurs is immediately exploited. By both sides. It's just as exploited by the radical movement as it is by the establishment. And the people who happen to be making these little budding gestures for themselves, are not conscious enough, aware enough of what they're doing to be able to defend themselves.

Grape: So you feel the left is opportunist, then?

Diane: Ugly, really ugly, yeah. Down there, anyway. I don't really know about up here.

They're constantly talking about "What program can we make up to take to the people?" Shit, that's not what they should be doing. They should be finding out what people want and need right now, 'cause they know, they don't have to have any program drawn up for them. They don't need that kind of game. My next-door neighbor knows exactly what she needs.

Grape: What follows from that? That is, you're making the supposition that consciousness of the social needs is present in the population at large. What follows from that?

Diane: I think that the development of a means to get to it should also and could also come from them. But instead of providing places for people to get together and have things out themselves, they, the movement (usually a bunch of kids out of some silly university), deciding what these people need, the kids have never lived those lives. The gap is so big that it's all totally boring and nobody cares anymore about it. And apathy is on all levels.

Also, I think maybe things are really too drastic. The place we've been put into on the planet is a little too drastic by now to be dealt with by slowly organizing and getting our thing together. And I don't know any real answers, but I have some suspicions of areas in which answers might lie.

In terms of things like unpoisoning oceans, because within about twenty-five years we may be faced with very simple things like a dead Pacific Ocean. The answers don't lie in the area of what we call science, in the realm of what we've allowed, slow understanding . . . but in intuitional leaps. Hugeness. I suspect that there's a lot of information in homeopathy that could be applied to the planet, as simply as it's applied to people. If you consider the ocean as one organism. So I've been studying, and learning, and trying to get my own thing together.

Grape: Yeah, but as long as the people who are exploiting the oceans and exploiting the planet are allowed to continue, I don't see what good those explorations are going to do, because it seems ultimately you're going to run up against those people.

Diane: Yeah, except that you won't run up against anybody much when it's a question of a dead ocean. At that point you don't have to worry about anybody much because it's going to be a question of oxygen.

Grape: Okay, but a lot of people foresee this, like in the Pacific, in this area, with the shipment of oil off the coast, there's an incredible amount of social awareness, more every day, and people are voicing their frustration, but the point is they run up against Esso, who say "Yes, we're going to do this," or they run up against the US government, or whoever it happens to be. And it's entrenched power, and they're a lot less likely to see this thing coming, because it's gonna cost them money.

Diane: Yeah, people have that awareness now. I think it's going to come to such a point that not Esso, and nobody else is going to be able to hang onto it and maintain control.

Grape: In what way? I don't understand.

Diane: Well, Esso is still made up of people, and people have to breathe. Unless you really postulate, as Burroughs sometimes does quite seriously, that they're exploiting this planet with a base somewhere else . . .

Grape: It seems to me that there's two sides to the Pacific Ocean, and that what's being dumped on our side of the ocean is drastically different from what's being dumped on the Chinese side of the Pacific Ocean. That is, the Pacific Ocean is not being filled up with shit from China, the Pacific Ocean is being filled up with shit from the United States. And both literally in terms of human shit being used in China, and in terms of industrial waste. There's a clear difference, and so if you ask, well, how is it that the Chinese are so hip to that, it's not merely a folk culture that makes that possible, it's a certain form of political organization that makes that possible.

Diane: Well, you know, my hope is that we deindustrialize and decentralize to such a degree that the political organization will reach a new low, a new minimum.

Grape: What that shows to my mind is a more insulated view. Because a lot of people don't have the things that we take as extra and they really want them. Not that they want them as consumer items, but just the fact that they can, they can't . . . the average person—90% of the people in the world can't sit in a house like this and just rap. The image is always striking them that these things exist. And yet they're stopped in every way . . .

Diane: No, you see soon they won't exist, and these people will forget about them, and go back to the old way.

Grape: The point is you can't go into a refugee camp in Bangladesh or Palestine and tell the people the world's going to die in twenty-five years.

They're going to say, "Shit, I gonna die tomorrow if I don't get something to eat."

Diane: Of course. What does that relate to? How does that follow from what you're saying?

Grape: Well, I think what you were saying is, the question I'm trying to relate myself to is: I agree this is on the agenda, possibly the Pacific Ocean will die, among other things, but I'm saying how do we stop it from happening? What Stan said is that the main course of action lies in the political organization of any society—

Diane: Well, I don't agree with that . . . It was that way from the start.

Grape: That's why you take it apart. You must have a model . . .

Diane: No, see, I don't have any program. I don't have any model. I'm trying to apply my head to specific problems of the immediate future. Like, different kinds of sicknesses, these are the kinds of things we're going to have to deal with in the next twenty years. I'm not thinking in terms of social organizations, I'm not thinking in terms of models.

Grape: But I think you are thinking from a, if not a white, it's a North American perspective. There's a whole mass of people who aren't from North America to whom you can't really attribute what you're talking about because they've had little say in developing these types of problems, short of being exploited in so doing. I'm just wondering where do they come in?

I get the implication from what you're saying that it's a problem that we have to solve or else the world is doomed.

Diane: No, I have to solve the problem for me, and each person has to solve the problem. I don't think that anything we know about where they come in is going to have any relevance to where they come in. They're gonna come in when they figure out how to come in. That's your thinking, still. See, you're asking me for a social organization. I don't have any of those ideas. I don't have any kinds of plans and programs for anybody else. All I would like to do most recently is my writing to bring up a bunch of questions that I don't know the answers to. And I hope that a lot of people will poke around with the same questions.

And all I would like to do specifically with writing and in my own head is to get together as much concrete information about healing and things like that. I'm not into agriculture, so I hope someone is getting it together there, and so on. So that we can go on from here and we'll have a new thing that transcends all the old things, including all these terms we're thinking about now.

Grape: Well, if you have two societies, one that's fucked up and one that isn't, what are the characteristics of those two societies?

Diane: I don't think we can bring it down to . . . societies is like too big a thing. What are the characters of the people that control the economy. This is something that hasn't happened through a mass organization of people, but through the preempting of control by a few people. The whole development of this country was set up to let that happen.

But I foresee a heavy time with a lot of immediate problems that are going to require a lot of immediate solutions of some sort. Like there's a flu epidemic constantly in San Francisco now. And I know how to deal with that for myself and for the people who want to take what I've got. I'm importing stuff from England 'cause they have medicines that aren't available in America and so on. That's a very minor attempt. There's a lot of stuff that one gets to know about on how to get through the next twenty-five years.

Grape: It seems to me, to a certain extent, that you do have a rough model for society: tribalistic, decentralized, deindustrialized . . .

Diane: Yeah, in *Revolutionary Letters* there was that. And for a long time there was that feeling that one wanted to go back to older models. But I don't really have that now. Because most of the ways that I've watched that work in California have been totally reactionary.

Grape: Why is that?

Diane: I don't know. It's easy to blame this or that. The most facile explanation in California is the consciousness of California men is so incredibly macho and rotten. It really is. I've never met men anywhere in the country that are like that.

But that's a nice, facile expression that doesn't say why at all.

Grape: Could it be that that whole movement, that all the energies that went into it, were tainted from the very beginning? The whole leap that people made into survival was a big catastrophe, ecological collapse, we're going to survive, we're going to learn the basic needs, that that was to a certain extent a sick motivation to begin with.

Diane: Uh-huh. You think it's sick to just want to survive. I do. I never wanted to survive if the terms of it were that there were no surprises. In '67, when I went out into the country, I wound up for a while in New Mexico. And I watched people there who had years before in the early sixties dug in there.

First of all, it's not very important to survive. Nobody survives that long, anyway. It's important that—maybe it would be nice if a bunch of humans survived. But it's not important that I survive.

I used to always know that with my head, but I started to know that with my gut about a year ago, when I started thinking about writing shit that was probably gonna get me in a hassle. And then I stopped writing it. One day I had a dream in which I was getting executed with a bunch of people. It was very realistic. There had been a riot the day before, and they had gone out and taken twelve people up the street the next day and executed them for the riot. It could happen in five years in America. The only total feeling I felt about waiting to get shot was this incredible rage that I had known or suspected more about the structure of the controlling factions of the country than I had said. It was total rage that I hadn't said it for fear something would happen to me. Survival—yes, I think that's maybe a bad motivation.

But I think there is something else there, too, which is that I watched two basic forms of romantic image going down that I saw all the time. One was the staunch pioneer. The staunch pioneer walks to the campfire in the morning on the commune, right, and says, "The cows got into the corn last night." And you're supposed to know, man, that this is catastrophe, the world's gonna end. And actually you know perfectly well that they're gonna drive to the city and get a truckload of supplies for the winter, anyway.

And his woman carries her baby on her back and works in the fields. One time I was living with some kids and left to drive some other people over the border and he said, "You're taking the kids with you." I said, "No, I'm not, you guys can take care of 'em." He said, "My woman," he actually laid that on me, "MY woman takes that child with her into the fields." I said, "Far out, I don't." But that's one consciousness.

The other consciousness is the super, super, super primitive. Those guys didn't even want to go back to tribes, they wanted to go back to real cave kind of situations. Long, long, long hair tied with a shiva knot, a loincloth, eating raw vegetables and leaves, those are the two most basic romantic images that I saw that people had in the country.

There were a couple of others. Like there's the hunter—the really primeval archetype hunter type. He decides that he has to have meat every day. His whole trip is his guns, and he stalks around the commune cleaning his guns, and he goes around and shoots, and if he doesn't eat meat for a day he freaks out, and he's very lean and pointy, he has a wild look in his eye.

What I'm saying basically, is that we were all taken in by a bunch of bullshit. And we all picked up the pieces of it we liked the best, and dressed it up in our new clothes, and took it somewhere, whether it was the country or city, acted out some role that somebody had made up from some book they'd read or some movie they'd seen when we were kids. And since the people who made those up were sick in the first place, naturally they were sick jokes. Some people are caught in that.

I also think that some communes in the country in California are working their way through to something else completely. And the struggle is incredibly difficult. Because, you know, the old patterns are very set by now. And a lot of the struggle has to be done by women because of the fact that the men—there's a lot of men that want to play out the return-to-wilderness game. And the women go along because they've got some thing in their head about "He's her man, therefore she's gotta go with him."

But the women wind up really struggling and bringing it through to a new place because they can't survive—the kids can't survive.

Aside from that, I've been in two religious, and one quasi-religious commune. Tassajara, a Zen place, that has a very set practice and schedule, and an ashram in New York.

And Millbrook, where Tim Leary ran his madness for a while. That was like mostly all super-money. Super-money and weird models. It was weird because you had the sense that you had completely lost touch with reality. You just didn't know what was happening anywhere. I mean, I used to play Bob Dylan because he was the nearest thing to reality that I could get there. I always meant to write him a postcard and tell him that. But it was like, it was interesting. You know what was interesting about it? I have never before, or since, been in a situation where I had absolutely no worries. I had absolutely nothing to concern myself with. It's interesting to find out what your head does if you don't have to worry about food, clothing, shelter, the police, anything. One day you said, "I'd like to try watercolors." The next day you had a resplendent set of watercolors sitting there in your robes and jewels . . . any little whim that came into anybody's head . . . it was frightening [*laughter*]. Tim had only one rule, which was that anybody who lived there had to trip every five days. And they didn't do it all on the same day, so you never knew when the whole orientation would turn around overnight. Every morning you came down to the kitchen it was all news, you know? Somebody had just moved forever into a tree. There was one guy who for a long time said, "Human beings are meant to live in trees." And he wanted to get us all to live in trees. Things like that were happening all the time. Somebody would spend all their reentry time sitting on the counter in the kitchen and for the next five days until the next trip, he'd never leave that counter.

Most of the left in the United States is weird, elitist, and boring. It's very, very structured. It comes out of books and not out of the streets. It just doesn't see what's going on in the area I live in.

But I have the feeling that there's something going on on my block, to put it very personally, that I don't know about. You know when the Panthers began they had the Black people really behind them. Because they were out on the streets and watching arrests and doing that whole number. And now they just sort of disappeared. They've made some kind of deal, obviously. They had been off the streets for some time before they started getting wiped out. Maybe if they'd stayed in the streets, it might have been different. Maybe. They got off the streets and into their own political organization games. They started doing this whole number about . . . there was that big coalition, that five-day conference in the Bay Area that was absolute shit, and then there was a rewrite of the Constitution thing that never happened. They really convinced themselves that they were leaders of the whole left movement in America. And at that point, when they started to see themselves as leaders, they were no longer on the streets with people. As soon as that happened, apathy entered the Black community. People lost that particular thing that they were getting. A real sense of something happening for them. And by now, I'm saying, possibly deals have been made, because otherwise why are Huey Newton and Bobby Seale walking around?

Grape: I think the Yippies blew it up. They blew up the political hero to absurd ends.

Diane: No, I don't think anyone ever took them seriously in the first place. They weren't really fun, because from the beginning they were tossing people by the dozens to the wolves in terms of setting up things like kids getting mauled marching. You know that love-in in Grand Central Station? They set it up so the kids couldn't get out. Many of them were beaten up, had arms broken. And do you know what Abbie Hoffman said after that at a very small meeting they called at his house the next day? (That was way before the Chicago Convention.) He said, "Now they'll have to give us some loudspeaker trucks, they made such asses of themselves, breaking all those kids' heads." They were trading in bodies from the beginning.

There's going to be a great big fiasco in San Diego. There's something called SDCC?

Grape: That's the San Diego Coordinating Committee.

Diane: Right. Who is it?

Grape: Rennie Davis is on it. Jerry Rubin's on his way there, if he isn't there by now.

Diane: Well, it all smells.

Grape: Why?

Diane: The whole thing sounds like a put-up job to get a lot of people messed up. Even the way the literature reads, man, it sounds so . . . no real freak writes like that . . . the San Diego Coordinating Committee, for Christ's sake, call it Anemone Incorporated or something. It's very weird. All the literature I get sounds like the CIA or somebody is behind it. And you know what Tackwood said about San Diego . . . he claimed they were planning on having some prominent Republicans killed in San Diego so that Nixon could declare martial law before this election. So everybody is just blindly going ahead and setting up the demonstration. Allen Ginsberg says to me, "We have to find some really positive way to do this . . ." The most positive way to do it is to get as far away from San Diego as possible.

You know, the kids in the States are getting to be, the kids I'm seeing more and more and more weak physically and in their heads, it's the food and television, and the whole trip. The schools are ungodly. Anything I can remember about school was paradise compared to what I see. I went and taught in a brand new high school in Daly City about two weeks ago. And there were no windows, and fluorescent light, green carpet, and yellow walls. And you can only turn the lights on or off, so you either have pitch darkness, or this incredible white glare. Usually what I do when I teach a poetry workshop is I dim the lights and put on some music the kids haven't heard before. Not rock, but anything that's gonna take them out of their usual context. But you can't even dim lights. By the time they get old enough to start shooting dope in their arms, they're wasted. They haven't been given anything in their bodies that's nourishing. They haven't been given any emotional nourishment. They haven't been given any touch. I'm teaching in a grammar school and the kids all want to be held. They just want to climb in your lap. That's a poetry workshop as far as they're concerned. Sit on your lap and hug you and hold you.

Apathy and cynicism, too. They don't believe anything. Don't believe anything good is going to happen. I was sitting around Berkeley High for a few days, and it wasn't so much the case, if you can make this kind of generalization with the Third World kids. They might have been into some weird, and in some cases, very reactionary trips like purple spats and straightened hair and eight layers of makeup, but they were alive. There was a lot of vitality. But most of the white kids I saw were sitting there. There was a different kind of life energy . . . just plain force . . . missing. It was really ugly. I don't see what they're raising that whole generation for except to kill it. What use are they? These kids can't work. They haven't learned anything, they have no hope, they don't love each other and themselves. Are they raising a whole generation to kill? They're not raising them to work in the factories. I don't know, man.

Grape: The dropout rate must be increasing, though, fortunately.

Diane: Oh, tremendously, yeah.

Grape: When you speak, it's with an amplified voice, and I want to know what you're going to try to communicate to people through your poetry?

Diane: Well, let's see . . . Most of the times when I write a poem, I'm not wanting to communicate a specific entity. Like the *Revolutionary Letters*, I wrote partly because most of my other stuff was too thick to read on the streets, and I was into a lot of that stuff at that point.

The only thing I can tell people is where I'm traveling. And hope they're all traveling in some direction somewhere. Because, I think it would be good if the human race made it. I don't think there's any really creative other species happening right now.

I am trying to tell people a lot of things. Like I'm working on a long prose book right now called *Blessed Are the Meek, Baby.* And it speculates about a lot of far-out stuff. What is the energy rip-off and where does the energy go? It gets into specifics on facts I've gotten my hands on about the CIA backing Scientology, a lot of shit. I want to do a chapter on Christianity being a colonizing force that wiped out Europe.

What I want to tell people in the book, finally, is that whatever's going down, like be hip to the fact that there can be more ways out than we suspect and also be strong. Get yourselves together physically, get your heads together, find out how your body functions. Trust it. Get so you're free as much as possible, so if there's no food today, then you can say, "Okay, this is a good day to fast." And then, find out as much as you can about what people used to know. Not because we're going to go back, but because most of the real information has been taken away, by people like the AMA. Forget about the fact that you're not supposed to take things literally. Start to take things literally like myth and symbol. Just believe 'em. Try them out and see what happens.

Mainly, just get strong and get a lot of courage. Make big jumps.

Diane di Prima Interviewed in Great Falls

Anonymous / 1974

From *Borrowed Times* 2, no. 8 (January 1–14, 1974): 6–7.

Diane di Prima is a poet of the Beat generation and style. Her contemporaries—as well as friends—include Ginsberg, Rexroth, Gary Snyder, Kerouac. She is from New York. She was there when that's where it was all happening: the Beats, their kinky lifestyle, their new art, all those changes.

The *Borrowed Times* is grateful to the Montana Committee for the Humanities for bringing Diane di Prima to Montana. Thanks to Barbara Koser and the Great Falls Women's Center for arranging the November 29 interview and putting us up for the night. The two staff members who did the interview would like to thank Diane for her patience at our lack of professional expertise (she helped operate both the camera and tape recorder), and for just being a good person to spend time with on a drizzly afternoon in Great Falls.

Borrowed Times: We heard you went through quite a change in consciousness. I don't know if that is correct or not—about becoming more radicalized. I wonder if you could talk a little bit about what happened—how you feel politically now.

Diane di Prima: I don't really think I went through a real change. I think what happened was that I realized what I was doing anyway. Because you know I never really understood that was what I was writing. I never really thought of it as a political involvement. I just was living a certain life and I was reporting on it all along in my writing.

All the things were reports on this incredible poverty and ridiculousness around me. The first political poem I wrote was, "Goodbye, Nkrumah" in *Revolutionary Letters.* I heard this report, "There is dancing on the streets of

Ghana today!" Okay, and what else is new, you know. And that's where that kind of thing came from.

After the first letters were written, and the poem for my grandfather which begins it (he was an anarchist from Southern Italy), I went out west with a friend doing readings and concerts. Don't forget, '68 and everything was mixed with it. The Diggers were into the end, really, the end of the free store thing. The Digger movement had become the free city movement which was really a lot more specifically political. It was going strong in April and May of '68.

There were readings on City Hall steps every day and songs and I went. Then I went from there to LA, and the culture shock between those two cities was incredible, anyway. There was a TV in LA. I was at some Hollywood movie writer's house, and on the TV comes a program about, "Bring your industries to the Navajo reservation because we have the cheapest labor in the country."

I just left the room—it was full of people drinking. It was like "a poet has come to town and maybe she has something we can exploit for the movies" kind of evening. I went out on this little balcony and I was looking at this one tree and it was sort of like me and this tree were in it together—the whole thing. I had to take care of this tree forever. I started to cry like a kid, you know, and I hadn't cried like that for a long time.

I realized that I had always been sort of involved in this—but the thrust had been my own life. My own affairs with people, the children I wanted to have as a result, the actions I wanted to take as a result of that. I realized that the other concern couldn't really be peripheral anymore. Ever. It had to be the main thing because there was almost no time left. I really felt like time was running out for sure, you know.

That was like a sudden kind of realization. There have been other sudden realizations since.

I realized a couple of years later something that makes people feel that maybe I have abandoned the political thing. Which is that I don't want to do anything that is going to push people into a head-on confrontation with the establishment because I don't want to watch what's going to go down. I don't think they are going to hesitate to bomb the slums. I don't think they are going to hesitate to napalm their own people. Because it's not there for them. It's not their people at all.

So around '70 I kind of pulled back from pushing fast forward in political statement. I still do as much as I can along that line—like I go to Flamingo Park. When there is a specific action I can take, I'll take it, but being inflammatory for its own sake I am very very leery of.

BT: Do you feel the time is just wrong for that or . . . ?

DdP: No, I think there has to be a way to get around—an outflanking movement or something to get around the backside of it. Sure a few of us will get killed, but mainly it is those folks who don't even know what they are getting in to. I lived in the Black ghetto in San Francisco in the Fillmore for about four years and I sure don't want to be pushing people blindly into anything.

What I mean by outflanking movement isn't as vague as it sounds. I think we are starting to figure out and we have to figure out a lot more about what the forces are that are keeping the whole thing going. I don't think it's as simple as the analysis that was set up in the nineteenth century. If you look closely at Washington you see two kinds of mechanics that I have seen before. One is the thing the CIA did in Chile that they are doing here. Inflation, scarcity, all those things so the people are feeling:

"What's happening?"

"I can't find anything in the stores that I'm used to eating."

And then next, "Well, here's a strong man who will straighten it out for us."

You know, they've done that in so many countries. That's one thing I see.

The other thing I see is *what are all those guys doing there who look exactly like the faces around Hitler?* Like what game is that? We know that Von Braun was NASA, right? Oh, that's the space program. You know how attached he was to getting a space program started in Germany. I mean there's a whole mystique in this. It's not as simple as just greed. Something more involved is happening. And we speculate.

I think that we are really starting to get a sense of what the forces are, like how money is manipulated, which is a lot more complex than the analysis of Lenin or Marx. It is very complex by now. Like it would be nice to really know more about the Federal Reserve Board. Twenty people decide literally how much money is in the country. And they manipulate all those things— all these scarcities we all suspect are made up. Not that we aren't someday going to run out of oil, but that we so dramatically ran out of everything at the same moment, right now. It's a little weird.

BT: I would like to ask about your novel, *Memoirs of a Beatnik*. I really enjoyed it because I had never read any pornography written by a woman and it was really different and really enjoyable for that reason. I wondered, you are a poet, so why did you write that book and how do you feel about pornography?

DdP: I will tell you very simply, I wrote *Memoirs of a Beatnik* because we moved to the West Coast and we needed some money. I really enjoyed writing about and getting into recreating the flavor of the sixties. Like the reticence of love affairs where you didn't say too much. You could probably pick them out if you read it, but there are about seven pornographic scenes extra to the book that I wrote in later because they said to me, "You need more pornography to sell this book." Well, specifically, the scene between the girl and her brother. You can see how that is extra to the whole thrust of the thing. I enjoyed writing it. What I enjoyed doing was actually putting on those sixties records again and remembering what I was like.

About pornography, well that's an interesting subject, because like, I think there's an area in which it is really useful. I suspect that, however dumb and stupid those sex movies in San Francisco are—I haven't been to any of them—they're useful to an Ohio couple going to the movies, somehow giving them, in their heads, permission to try something a little bit different than they've ever tried before . . .

BT: Could you talk for just a moment about the controversy of art for art's sake versus political art. Your art is political, right?

DdP: Some of it—some of it is definitely not. I mean not in that immediate narrow sense of political. I have been working on a long poem for two years. It's called "Loba the She wolf."

In the broad sense, it is a political poem. Because I am exploring as much as I can from inside myself, all kinds of female consciousness, like exploring me as animal and me as goddess, but also exploring the goddess and then making the trip within myself and saying, "This is also me." That in a narrow sense is not political art.

It does eventually change events. Inevitably really great art changes people's consciousness. Everybody's consciousness. But not an immediate process like getting that crowd to go down that block and burn that building today. What I think frankly about art is that it's okay to do whatever you feel like doing, but not to pretend that you're doing something else. You don't pretend that you are setting a standard for what art should be for everybody. That's all. I wrote *Revolutionary Letters*. I wouldn't even argue if someone told me they weren't poetry. What the hell does that mean? I wrote them to do a certain job and they did it.

I am writing "Loba" to explore a whole lot of my consciousness and a whole lot of the possibilities for women right now—not in terms of social options but in terms of mythological, spiritual, psychic power that we already have. Okay, that's what I'm doing.

If somebody tells me that a poem is not going to move that crowd down the street, that's not what I am doing it for. I think you have a right pretty much, still, in whatever aims you pick for yourself, but then you have to take the consequences of being either relevant or irrelevant to the rest of the people.

BT: Is this different than in the past?

DdP: It is definitely different than even three years ago. That is what I mean by art and also the movement—whatever you want to call it—changing everybody finally.

People should have the right to feel that they are not involved at that moment in moving the crowd down the street because that might not be their moment to work on that. There are public and private moments in everyone's lives. The possible danger of the movement is if it finally demands that you make all your moments public. It happens less with women working together. Women seem to understand more that a lot of stuff is private.

There is also the fact that some artists are being used by the whole huge establishment that has set the standards for art in this country and don't even know it.

I come from New York. I have watched over the years a very specific kind of direction being given to both art and, most recently, literature. I suspect basically that it is the fine hand of Rockefeller behind the whole thing because he's pretty much behind the Museum of Modern Art, that place has set the standards for, I won't say the whole country, but definitely for the East Coast and Los Angeles, which are the two big art markets.

BT: But how does it set standards?

DdP: By who gets to show at the museums. Who gets to be shown in the museum can be sold in the galleries. Who is bought by the museum, even. People who aren't bought by the Whitney and are contemporary modern painters, can they be any good? Or if they aren't shown in one of these collective shows at the museum, are they any good? So that stuff is the only stuff that finally the big chic galleries handle. It is also the only stuff that Los Angeles handles in the County Museum, which governs its whole gallery scene.

These are the two big money places for art. What you have them buying and doing is very interesting, because it is the most non-concrete stuff you can get. The most contentless art you can find. I don't always necessarily believe it is "not good art" or that it doesn't eventually in spite of itself make interesting changes in people's consciousness. But a lot of it doesn't do anything.

I walked into the LA County Museum and there was a chrome cube sitting in the middle of an empty room. That's Robert Morris. I know Robert

Morris, you know, and his intent in his personal life is to work toward true asceticism in cutting down to sparseness of everything in a certain Zen trip. But the idea that he's being used would be absolutely obnoxious to him.

Meanwhile there is an incredible burgeoning art all over the country that nobody is seeing, nobody is buying. Like on the West Coast there are like in San Francisco visionary painters doing beautiful things that incorporate contemporary man and old alchemical symbols and a lot of psychedelic junk of the sixties in huge canvases that sometimes take two years to paint that are just mind blowing.

This stuff isn't fashionable. And it isn't fashionable, I think, partly because it has a content. It doesn't even have that strong a political content, but it moves in that direction. It moves toward a freer man.

I watched the same thing happen in the literary world later, and again they would really die if they thought they were being used. The thing was set up after we got rid of our beats. We got them all scattered all over the country so they weren't a big thing in the big cities. Then we started this thing called the New York School of Poetry.

The New York School of Poetry has some very sincere people in it and it has some quite good poets in it and the basic thing it started with was a kind of surrealism. It has moved more and more toward a gross realist poetry, you know. Like, "Oh [yawn] today I got up and watered my snake plant and now I must buy a tube of Crest." It is okay, but it's not okay to be set up as the only school of poetry happening any more than that art is the only art happening. It has effectively silenced a lot of voices.

There's a guy, Stuart Perkoff, down in Southern California who has several books of really strong street writing, really good crafted poetry, and it's got that punch of being street writing. Stuart spent five years in jail for selling grass and Stuart cannot get a book out anywhere. Anywhere. It's the same all over the scene.

I have a Black lady poet friend, Audre Lorde, in New York. Her work is stronger than the Black lady poets they are publishing who are bitter, but not warrior bitter. I published one of her books, and somebody else published one of her books. She has received large grants. It is recognized that she is a good poet, but she can't get a book out with a big publisher. And she wants to.

I guess finally it makes me pretty mad, because of what I watch happening right now near the town I am living in. The East Coast money is definitely right now in the process of buying San Francisco. That is the last stronghold for deviant art in the country.

An Interview with Diane di Prima

Bill Tremblay, Kate Mele, and Russ Derickson / 1976

From *Colorado State Review* 5, no. 1 (Spring 1977): 4–13. N.S. Reprinted by permission of Bill Tremblay.

Bill Tremblay: Is there one thing you start with when you talk poetics with young poets?

Diane di Prima: I think that at this point in history I would emphasize things that aren't usually emphasized except by a half-dozen other poets maybe and a few metaphysicians, which are things that don't deal with "the objective world" or daily life. Not that these are to be underrated, but unless the attention is constantly brought to bear on the fact that these are just one of several alphabets which are there to be read, one never gets farther than the realism which was exciting maybe in 1920, but which is kind of dull by now, as that view of the world is dull by now.

Tremblay: Are you reacting against Williams's "no ideas but in things" as a dictum which is perhaps too narrow, not suggestive enough for today's poets?

di Prima: I think "no ideas but in things" is fine. But finally we do understand that that is like one of many possible approaches. I think that in that sense, yeah, I differ with people like Ginsberg in that I don't see reportage is an end in itself. He's claimed he does, but when he gets going you can clearly hear in his poems that he doesn't; I mean, he's perfectly happy to star-travel and come back to a hard-core description of the hotel room at the end of it.

But I think that taking off from "no ideas but in things" you sooner or later come to that moment when you understand each thing and the arrangement of all things at any given moment is indeed simply something to be read. I keep coming back to the analogy of an alphabet. 'Cause finally all we deal with in poetry is the alphabet. We have our vowels and we have our consonants. One time I had a dream in which I was told that vowels are for traveling on but that consonants bound you to the Earth, but taught you "difficult variety." And in the same way, the material world or any other world you choose to use, the world of math, any world, is merely an alphabet and it does contain its consonants and its vowels, its traveling places and its difficult stoppages where the tongue is in trouble.

Tremblay: Is what you're saying similar to the Tarot deck where the Major Arcana represent the archetypes and the Minor Arcana represent the infinite variety of the phenomenal world, and the whole deck, therefore, is the varieties of ways the archetypes work through the ordinary world?

di Prima: So, like what you're saying is that you have the Major Arcana as the vowels and the Minor Arcana as the consonants—and again, an alphabet. Yes. But what I'd like to point out here is that's why there's a big interest right now in I Ching, in Tarot, in anything that teaches you to read the phenomenal world because picking our way through it, the multiplicity, is finally only useful to us in terms of our own primal unity. Finally, if you go out towards the multiplicity it becomes a unity of not "me against that" but "me and that" which is apprehended, and that's what all these different systems from these different cultures teach. I think one of the big movements in poetry is the movement toward that total apprehension by the poet of the multiplicity, so that finally there is that unity achieved in the work, and hopefully, in your life and your self.

Kate Mele: What I'm thinking about in terms of the poem is the voice in the poem, and, being one of the very few women in the workshop, I'm wondering about the difference between the masculine and the feminine voices, and whether that can be defined.

di Prima: Of course that's one of the things endlessly being debated right now everywhere. A lot of women's liberation people really don't want to admit a difference, which to me is an odd way of being liberated. It destroys again that "difficult variety" we do live in. Maybe not just a male and female voice but maybe twenty-two archetypal voices, or maybe one hundred and eight, like in some kinds of Buddhism.

I've addressed myself over the years to the question of whether there is really a different field, almost, of play in which the female writer more delights than the male. That came from starting not as a theoretical question, but looking at the works we all look at—Djuna Barnes, Virginia Woolf. There seems to me a different portion of the psyche that's being minutely described; not necessarily better, just different. I think as more women writers get published and get the courage and the skill to write clearly what they know, this will again become more the property of everyone; become common speech like the clipped speech of Hemingway or the metaphysical questions of Galway Kinnell. It seems to be dealing with what I would loosely call the dream, or what Jung relegates to the subconscious, though, once you are aware of it of course, as Robert Duncan once pointed out to me, it's no longer subconscious, it's the other-conscious. As for actually the voice which is the breath, I notice a certain shortness of breath in most women who try to read, which is actually their own apprehension and nonbelief in themselves and that's another question—one of the things in working with women in workshops is actually getting them to breathe and getting them to speak.

Insofar as we are all very messed-up physiological beings (witness Reich) and the particular problems and the particular knots we've made ourselves into are quite different for women. I mean, what you're supposed to be, which is how you form your body-image, is different, so that your actual voice, to be true, would have to express those knots and hesitancies. I think you're going to see a lot of changes in poetics as people begin to repossess their bodies and move toward a freer (I don't mean just sleeping with more kinds of people) body-self.

Russ Derickson: I read an article called "The New Narcissism" in *Harper's* which notes how much of what we're reading these days, like Castaneda, stresses the individual as isolated. The article says we experience a pang and it's because we've disregarded the social thing. Are you, in effect, preaching the individual?

di Prima: Well, if you'll pardon me, I think the *Harper's* article sounds like a load of bullshit. The only way we're going to experience the communal thing is to get back into knowing who we are. Separately. There's no social unity out there that you would like to join. We are slowly and painfully in the beginning stages of forming these possibilities, which will probably be a process of several generations. The thing that's being foisted on us as a social unity is a crumbling, superimposed piece of nonsense that we still think of as a nation. It's clear to me that it's not there as a single nation.

There can be a social unity, for individuals if we really go about forging it. Like up where Gary [Snyder] is, there's maybe forty or fifty small communes joined together for . . . mutual aid in the old Kropotkin sense, because that's the only way for animals and man and plants to survive, not "the survival of the fittest."

Tremblay: Is there a connection between what you've just said about American society and its lack of any real existence and, let's say, the differences between your *Revolutionary Letters* and your more recent *Loba* poems?

di Prima: I have to say there's always been two kinds of writing happening for me. Slowly, I hope they are coming together. There was always the more esoteric "secret language" that I wrote in and that was mine; a kind of apprehension that's reaching some kind of culmination in *Loba*, but was already present in *Calculus of Variation* and *The New Handbook of Heaven*. And then there's the work that was always more explicit. Like *Dinners & Nightmares*. It's just "laying down what was happening." I'm still writing it, there are still sections of it happening! I just shipped off four or six more "letters" to City Lights to put in their files before I lose them for when the next edition happens.

That book [*Letters*] was started specifically for use in the streets. In that sense, it's street theatre or guerrilla theatre. It started right after Martin Luther King died. Sam Abrams hired a flatbed truck and got a bunch of us poets, folk singers, some guerrilla theatre people together and we were touring the East Side with songs and poems and short skits and inflammatory material in the form of speeches and impromptu blues. I found that my stuff like "Goodbye Nkrumah" had too many outside references. People couldn't get off on them the first time they heard them. That poem, for instance, refers to Shiva and Miles's rendition of "Bye Bye Blackbird" and the fact that Buddha died by eating a mushroom. Then, the *Letters* began to come shortly because after that I was out west and was really blasted by what I was seeing out there where they had free readings out in the streets, the same as New York but a lot more theatrical. The *Letters* began specifically to use in those places and on those occasions and they just continued. I have that particular heritage of being born in an anarchist family.

Directly out of the *Letters* and the form of the work I was doing with the Diggers and the Free City People, came the point where I went away and taught in the Poets-in-the-Schools for the first time. I was also doing at that point a very lot of sitting, *zazen*, at The Zen Center. I came up against the familiar paradox that on the road in places like Wyoming, I found more human suffering among children than I'd ever seen anywhere, and at the same time found no one to blame it on, since the most unpleasant of those folks were the most suffering of those folks. The whole thing was based on alcohol and anger as far as I could see. I went home from two weeks on the road and got sick for a month. Just trying to take in the experience. And the way I took it was that my body said, "I'm going to lie flat for a while, while you think this over." And a series of dreams occurred which involved the inclusion of all these possibilities of so-called "evil" and "good" and the movement toward change, and in the last dream of the series, there was a she-wolf. She was supposed to hunt me through this labyrinth. When I decided to split and not wait to be hunted, she turned into a guardian who just followed behind me. When I turned to face her, immediately, from some really "back there" DNA place, I recognized some kind of wolf-goddess from northern Europe. She didn't figure into my poetry for fourteen, sixteen months. Then I started writing about Loba—one of those dictated poems.

So, in that sense, yeah, *Loba* moves out of the *Revolutionary Letters*, moves out of the attempt to deal, externally, with the problem of evil, or, rather, change, especially necessary change in the human species. Charles Olson, in *The Special View of History*, says that human beings gave over physical change in the evolutionary process for cultural change, some time around the Pleistocene. Now, the two have become inseparable again and so we feel vaguely threatened on every side because everything we've been for so long is undergoing a deep revolution.

Tremblay: Ginsberg once said that Reich was one of the sources of this "spontaneous bop prosody" in the sense that breaking through the body armor was like breaking through writer's block. The way to do that is just keep writing and forget about revising. Do you go along with that?

di Prima: For me, the work that counts most is revised very little and if I revise, it's simply to go back to the places where I dropped my attention. Like we're primo receivers, even in cosmic terms, and when you're really blowing as a musician of any sort—in a piece of writing, in music, in response in love-making—you're receiving and giving out without interfering thought processes. That's what I mean by total attention or staying-in-the-moment. There are times when you want to go back and say, "There is where I really lost it," and if you can bring some of the original force again, you can find how to rectify that spot. I do some revising in terms of notation, how the lines look on the page. Because I want the original rhythm to come through.

Tremblay: Do you have an overall view of where you think American poetry is or should be?

di Prima: Certain advances were made from the late forties to the early sixties on how you play with things like syntax, and how you notate the line on the page and what is possible with an open-ended sense of the poem, and of the cosmos and of society. Then, too, there's this alphabet I mentioned earlier that we're relearning. All you have to do is go back to Robert Fludd in the late sixteenth century and you see people still interested in the translation of that alphabet. Folks really lived in that apprehension of the spiritual world being as palpable as the material, not only the Jewish Cabbalists but folks all over Europe fancied themselves magi who were working in the process of creation along with God, because they were parts of the many thousands of limbs of God making the malleable stuff of creation into the stuff it was supposed to become. When you see that people really felt the spiritual world as palpable even so-called "uncultured people," then you get another view of the Dark Ages. They believed the material world was in process, transmutable, becoming something more perfect. So if you saw the alphabet and the technical advances in poetry together, then you'd have an idea of where I think American poetry should be. The changing of the concepts of what the poem could be in such things as "composition by field" that Olson talked about and that Duncan moved into other directions is still with us as possible techniques that have only been scratched on the surface. *The Maximus Poems* is only a beginning. All that is just in the beginning stage, and yet now set aside for these other urgent discoveries of reading this alphabet and immediate social change, that is, revolution, which is the urgent voice of the Black writer, the Indian writer, the Chicano writer. Both of those two more recent and urgent concerns could do well to incorporate joyously the techniques and ways of perceiving reality that were developed from the forties to sixties. I'd like to see all that come together. Plus all the information that keeps bursting upon us from the sciences, from physics and biology.

Tremblay: We here have been discussing lately the *New York Times* review by Louis Simpson of Dan Halpern's anthology where he says, in effect: "I don't know how to relate to these poets under forty because they seem to be in a state of withdrawal from the political frustrations of the early seventies; that sounds a lot like solipsism."

di Prima: Simpson doesn't know how to relate to those people, but then when I come down to talk about what's happening in writing, I don't even think about them—the people included there in that anthology. When I think of new people writing I think of Leslie Silko, Simon Ortiz, some of the West Coast street oral poetry that has no written technique to it, Chicano poets, and so on. What I'd like to point out is that both the *New York Times* and *Harper's* have a vested interest in the "closed" poem, as in the closed society, as in the closed universe, because that's the only way this crumbling economic system in this nation is possibly going to sustain itself a little longer. So Louis Simpson never gets the chance to react to anything beyond what he's shown. Don't get me wrong: there's a lot in, let's say, Jim Harrison's work that I think is very deep, but it presupposes axiomatically the existence of certain external structures that are not necessarily "the way things are." He's still working within the "closed" poem and that implies something about a sense of the closed organism, as having hard edges like the nation holding itself together at this moment. I got invited to the International Poetry Festival in Rotterdam and didn't know the names of most of the poets! They're poets all over the world writing poems that we never see. Obviously, we've been really closed off as that hard edge holding itself together has gotten more and more necessary to the maintenance of what is already an obsolete structure. I'd also like to point out that *Harper's* and the *New York Times* are going to want to print anything that will foster despair because precisely what the Establishment needs is a lethargic and totally despairing generation. And if it looks to the universities, it might find it; but if it looks to the streets, it might shit its pants. I'm not saying, "Yeah, yeah, hippies and freaks." I'm saying Chicano women learning how to write, learning how to paint, for the first time, I'm saying just ferment and people saying, "Give us what's ours!"

Tremblay: There's a lot of anger in the critical voice that upholds this stance of despair. Someone talking the way you're talking, I can hear a New York intellectual expressing disgust that you're still using terms like "the Establishment" and saying something like "Despair is the only respectable position to take and you are a pollyanna."

di Prima: It would be more accurate to call me a "dago anarchist." [*laughter*] Well . . . but if you translate "respectable" to mean "white middle-class" it is the only position to take. That particular anger is in their bodies from that stance or posture they hold themselves in, so there's nothing else they can have but despair. But I don't know if it's just New York. I think that New York still thinks it can arbitrate the tastes of the nation; like the ground-rules they lay down are the ground-rules for art all over. The "moneyed" people feel that, so a lot of pressure is brought on the New York–based media to hold that line—called the "avant-garde," or called "minimal art." I'm saying that those newspapers and magazines are the voice of that position, as the Museum of Modern Art is, which would like to pretend that there's no other art happening in America but what they show.

I saw a process go down when the New York School of Poetry was being invented, which was '68, in which, within two weeks they hit three or four levels of possible audience. There was that article on what they dared to call "white writing" in the *Times*, which they defined as writing with no particular context of content. I think they were making some simplistic assumptions about Ashbery and other folks. At the same time people that were mentioned as "white writers" were reading for free in Bryant Park, together with Mayor Lindsay. Then, a similar reading with some of the fancier names was billed as a benefit for Robert Kennedy, and was to have been emceed by a lady named Marietta Tree, who was connected with the CIA. So, at once you hit three or four different kinds of people with the fact of a particular writing occurring in New York which is "the new writing," and cast a blanket over everything else that's being written.

If you think of all the rich folks you know (this is very personal) and think of their lives, you see their despair and the inevitability of that despair. Because finally there's so much to defend, there's no way to defend it. We in America all share that to some extent. There's so much we don't want to share that finally there is nothing left but alienation. That's why we need to relearn this alphabet and get back into working within the "open" poem, an open which implies an open society, and open universe, an open body.

Diane di Prima: Poet

Ellen Zaslow and Alan Kuchek / 1976

From *Psyclone*, 1976, 10–12, 27.

Alan Kuchek and I drove up to Marshall to talk with Diane di Prima at her home, one of a short string of houses literally overlooking Tomales Bay. She met us at the door in her bathrobe—she had forgotten all about the interview. Nonplussed, she sat us down to coffee, joining us after she finished what she had been doing in the kitchen. Our initial question about her work-in-progress, *Loba*, led into talk about the writing process itself, and particularly the poetry of dictation.

> D—Diane di Prima
> E—Ellen Zaslow
> A—Alan Kucheck

D: Okay, what did you want to do? You wanted to come to the country and drink some coffee and see some birds, get some fresh air . . .

E: Maybe you could talk about *Loba*, and what you're working on now.

D: Sure. I don't really know what I'm doing but I'll be glad to talk about it. *Loba*'s about four years in the writing now, and I'm not writing it at anything like the intensity of the first two years—the first two years I didn't do anything else. What happened was that for the first two or three sections I had no projection at all. I just wrote, and although looking back I can see that certain things got developed in each section, I mean I can rationalize and say, well, this is the structure, there wasn't any planned structure. I don't usually make plans when I write. I can do whole books for three or four years that later seem like they were outlined in front. But now I more or less know what I want to do with the next part, and that's somehow a slower process.

After the "Eve" section I wrote something called "Lilith, an Interlude" that's part of *Loba* but separate—she's not exactly a portrayal of the wolf-goddess-moon. She's more about what happens when you let sex take precedence over your feelings, when you're completely based in a materialist sense of the physical. And then Part 5 wanted to be "The Seven Joys of the Virgin," taking off from a Hans Memling painting. It's not any Christian type of Mary that's ever happened before. I have the first two parts of it—they're not very joyous.

A: When did you start working on *Loba*?

D: January of '72, four years ago. "Ave," which was published with Part 1 of *Loba*, was December of '71—it happened while I was traveling. It's partly a New York take of remembering the various street women I had known over the years, you know, beautiful brilliant women who got caught up in the smack thing, or the hustling thing, or both, or just disappeared into the woodwork, or finally wound up with seven kids living in Santa Barbara on welfare, whatever. There was no intention of making it into a long thing. The first parts of *Loba* happened like dictation—they would just come. I would start hearing words, which I do a lot when I write. You get the first words down and then the next ones come.

A: Do you feel you know where it comes from?

D: At this point, when I'm first getting it?—No. It just comes in like a radio broadcast. It's a phenomenon that doesn't always happen when you write, but when it does, you have to stand ready for it, open to that possibility. Well, after two or three of these sections I began to see that they were connected, that there was this thing about the wolf-woman.

E: Does something different happen when you try to plug into a specific image or person, as in the "Canticle of St. Joan"? It has a similar tone to *Loba*, but a very different tone from, say, *Revolutionary Letters*.

D: Well, you see, *Revolutionary Letters* were deliberately written. They were designed to be guerrilla theater, street theater—that's what I was doing at first in New York. Sam Abrams had this flat-bed truck and we were taking it around up to Spanish Harlem and the East Side. And out here Peter Berg and other people were giving free readings on the steps of City Hall every day during lunch hour when the businessmen and secretaries were out. They were written as street theater because my other poems on the subject were too thick to catch in one reading—people passing by wouldn't know what you were talking about. So I wanted something direct. They're still happening from time to time. I did one recently that's dedicated to Inez Garcia, and there's a famine piece I wrote in Wyoming called "Another Wyoming Song." These weren't received as dictation in that sense, they were something I set out to do.

E: Right, well all those themes are political.

D: Yeah, but not only political. I mean "St. Joan" is political. *Loba*'s political. But they were directed to a particular tone that could be easily accessible to a large audience. I think you know that as far as I'm concerned you can do anything you want legitimately in a poem. Like, Jack Spicer felt that the only poetry worth being bothered with was the dictation. It depends on what you're after, and you can be after dozens of different things in one lifetime. But it's important not to confuse what the different things are, what they do, what they're for.

E: Did you first start writing poems by dictation?

D: I started writing when I was six, so at that point I was driven by a whole other thing, which was simply not wanting to lose the moment. Obsessed as kids are with the sadness that everything passes—I wasn't thinking about it as writing. Then somewhere around fourteen I got a much larger sense of what poetry was about because I got very much into Keats. Actually I was reading one of Somerset Maugham's novels and he quoted Keats, and I thought "Now there's a line I can relate to!" I went looking for who this Keats was and I found Keats's letters. Up until that point I'd been preoccupied with philosophy—I had discovered in the library that there were all these guys who were worrying about what was real and what wasn't, and that's what was on my mind, you know it's on every kid's mind at ten, eleven, twelve, even if most people don't get around to articulating it. So I had plowed through the entire *World as Will and Idea* by Schopenhauer, books like that. I couldn't do that now, but at twelve you have a lot more persistence. But when I found Keats, I couldn't see why anybody bothered with philosophy when there was poetry. So I spent a lot of time in those years with the letters, with Shelley, Blake, Coleridge, all the Romantics. And then that whole sense of it being dictated was also starting to come in by then, experiences of that nature. You know, those moments when everything stops and a certain voice or a certain clarity appears, which is after all what you do it for. It's not different from meditation in a sense.

E: Does it ever go away?

D: Oh, well, it goes away for periods but it always comes back. The other day in writing class someone said she used to be a writer but she hadn't written for a very long time, and I said how long, and she said seven months. So I said listen, you can let it go for up to two years! Yeah, it goes and it comes, your life has its circumstances, your whole biology too has its own rhythm, when it's open and when it's not.

E: Was there ever a time when you rejected writing?

D: No, by the time I was fourteen I knew what I was going to do, that was clear. There was one year when I wanted to write and couldn't, that was when I tried to go to college. Going to college didn't work at all. The approach was completely analytic, with Poetics and all that. There were three or four teachers who really wanted to be writers but weren't able to write—a stifling, horrible experience.

A: Were you getting any flak from your parents about writing?

D: Yeah, well it was more than writing. I brought home Nietzsche and my mother burst into tears. Also, when I was six or seven, I was separated from seeing my anarchist grandfather because they felt he was being too deep an influence on me. Before that I remember hanging out for a couple weeks at a time at my grandmother and grandfather's house in the Bronx. He used to tell me stories, parables about society. And I remember him reading Dante to me in Italian then explaining it in English, and showing me his copy and saying it had gone around the world, and me thinking this one book had been handed from window to window across apartment houses in the Bronx and that one copy had gone around the world—that's how I saw that as an event. Interestingly, I don't remember much at all about my life from age seven, when I was separated from him, to age twelve when I found Plato and Schopenhauer—and that was a general freakout in my house.

Anyway, I want to finish "Mary," in which I thought I'd correlate the "Seven Joys of the Virgin" with the seven chakras of the body, and then what I'd like to do next is a part where she turns back into a wolf and suddenly finds herself chased around the Zodiac, which could be correlated with the twelve alchemical processes as it is in a lot of old texts. But I don't know if that's going to happen or not. I know that those two things have to be dealt with at some point: the actual alchemy of transformation and the actual physical experience of opening different pieces of your body. Of course since both of these things are in process with myself, they aren't complete, so the poem also slows down, goes into slow motion to keep pace with my own involvement.

E: How does that work out when you more or less distill where you think something is going, and then what comes out isn't that at all?

D: Oh, I just always let what happens happen to a poem, that's no problem. It's more like having this momentum. I wrote a prose book once on the eight trigrams of the I Ching, but that didn't mean I was actually going to write about them—but more get the feeling, the texture of the Creative and the Receptive into the different pieces. That's all I needed for a structure. The book [*The Calculus of Variation*] took three and a half years to write—and yet things toward the end of it recapitulated things in the beginning with no outline at all, I didn't even read the damned thing over till it was done. Just piled up this great stack of papers. So I let *Loba* happen now as it happens. There's two more parts of "Mary" in this notebook that were finished earlier, but nothing on "Mary" recently because last December a very close friend and teacher died and I got involved very deeply in why and how I was so affected by his death, and then into writing about it, which was only finished last month: it has nine parts.

E: How do you know when you've finished something?

D: Well, it stops in a way that, although it may not at all be what you expect, it feels like a whole organism. This piece I just finished stopped in a place where I would have sworn you couldn't possibly stop something like that, but it became obvious that I couldn't go any further and that was it. Only thing I don't have for that is its title. I wasn't aware that I was doing this until I wrote the last five sections all at one time, but it was like I was following the soul or spirit of this dead person on its journey until I couldn't follow him any further, and that's where the poem stopped. The mishmash I made of mythology is ridiculous from a logical point of view: I went past the various Gnostic archons, past various Tibetan-type snake-headed and pig-headed goddesses and frightening buddhas. I mean I wasn't worrying about it, I was just seeing what I saw.

So it's not really planned. Sometimes you write what you need for the occasion, sometimes the poem uses you to get itself written, sometimes it's a purely personal occasion, like making a poem for a person you're with. I don't try to say only this kind is good. Maybe you can do good stuff in any of those fields, but then also there comes a point where finally good writing isn't really what you're after. I mean there are rules, let's say, by which writing can get good to a certain point. And if you follow those rules, you can make anything good. But that's kind of boring. Like when I finished that stack of a papers that was *The Calculus of Variation*, I knew exactly what I had to do to make that a work of great pyrotechnics. I could cut off this beginning, cut off all explanation of how you got to the space you're writing in, cut off certain ends and don't let things taper down but let them stop at a high point and all that. And fuck, I decided to do none of that—this was back in '64. I decided that I wanted to take people all the way in by leaving all those more obvious remarks and more clumsy parts and leaving all the awkwardness. So, you know, in that sense anyway, good writing just doesn't get to be important, I mean you know that if you do anything. I use this example in my writing workshops: I went to two photo exhibits in one month once, one was Minor White and one was Atget. And after maybe ten photographs of Minor White's, I was just bouncing off the surfaces—they were all perfect. But Atget's work, which was awkward and never perfect and full of little jerky dissonances, pulled you right in every time. I don't care if my writing is ever admired in the universities, you know, it's just got to have the urgency of where my life is at the moment, and it's got to leave those mistakes that are my mistakes, my personal mistakes, too, not just my writing mistakes, because that's how people can get into each other. And at this point I feel that's what we're all really after.

E: So you don't work to polish your stuff?

D: Well, no. I get it where I want it. I mean I do do that. I'm not into Allen Ginsberg's thing of "don't change anything," which is a lie—he changes stuff. He advises the young never to change a line, but at one time he took all the "the's" out of his collected works, then he put some of them back in—I remember that! What I mean is that the whole idea of a perfect poem or "good writing" isn't part of my projects at the moment and hasn't been for a long time.

E: Did you work on *Revolutionary Letters* a lot to get that directness?

D: A lot of them came out whole and some of them got worked on. I remember writing seven of them in one day in the Long Island Railroad, going to read at Stony Brook. I thought (this was '68 now) the people at Stony Brook need some new stuff that's never been heard before, and I sat there writing next to this man who was reading the *Wall Street Journal*, and he's reading over my shoulder and getting very upset! Now, some of the more recent ones I've done specifically to get certain information out, and in those cases it's more likely there'd be some cutting and revising. Over the last couple of years I've tried to write about how our culture as white Europeans is still being hidden from us, so that all us white folks think pitifully that we have to look to the Black people or the Chicanos or somebody else for roots instead of looking back to when Europe was a big forest full of fur-covered shamans. Which wasn't that long ago. St. Ambrose in the year 1000 cut down the holy forests in Germany, so that's not that long ago. But it's much more closed a book than the cultures of what we've been taught to consider more primitive peoples. That's what the "St. Joan" poem came out of. It was a complete dictation, I didn't have to revise that at all; it took about two hours.

E: It's really powerful.

D: Yes, it was a very powerful experience to write it. On those levels, writing for me is a question of how much charge you can carry and how long you can sustain it. It's similar again to meditation. But not that simple moment of opening up that happens to you after you've sat zazen for a couple of years; this is more like if you can get to a high place and stay there, and how long you can stay there before you have to break your attention, or before it's too much for your body. Like when you first sit a sesshin you got wobbly, you get chills and a fever because energy is trying to break through places in your body where it got stuck years ago, as Reich well knew, and has been stuck culturally for generations. Okay, so when you're taking dictation on a really powerful level and it's very condensed, the problem gets to be how long you can stay with it. All the time you're not actually writing is potentially time for building up your capacity. When I began *The Calculus of Variation* it was clearly for me an exercise in staying with, not so much dictation in that case if I can make these distinctions, but the series of images, like a movie, that's always going on in the back of your head only you're in a lighted theater so you don't see it. What I tried to do in that book was jot down the movie as it was happening without extending any of the images or trying to make logical sense, without trying to make the dream have a good ending. So at first I could only write it for ten, fifteen minutes at a time and then it would trail off into trying to make sense. Later I got so I could do it for a couple of hours. Dictation feels more like charge from the outside coming through very fast, and again it's a question of building up your capacity. For me that's what the body is, it's an instrument for receiving that kind of current. Carry as much of it as possible, as much of the time as possible. I'm not saying I'm doing this every minute, but I think of my time as potentially time for getting not only more open, but getting that kind of tensile strength that you think of a good wire as having. So, for me the practice of poetry is that.

A: So would you say that your poetry synthesizes your experience for you, that it tempers you?

D: I'm saying that you temper yourself, so you can receive more of that dictated kind of writing. As for synthesizing your experience, it starts to be part of the process at some point, but it becomes a process the same way it does in meditating. I keep going back to that. It's like at any given moment you're not with the people going into the spaces you may be writing about, and what you have of them is something other than the experience itself was. And I'm not at all into this Wordsworthian thing of "emotion recollected in tranquility"—that's what he said poetry was. What you're synthesizing isn't really the experience but the residues of the experiences. Maybe it's more whatever afterimage you have of you, you know, various egos that you want to promote in yourself at various points in your life. And what the residues of those egos are and how to strip them down to some kind of true seeing of yourself in the world, that possibly—that happens in some poems. But I think the dictated poetry is finally the most interesting. Then those residues are more like information, handles you have to apprehend with. Say the current or that radio program coming through; depending on how much information the instrument already has, that determines how many strings it has, or how many overtones it can carry. It becomes a question of not only how much you've purified the instrument but how much information you've fed it. It's not only an instrument, it is a computer too. It's like we're very fine transformers, maybe one of the best of this planet. So I see my life experience as part of what helps me interpret the current that comes in, that's all.

E: Well, it seems that kind of dictation obviates psychology.

D: Yeah, well, it adds a new twist to whatever it was you thought you understood each time. One of the main things I learned in my life was to suspend the critical/analytical person in myself while that was happening, so that I didn't censure it. So what else?

A: So how are you doing financially as a poet these days?

D: Oh—terribly! I do an occasional reading and I teach workshops at Intersection once in a while. And a few years ago I went on the road a lot and finally decided not to do that anymore. I made a lot of bread but I was never home and the kids were getting crazy and I was getting crazy. Most of the jobs were with Poetry in the Schools in places like Wyoming, which were heavy places to be. There's just so much pain around. You go into a class of third-graders and have everybody make up a planet, and one little kid makes up a planet named Dad that has belts hanging off it, and the spaceship that's near it has welts all over it, I mean that was daily life in Wyoming. So after two or three years of that I realized I couldn't do any more there.

E: Is reading your poems part of it for you, or is it an incidental thing that you might do?

D: Occasionally, very rarely, there'll be a reading that's really part of it for me. In general it's just something you do, that's all, when I'm asked to, and if I can, and if it's worth it one way or another. Where the reading is really great is right here, if a couple of friends who write are over, and the kids and the guests and I each read one poem, going around the table a few times— that's good. And I did a reading at Sonoma State a couple of years ago where lots of folks came out of the woods, and I read all of *Loba* that was written at that point, and it was the only place I read *Loba* where I didn't have to explain anything. I realized in that sense it was a local poem. When I read

Loba in New York City, I had to explain for hours what I was doing. So in a way it's like being a bard for a particular area, which makes sense.

I think Poetry in the Schools was really useful to me when I did it, because I'd never ventured into the wilds of Middle America before. On one of those trips I did seven Indian reservations in twelve days. The thing that's really ugly is the Indian boarding school thing. Kids fourth grade on up, some of them taken a couple thousand miles from home and jammed all together with completely different cultures and languages. One was on an Apache reservation, so of course the housemothers were Apache and spoke Apache, and you had kids from as far away as the Hurok reservation north of here. The running-away rate was phenomenal. When I was there I think there were six kids missing out of two hundred, and that was about average. There was one kid in my class sleeping, looking completely like parchment stretched over bones—they'd just found him the day before living in a cardboard box by the roadside somewhere. And they wouldn't send him to the infirmary, because "that's just what they want." Some kids, nine-year-olds, not just teenagers, freeze to death rather than go back. Fifty miles in any direction from that boarding school is nothing, so to hitch out of there takes a hell of a lot of guts, especially in the winter. The poems that got written were all obviously about home: "My Grandmother's Break," "The Tree Near My Hogan," that kind of thing, they were really amazing.

E: Does dictation happen just with words, or can it be images or what?

D: It's usually words. Even if it's pictures, it's usually pictures and words together, almost simultaneous. It's very rarely that it's an image that I have to translate into language.

It's different from when you're sitting zazen and it's empty. You know, I wish I could clock the physical state—it happens so fast and then it goes, you know. I wonder whether there's a change in breathing, a change in physiology when you're receiving in that way. Because I have a distinct feeling that there is a particular physical state that goes with it, as there is when you're sitting and really start getting empty, or getting into what they call an alpha state now.

I can say you get a lot more dictation happening if you're opening yourself to it every day, like if you propose to write from 8:00 'til noon every day, even if you're not writing a word, just keeping that space open for puttering and writing. Like when *Loba* started and was happening heavily it was a period in my life when I was living in San Francisco and doing a lot of work, so I had a fair amount of bread, and I was paying somebody to come in 8:30 to 1:00 every day and straighten up the house and take care of Rudi, who was a little baby. I'd just shut myself up in my room and . . . not always write—read, putter, cut out pictures, burn incense, play a record, sit—but it was my time. And stuff is more likely to come in if it knows it has space to come into. But if it's urgent enough, it doesn't matter.

E: Does the sitting help tune you, increase your capacity?

D: I think it's more like where you recharge. You could think of dictation as sleep with dreams, and sitting as sleep without dreams. Sitting gives you a lot more staying power, not only for writing though, for living too. We haven't talked about one thing I think we should, which is that what I dream is totally important to me, I mean I take a lot of my direction from what I'm told in my sleep. I accept certain kinds of dream information as literally true. Like if a dream tells you that some fine point of Egyptian mythology is this way instead of the way it was in the books, I'll always believe it above the books. Recently my dreams have pretty well been dictating what I read next.

A: Do you keep a dream journal?

D: Yes, I've tried to write down just about every dream since around '71.

E: I remember reading somewhere that some Zen roshi said that feeling the need to describe one's experience was suffering.

D: Well, I think the only thing you need to know is that you can go where it's empty, you don't need to live there. The word they translate as suffering I think I've heard better translated as unsatisfactoriness. That's really closer, I don't think that it's always active suffering. You constantly remember a perfection you never see, right? But I think the thing about sitting is that it maybe gets you more into being able to enjoy it or relish it as it is. If you can build up your ability to go to that empty place when you want to, then finally there is no suffering if you know you can split. Obviously we all have these problems where you have too much anger, or too much this or that, and you can't find that empty place, but I don't really believe that like when somebody gets totally enlightened they go away to Nirvana and never come back. Obviously what you do at that point is you keep arriving here, right, what else could you do? So like in the same way I don't think that there's anything to go away to. Just to go away for refreshment, you know, to remember where you really live.

. . . Well, I'm glad that we talked about the stuff that we talked about. I was afraid we were going to do one of those endless numbers about women and the arts: ". . . and what was your struggle like to be a woman artist?" Well, first I had to buy paper, and a pen, and nobody would sell paper to women in those days!

Interview with Diane di Prima

Anne Waldman / 1978

From *Rocky Ledge* no. 7 (February/March 1981). The interview took place in July 1978. Reprinted by permission of Anne Waldman.

Anne Waldman: How did you write *Loba*?

Diane di Prima: Well, it happened in many different ways. There was a period of time when I made time every day to write, or three days a week, sometimes, or four, and how that was for me being the mother, as I am, of five kids and so on, was to have somebody come to the house who covered doorbells, phones, and all sorts of exigencies for certain hours of certain days. This made a space. Sometimes the poem filled that space, and sometimes it didn't. Most of the time, of course, it didn't, but it was an active emptiness that things could come into. Some of the first parts of the poem happened in that manner. I wrote the Helen sequence on an airplane on the way back from a reading trip. As a matter of fact, I was in the middle of reading *The Truth and Life of Myth* by Robert Duncan and the whole Helen sequence happened to be written out in the back of that book. And then there were other parts. Twice it happened that I was in a car with someone who was talking insistently to me while I was writing the poem. And the poem kept happening. I was keeping up a conversation and writing a poem, at the same time. One was the first section of part 2, "The day lay like a pearl on her lap." I was talking to a friend who was sweetly and obliviously chatting on about some boat he was about to buy and I kept answering him and chatting at the same time. And the other is a later part where Loba recovers the memory of a mare. We had gone to the airport to pick up something, I was writing, a child was climbing all over me, and I kept writing. It seemed a continuous stream in both cases. These pieces didn't come out needing a lot of other work so it was some division of consciousness that other parts would come out very whole and very suddenly, you know, and then in between nothing would be happening. The whole Lilith section of the poem was written in one afternoon and evening, started at 2:00 in the afternoon and went until 10:00 that night and under the most ordinary household circumstances of phonograph on, the kids around, everything going on and it just kept going on. The sensation isn't different from tripping, from being on a trip of your own so that the life of the family or the body of people continues and you just stay with one thing.

AW: What about the "Annunciation"?

DdP: The "Annunciation" was written in a workshop. I gave everybody an assignment, which wasn't anything like the Annunciation problem, but while they were all busy and I had a few minutes to myself, I wrote that. I had had it in mind that it was time to begin the Mary section for some time. I often let an idea sit until the poem material starts coming through. The "Visitation" was written at Keystone Korner, in the middle of a Cecil Taylor concert.

And then the Nativity—well there is so much Christmas material in the world that I waded through thousands of very poor poems, and a lot of copying of other people's visions of that, and then one day I was very sick and hanging out at home and the Nativity came through as a kind of reliving, the first part of it at least, as a reliving of the circumstances of the birth of my daughter Jeanne. I was in one of the charity wards (I don't know what they called them in those days), of a very poor hospital and the whole experience of having insistently not used drugs to experience this birth all the way through, and then strapped to the delivery table, having a gas mask forced over my face, and somebody, you know, through all the sentimentality of Mary, and birth and all that, the horror of what it often is was the predominant thing, and then other overlays on that: the horned God-King which I think Graves's *King Jesus* talks about as a possible father of Jesus and other overlays came through that, but that's how I broke through all the Christmas nonsense.

AW: You obviously weren't discouraged by this experience to have more children.

DdP: Oh no, the having of the child was not the problem. It was the people of the hospital and so on. And there was another layer, however, an incredible beautiful layer to all of it which was in this ward the persistence and power of those very poor women who were there as well. In one case I remember one woman was being visited by a bunch of little kids, and the oldest kid couldn't have been more than eleven, and he obviously was running the household—it was a Black woman—while she was gone and she gave him instructions from the bed every day: fifty cents for beans and stuff like that and laid it out very clear, and he'd go away and do it, and just the beauty and the spirit of people more than compensated for my bad experience! But it came back at this point in the writing with its full power and rage, and I guess it had been kind of waiting its time all those years. But what I did do is, look at zillions of Nativity paintings, especially pre-Renaissance, earlier pictures.

AW: I get the feeling in some of these poems that you are possessed.

DdP: Yeah. It's almost as if the circumstances of your life are simply the catalyst which allow a particular form to possess you at the moment or something.

AW: Do you have writing rituals?

DdP: Well, I'm doing a lot of work with visualization, but I haven't done it in relation to doing a poem. It's more the material that comes through in visualization, comes through there as whatever fact and image and then cooks for a very long time. There's a process of internalization of that material so that it is truly your own, a long slow process. I imagine that everything that comes in as visualization probably eventually works into a poem just like the rest of your life does, but it's not that direct. It's like in one case with the Iseult poem, "Iseult on the Ship," it was based on a drawing by William Morris, *Iseult on the Ship*, where a woman is leaning her full weight on the mast that holds the sail, it's as if the whole power of the weightiness of the body, the weightiness of death is moving her forward. I saw the drawing, it struck me, really hit home, and then came back two or three weeks later to Berkeley and bought the book with the drawing in it, and then that just cooked and hung around for quite a while, and then one night the poem came out whole. But I didn't sit down that night to write that poem. Yes, there are periods in my life when I have writing rituals, as when I had that space three days a week or every day. And I will burn some incense, meditate for a while, put on some music—sometimes it can be the most off-the-wall stuff—that just resonates with the writing I'm working my way into. But, at a lot of other points in my life, that is sheer luxury because I have five children and I'm supporting the household, so that the poem comes when the insistence is such, when its power is such that I have to put everything else aside. It has to woo me, sometimes, instead of me wooing it. I used to worry about that years ago because I wanted to be able to write more, but I realize that somehow pieces that have a compression have a certain power to them, too, that doesn't happen until when you can't help writing them! There are occasionally days that I'll wake up with a certain feeling and just cancel a day. Sometimes I'm gracious enough to call everyone up and tell them I'm not going to work, or whatever. Sometimes I just unplug the phone, there's too much urgency. And in some of those spaces it feels often like I'm just hanging out. I'll put on a piece of music, read a piece of a book, and then something wells up and it's a physical sensation almost, and the work begins. I wrote a love story in two hours one night that way. It was just ready, and I had taken the day off, didn't really know why, but I wanted to stay with whatever the dream fragment was, probably didn't even remember what it was, or what it was like.

So a lot of the time I long for the kind of time and space where you can make that kind of thing happen, but most of the time it's not so.

AW: And yet you have a very substantial body of work.

DdP: Well, the work that has the insistency is written, and there have been periods where I have been able to do that, but not that many.

AW: Maybe you can say something about raising five children basically on your own, without a strong father figure. It's rather unusual. Also, your children are quite extraordinary and you've come through with tremendous energy and work.

DdP: Well, I think I probably arranged, I mean I know I did with the first child, but I'm realizing now as I think about it, I probably arranged to not have too strong of a father around altogether, because I didn't want the interference in my own life and in my own process. In some sense, children never were that interference because they come into the world without any particular expectation. They expect to be fed and held, but they don't have expectation about role. So you don't have to play up to someone's notion of what time dinner goes on the table. Whatever time dinner goes on the table, they'll eat it, and if they're hungry before that they learn very early to open the refrigerator. So, what happens is that given any man I've ever tried to live with there was always some particular notion of how we were going to do it, that I had to work with, or against. And I never got that kind of flak from the kids so I realize now I've probably from the beginning had a sense to avoid strong father figures, to avoid the patriarch. In the first case I simply knew I was ready to have a baby. My body was ready, and emotionally I was ready. I was twenty-three and I really wanted a child, and didn't especially want to live with a man. I was in a state from eighteen to twenty-three of relative sexual freedom. I had the lovers I wanted, male and female, and there was a kind of coming and going. No one tried to own anyone else. This was '53–'57, or thereabouts, and at that point I knew the last thing I wanted was to try to do a one-to-one relationship, so I got pregnant and I had a baby and let the dad know when the baby was about four months old. Being alone with one child was no trouble. She just went with me everywhere. When she was two, I was doing the stage-managing of the Living Theater for Jimmy Waring. She came to all the openings and all the parties and all the readings, that was no problem. The second time I had a child it was because I truly loved the man, and wanted that man's child. And so, against his will I brought a child into the world, a child that I very, very much wanted and have never for a second been sorry. But it was overwhelming to be alone with two children, in the sense I was also ill right then. In the sense that the relationship itself was overwhelming, in the sense there's a lot of repercussions in the world we both shared, the writing world in New York. So after that I married. I lived with a married man who was gay and had two children with him. The relationship was more or less matter of fact, almost a contractual relationship, and a warm friendship. He's a very erratic man, but a basically warm person. And we'd made a whole lot of things happen that we really wanted to do. We did a theater together for four or five years in New York, bought presses and began the Poets Press, moved a lot of work forward in the world, and that was one of the only times I did indeed have space to make writing rituals. I wrote a book of prose called *The Calculus of Variation* and then another one called *Spring and Autumn Annals*. I also began some religious practices at that time, meditation and so on. If I had had at that point no children, I probably would have gone off to a Zen monastery or something and a viable solution was this marriage with a gay man, where the sexuality was very seldom, and was intense when it happened, but in between I led a celibate writing life, which was exactly what I wanted and got a lot done in the arts I really cared about. And I think, moved some things forward in New York at the time, especially in theater. So that's two more of the kids, and the last of the kids, I had with a man I loved—a young poet—and we had a very tender relationship. It wasn't a very visible one as time went on and so it came easily to an end at some point for me, and so that's five kids. One of the most amazing things for me was being at the birth of my grandchild, assisting my daughter while she was in labor and beginning to understand the kind of link that that is. The kind of link between mother and daughter, and what that is that you pass on and what that is that binds you together in way of common experience and support. At one point when the baby was crowning, he was just about to be out, Jeanne suddenly had a moment of panic and said, "I can't do this!" And of course, the various folks were rushing about and doing one thing and another, but, well, it became so clear, I simply said, "Your body already knows how to do it. Just let it." And this is the information I have, finally, you know. And this is what

I pass on to a daughter, and this began for me to be a whole different understanding of what is between us—not that I didn't always know that we had childbirth in common and all that, but somehow the mother-daughter link is very interesting to me now.

Part 7 I think came out of that experience, the refusal of pain and getting reborn kind of uniqueness. Not that pain has to be our identification, but rather an ecstatic experience we share.

AW: Could you talk about that period in New York when you were running the Poets Theater and doing plays by Frank O'Hara and others? Had you worked in theater before? What inspired you?

DdP: Well, see, what happened for me was I began by being very interested in dance. I'm second-generation Italian American and my world was very restricted physically as a child. Girls didn't go out and play. When in my teens I came upon dance, it was an incredible release and it was a permitted physical activity. Up until that point I was really limited in my range of movement, I mean, I spent my life reading and doing housework. Girls were supposed to be very smart. And there was no question about college and blah blah blah and careers, and final subordination to marriage. But, girls didn't do anything physical, the streets were for boys, not girls. So dance became for me a primary kind of release of my body, even before sex or any of that. Then through dance I met James Waring, who became a teacher of mine, both as a dancer and generally in terms of how do you compose, how do you make the creative work happen. And he was working, making plays at the Living Theater on dark nights, which were Monday nights.

The Living Theater was then on 14th Street and was very active, and I began to be a stage manager and helped him do a Frank O'Hara play and some other plays back then. So I had had that experience in theater, and when we made the NY Poets Theater there was Alan Marlowe, my husband, myself, James Waring, LeRoi Jones, and a dancer named Fred Herko. We were the founders of the theater. In '61 what we had was a gallery on 10th Street. The back part of this gallery had a stage. Anyway, we did that season a piece of a book by LeRoi Jones. It was called *The System of Dante's Hell.* This was before he'd written any plays and I think it's what got him into starting to do that. He spent a lot of time watching the rehearsals, figuring out theater stuff. And we did a verse play by Michael McClure called *The Pillow*, and a play by James Waring, and one by myself, and several other pieces. Six plays that season—one-acts mostly. And then the following year we were away, and then the year after that we got a theater on the Bowery, which we kept for a year or two, where we did many plays by Frank O'Hara, Michael McClure, Wallace Stevens, an opera by David Walker, and others. We kept mostly to plays by poets and we didn't get set builders to build sets, we got the painters. We had a set by Alex Katz for a play by Jimmy Schuyler. And we used a lot of dancers and choreographers—dancers as actors and actresses, and choreographers as directors, and so on. We were thrown out of one theater for showing Jean Genet's movie *Chant D'Amour*, which led to a whole court case, where the court upheld the right of the landlady to throw us out because we were obscene.

AW: What year was this?

DdP: 1964. We moved to a theater we built ourselves in a loft in the Village on Bleecker Street. Now, in that case, we had to pretend to not be a theater because there were strict rules governing what the building would have to be like if it was a theater. So we called ourselves a club, an arts club, and issued membership cards, obeyed all the rules for clubs, which were that you had to sell your memberships otherwise than where the performances were, and keep a membership book, so that was easy. We worked there for a year. Red Grooms did a set for us there for a play by Kenneth Koch. And then we moved out from there to another theater, the one last theatre, which had a Ukrainian bar upstairs and was on E. 4th Street. We mainly did plays on the weekend, and during the week we'd have other activities. Tuesday night would always be, for instance, dance, and Wednesday movies, and Thursday music. Devotees of one thing knew when to find it there. The people only in the plays, only were working Friday, Saturdays, and Sundays. We had a lot of poetry readings, too.

AW: When were you first writing?

DdP: Well, I guess I first wrote when I was six years old. When I learned how to write I started to write. I wrote little rhyming poems. And I was moved mainly by this thing we go through as a quest even now, and the religious thing, which is the transience of everything. I was very moved by how certain events weren't going to re-occur, so I would try to write them down in my cute, little way. Then, by the time I was fourteen, or thereabouts, it really hit home. I had been reading the letters of John Keats and at that time it really hit home that I was going to be a writer and that was it, I really had to do it. And it was not an exciting, happy thing. It was really heavy and sad. I remember I stood in my family's backyard and cried about it. It seemed I was going to be outside a lot of the ordinary things of people's lives. And it was almost sentimental, I guess, but at fourteen it seemed sad in some ways, and very difficult. It had to be done, there was nothing else, no question. And from there on I began to write every day in my journal, a poem, or something—no day without writing something. And that went on steadily until I was in college. And when I was about seventeen or eighteen I had written for those three or four years all the time. And at that point experiencing an American university English department stopped me dead, and there was about a year when I hardly wrote at all. So I left college and it all came back fairly fast after that. I became, I got my own apartment in New York and began to correspond with Ezra Pound and did a lot of studying. Tried to read a little Homeric Greek, a little of Dante in Italian, just enough to get the sense of the feel of the quality of the language and the work. So between eighteen and twenty-three there were five years of a kind of apprenticeship before I had any children and I was working a lot.

AW: Do you feel yourself part of a poetic lineage? You mentioned Keats as some sort of trigger . . .

DdP: I feel very close to H.D., but when it comes down to thinking of a poetical lineage, I get stuck because I think in the terms of how people classify people in schools. I can't say I belong to a Romantic school, and yet, there is certainly some of that lineage. I mean, as much as H.D. is definitely a gut connection, almost like a mother figure for me. There's a way in which Gertrude Stein is a teacher. Not that same kind of relationship, but especially Gertrude Stein filtered through James Waring in those early days. The understanding of her meditative thing.

But I belong to a tradition that maybe is more a hermetic order within the writing thing or something, it's like a particular tradition that isn't only amongst the writers, but amongst the alchemists, and some of the revolutionaries. And the tradition I belong to is somehow the tradition of the possibility of transmutation. A hermetic tradition where magic and art come together, in some vision of what the possibility is for the human creature. I don't know how else to put it. I see that part of my tradition is Pound and Keats, part H.D., and certainly Thomas Wyatt, Christopher Marlowe perhaps. But, also, I'd have to say my tradition includes Paracelsus, moves from there to Dante, Cavalcanti, that I feel certain visionary concepts of the Sufi tradition are in my tradition. Maybe it's a visionary tradition. I see it as hermetic in the sense that it's never really emerged as a single school. Perhaps it's what Robert Duncan would call the Romantic tradition as well, other than what we've thought of it as. And that one of the main moving things for it is love, Eros is a changer, not only connecter, but changer of the human possibility, perhaps. It's hard to explain. But it jumps the lines from one discipline to another a lot.

AW: You've talked of the luminosity and light that comes through paintings and how poetry can have that light as well. Do paintings feed your own work more directly, say, than music?

DdP: There are certain qualities I constantly look for, and you could use the word light. When I use the word Eros, it's like that description Don Juan has of the gold dust of moths, the golden light in the air. In the Castaneda books there's a description of a state of mind where it's like a fine dust of light in the air. This is an actual physical state, you know, I've lived in it for a while in Marshall, California, and that kind of quality of light and art, in a visioning of the world, is what I look for. Not only the Italian, but Flemish painting has that luminosity at lot. Also some jazz. Early polyphonic music, Palestrina sometimes. So it moves from place to place. I find it in Flemish painting, but I also find it in Pollock—that light. Painfully won in Pollock, harshly come to there.

AW: You've always been intensely involved with political struggles. In fact, the struggles of all creatures. There's that wonderful poem where you talk of freeing the creatures in the zoo, freeing the turtles. Could you talk about the writing of *Revolutionary Letters*?

DdP: They began just shortly before I moved to the West Coast. The business of struggle, and revolution, is to me not separate, is not different from the seeking of light, this visioning of the world. The heart of revolution is the visioning of a transformed world, a new heaven and a new earth. And so for me, the deadening of myself would be to keep these things separate and compartmentalized. You do the work that comes to hand. Sometimes it's the poem or the visualization. Sometimes it's getting some dissident over a border. Each time it's part of the same going forward of matter into a more amazing possibility. I think I moved to the West mainly to begin freeing myself somewhat. For me the West has been the experience of my body in a very large way, the experience of a whole lot more possibilities for the form of human relationships, for families, for community. It hasn't stopped when the psychedelic so-called revolution seems to have supposedly stopped. It's still in the experimental stage for lots of folks in California. I can't say everywhere.

AW: And yet, *Revolutionary Letters* seem to reflect a kind of paranoia and urgency that many people were feeling, that a revolution was imminent, that one had to arm and protect oneself.

DdP: The *Letters* began around the early part of '68, with the poem to my grandfather that introduces the book. I wrote a couple of the letters out of sheer, real desperation, and urgency—the first few—and then realized this was a form I wanted to work in because I was involved in street readings.

AW: They're filled with instructions, you're talking very directly to people out there in the street, people that you're actually meeting.

DdP: Yes. I was writing them for the face-to-face reading-encounter on the street, and I found that all the revolutionary work I'd written before, or what seemed revolutionary work to me, relied too much on bookish references—or on Miles Davis's "Bye Bye Blackbird," for example—for people to understand and grasp at a first reading. This stuff was written as guerrilla theater, it was written for immediate use. But I don't think that the urgency is any less now, Anne, and I don't think that the sense of urgency is less. I think that it's moved from the cortex, being thought about, to a more cellular place. I think people feel pushed now more than ever. We haven't got a whole lot of time to figure out what to do about nuclear power. In fact, we may be past the time already when we have any time. It's changed form because the whole organism is involved in the urgency now instead of just something we're thinking about. And when the whole organism senses danger it moves quite softly, you know.

AW: Do you still write direct poems that don't rely on mythic references?

DdP: Well, I'm still writing revolutionary letters. There are a few in my *Selected Poems* that will go into the next edition of *Revolutionary Letters*. One around the Inez Garcia case, and one around the issue of famine, and then there's a new one that I wrote when we were trying to pass the moratorium on the nuclear power plant building in California a couple of years ago—I believe it was Proposition 15—that is a kind of prayer. The refrain is "May it continue." It's a prayer for all beings that we continue on the planet. And it's very moving because I ask the crowd usually to do the refrain, and it becomes a ritual. I ask forgiveness of the fire and the water and the air and the earth toward the end of it. These kind of poems are still happening. And they don't seem incompatible to me to the other works, the same person speaks in different voices at different times.

AW: Maybe you could say something about the public reading phenomena, in recent years, the difference it makes in your work. You've worked a lot in prisons, you've worked with ordinary folks in Wyoming. You've had a lot of different kinds of audiences and experiences. Are you writing for an audience in a reading situation?

DdP: Well, that varies. When I'm writing *Loba* I really have no thought of audience. I've never really had any notion of what the audience for that was. And then it began to clarify itself. I read one time up in a small college in northern California and all these folks came out from the surrounding communities, and communes, and towns, and a lot of women with babies arrived and the reading seemed to reach everyone. Everyone was moved and it was a magical event and no explanation of all these so-called eclectic references was needed. It wasn't needed at all, it just happened. People just heard it and received it. Whereas I find that reading *Loba* to an intellectual audience up at one of the universities in Massachusetts or something endlessly requires explanations, so, I guess my sense is that everything finds its own audience in its own way and time.

The landscape of the American West has completely informed what has happened to me in the past ten years, that's one thing, and another thing is like trying to stretch myself to understand the circumstances of people's lives so that I don't enter them as an outsider with a preformed judgment. And especially when I'm being approached by, say the only woman in a northern Wyoming town who is an artist of any sort and is doing watercolors and had been committed once or twice by her husband because she gets freaky. I can't go in there with my idea of how she should live her life. So, it's not only the work—the readings and the workshops—but what spills over because if you're a visiting artist in these places, you're kind of the local healer, shaman, psychiatrist, friend—a friend who is going away tomorrow so can be told everything. And, so, I've learned a whole lot about the circumstances of people's lives, and I've also, I think, I know, been deeply radicalized by what I've seen at the Bureau of Indian Affairs schools, and I've worked at reform schools in two states. And from what I've seen, especially of the women's reform schools, they are painfully sexist. In Wyoming, I don't know if it's true now, but two or three years ago the only job training you could get was as a beautician or a secretary. That was it! Meanwhile, of course, everywhere you go you get to see and know a little bit more of the puzzle about the rip-off of the land for uranium, for example, what's going on along those lines. Nobody knows other people's pieces, but each little place has a piece of the puzzle, which for me leads me to the idea that it's really time for a newspaper, or a bunch of newspapers around the country that are simply devoted to news. And the way we get news is by hearing from people who've seen it happen wherever they are. And my notion myself in California is that I want to do something like that that receives articles signed by folks and asking them to state their affiliation, you know, whether they are Marxist or lesbian feminist, or anarchist, cynicalist, or whatever and that's because my assumption is that news can't be unbiased. So we should state our biases closely as we understand it and sign our articles. And I'm hoping to get that started soon. And the reason I want to get that in here is, if any folks are interested in working on something like that, or a chain of newspapers like that, I want to hear from them. Because I think the most important thing we can do right now is start getting some information back and forth.

AW: Has male energy and consciousness been dominating the poetry scene or do you find you can work with that energy? Have you had trouble getting your own work published in New York for example, in a big publishing house, which are on the whole dominated by male editors?

DdP: Over the years, let's say for the first ten or fifteen years I never really realized one way or the other or cared that much about what was going on in that way. It wasn't an issue for me. It's only more recently I've come to spend any time realizing or thinking about the fact that indeed if the body of work I had done, have done, or say had been done by the time in '63 when *The New Handbook of Heaven* was out and *The Calculus of Variation* was finished had been done by any of the male writers on that scene at that point, we won't name names, who were my close friends, I think that the acknowledgment that a body of work indeed was in progress would have been much greater. But, in those days, I was just expecting trouble all around, so it never occurred to me. I just kind of grew up with a tough back-to-the-wall, ready-to-fight-anybody attitude. I can't really say why. It seems that the particular kind of head I had and the particular kind of demand I made on the world having never been fulfilled as a child and so on, made one grow up fighting. So that I didn't distinguish which of these things is happening because I'm a woman, which of these things is happening because that's just the way the world is, and there was a lot of that's just the way the world is, don't forget, in the air in the fifties, too. We all expected the worst. All of us . . . it's the Jean-Paul Sartre era. But, indeed, yes, I'm sure that a lot of stuff, a lot of like not getting published, is traceable to that. There's another thing there, which is not only am I a woman, but I'm a particular kind of woman—I'm not apologetic. I'm not sad, you know, if . . . Maybe if I was drinking a lot and writing miserable poems about some man and trying to kill myself every three years, maybe that would be okay, because, that makes guys feel okay, too, you know. But, I think it is that I've actually had the balls to enjoy myself. I'm a woman, I've enjoyed myself. My politics is ridiculous, it's not establishment politics. And, although my parents were sort of on the lower edge of the middle class, I'm definitely a street person. All my first writing was completely predicated on getting the slang of New York in the period in the early fifties down on paper somehow or another. And to this day, *Loba* may go through several worlds, but my sympathies lie with the street.

I can't really untangle what's class prejudice and what's sex prejudice and what's the natural desire of the ruling class to maintain its position. All those things are in there. I didn't even go to college. I left after a year, you know. But, so then, the question is, it's a male dominated scene, the literary scene? Yes, and women are just beginning to get a place in it and I think your generation is the first generation of women that has had access to the information that makes you a proficient writer. Don't forget, however great your visioning and your inspiration, you need the techniques of the craft, and there's nowhere, really, to get them because these are not passed on in schools. They are passed on person-to-person, and back then the male naturally passed them on to the male. I think maybe I was one of the people to break through that in having deep conversations with Charles Olson and so on. And Frank O'Hara. Robert Duncan and I are now conversing on those levels. I'm learning a lot from him these days.

What I learned from Allen Ginsberg was to have confidence in my own spontaneity, more than technical information. I'm talking about things like what's happened with the syntax, what's happened with the line, and also stuff like how do we get to the source material that will shape the new vision for the time. Have you read Nilsson's book on the primitive orders of time? That kind of stuff was passed on mainly man to man. So, this is the first time there is a really skilled generation of women writers, I think. Not only with a lot to say, but with really the tools to say it. But in my day it was still a question of women just not writing as well. And the fact was, just like with the Black children in my neighborhood in school, they were never given the tools to write well with. So, it's a mixed question. I can't say a lot of really great women writers were ignored in my time, but I can say a lot of potentially great women writers wound up dead or crazy. I think of the women on the Beat scene with me in the early fifties, where are they now? I know Barbara Moraff is a potter and does some writing in Vermont, and that's about all I know. I know some of them OD'ed and some of them got nuts, and one woman that I was running around the Village with in '53 was killed by her parents putting her in a shock treatment place in Pennsylvania, that promised your loved one back to you in three weeks cured. What the parents really wanted was the illegitimate child she had had so they could raise it without making the same mistakes they'd made with her. This was the kind of general atmosphere we were up against. I don't want to rant on about individual cases, but the threat of incarceration or early death in one form or another was very real. A friend and a writer in my crowd were threatened with jail because the parent of one of them discovered that a homosexual affair between the two women was in progress. We were all under threat of being dragged into court for that. This was daily life. I remember sitting on the steps of a house on the Lower East Side about a year after I left school and hearing the news of the death of the Rosenbergs. There was a way in which we didn't even dare reach out for too many tools. We wrote the way Virginia Woolf describes Jane Austen hiding her papers under the table-cloth. We really wanted to stay inconspicuous. Most of us. I was a brash little brat. Probably why I'm still alive!

AW: I was just going to ask you how you survived.

DdP: I bluffed a lot. I was very angry. I had enough anger to carry me through almost anything, and I learned how to use it. I was real determined to survive. I never assumed a barrier because I was a woman with anybody that I wanted to know, or any group of people I wanted to associate with. And I didn't necessarily have to associate with them sexually. They were mostly men. I merely assumed I could go where I wanted and do what I wanted.

AW: Were you nervous or self-conscious about sending poems to Ezra Pound?

DdP: A little bit, sure. And they weren't very good poems. He was very sweet about them. This was in '52. I'm sure they weren't very good poems.

AW: How did he respond?

DdP: He wrote me back, right away, and wrote they seem (underlined) to be well written, but no one was ever much use as a critic of the young generation. And that was the basis on which we went on with our correspondence. Finally I went to visit him. I find now one of the most deadening, killing, and stultifying things that is offered is homage and admiration from the young as opposed to just love and peership and friendship. Duncan once said that if you want to kill an artist, flatter him, but I think if there's no homage, there's also no hostility. Most of the poets and dancers and painters were older than I in those days, and were a lot of my survival because they were a huge protective network. I think of Franz Kline as a hovering presence protecting all of us, young writers. I think a lot of what helped me to get to the place where I could receive protection and receive the information they had to offer was the love I had for them overrode any awe I had. So it was never just a question of admiration involved. It was a real hug and a shared dinner.

AW: But do you think the poetic community now parallels that community you had in the fifties and sixties? Doesn't it seem less intimate now?

Everybody's informed even in incredibly out-of-the-way places through the network that's been built up in the last two decades of reading circuits and little magazines, and so on. Don't you think that it might be a little discouraging for a younger writer, the overkill?

DdP: Folks really have to know themselves what to do. Who else can know for them, right? No one else knew for us, but I know that many writers are discouraged because although it's easy to be published, it's not easy to get read. Nobody reads all these magazines that everybody publishes. I'm sure you have students you feel are very fine; I do. And my sense of it is they shouldn't publish. They should hang back six or eight years anyway, of good writing's worth before they bust into that and then have something really solid—get a good book together and not worry so much about the magazines. But there isn't just a small elite creating art now and that's great! It should be that everyone makes art. It should be part of daily life in every village in America as it was in every tribe everywhere. That means that at some point some fine artist in one place emerges and goes to another village and exchanges songs with fine singers there. I urge people to form workshops and situations within their own community. Start working at home.

And I think each piece of this country has its own forms for all the arts. Certainly in poetry, the middle west the poetry is different than the poetry of either coast, and the two coasts don't have that much in common really anymore. That should be a local art, and I think there should be a universal attention on the part of the artists. I mean, they should read stuff from everywhere, but the art still remains a local art. How you filter that stuff back through is yours, you know.

AW: The tribal situation was interesting. There was a place for the poet, it was completely natural. And somebody else wove cloth or made pottery and somebody else gathered food and so on. There was a functioning mandala. And somewhere along the way that broke down. Ezra Pound would blame it all on "usury." But in the last ten years there's been more of a demand for the poet. Do you think poetry is essential to life? Or is it just some kind of refinement or distillation of life that can parallel whatever else is happening?

DdP: I think the poet is the last person who is still speaking the truth when no one else dares to. I think the poet is the first person to begin the shaping and visioning of the new forms and the new consciousness when no one else has begun to sense it, so that there's both of those happening all the time. I think these are two of the most essential human functions. Pound once said, "Artists are the antennae of the race." Whether or not we have an audience, this strong visioning and shaping of a master poem informs the conscience of generations to come. And we seek very dramatically in our time how without even reaching that high plane, like Dante and Shakespeare, the work of Allen and Kerouac in the fifties and so on has informed the seventies. And in the same sense, I think that the job for us is to get the vision clear and transmit it in its purity. First off, whether or not at the moment there seems to be a place for it, because there's no question that the old must give way to the new constantly and that the visions of the new forms of consciousness are the visions of artists. That's undoubtedly true to me. And the other thing is: poets speak truth. A poet that is a liar is very spottable, and you leave very fast. Poetry is not a place where you can bluff, so that you speak directly to the hearts of people. People are hungry for that directness. It's like days of dying in the desert yearning for a glass of water, for any speech that's speech of the heart. And there's way too much speech of the brain, and there's way too much information about what's going on and not anything of the gut and not anything of the heart happening. So whatever else we do, the first thing is we reactivate the feeling, we reactivate the possibility of living a life of emotion and of the flesh, as well as of the life of the brain.

AW: What about language being sound that can trigger transformations in the body, such as the way a mantra works? Or text as illuminated manuscript, actually coming alive and imprinting on you?

DdP: . . . and the various pieces you can't even name inside you that anatomically create, like we were saying that sensation of light as they move through your body, as they move through your body/mind, all at once. The thing about language is that, and to a large extent our consciousness, the consciousness of any group or community—that consciousness is shaped by the language they speak. And as soon as it becomes a dead language, which it can, very easily and quickly, now much more quickly than in the old days, in the hands of the media. Words lose their power because they are constantly formed into new clichés. So we have the art of the word, the job of the word artists, to stay two jumps ahead of that remaking the livingness of the word, making the words come alive again. Because without the livingness of the words, there's no living of mind consciousness. That's the element we move in when we quote, "think." There's that kind of constantly making the language new, which constantly makes the human consciousness new. And right now we are fighting an incredible dead weight of newspaper, television, magazines, movies, and so on.

AW: When do you know you're a poet and what do you tell students who have a fascination with the "glamor" or whatever of the scene?

DdP: It seems to me whatever you do, if you're a healer, if you're a true Eastern meditation teacher, or if you're a poet, or if you're a prophet, there's a time when the work moves through you, when you're pulling transmission and at that time you're much more than yourself than the rest of the time. Buddha must have picked his nose, you know, so there comes that point where what's the work and what's you, and what's up for criticism, you know? I think what's really up for criticism is that a lot of folks don't want to think of that power as there at all to move through you and make this work. I mean, I've seen it move through healers, and it's very awesome. And I'm sure it moves through us in much the same way. If your poem is suddenly there, if the moment comes you write it and that's it. The same thing can happen at a reading. I've seen you experience it and I know I've experienced it where the poem again relives itself through you and moves itself through you in that way. Whereas there's no question about who's reading, or whatever the limitations of Anne Waldman's or Diane di Prima's vocabulary, or voice, or pitch, it's just there. It happens like that, and that's that. Those are extraordinary occasions. They are not our daily lives, you know, and anybody can have those extraordinary occasions, you don't have to be a poet, but you have to be willing to pay the price, put in the time, prepare the instrument so the stuff can move through. And I think all these kids who would like to be poets are, most of them don't want to put in that kind of time. I don't know. Or, a lot of them are appalled when I begin to mention the first twenty years you do such and such, and then you learn how to do so and so, and you know . . .

My Work Is My Life: An Interview
with Diane di Prima

Phyllis Stowell / 1979

From *City Miner* 4, no. 2 (1979): 18–19, 21–22.

Diane di Prima has been writing poetry for over thirty years. She has been an editor, a publisher, and a printer, and she has had many volumes of her poetry published, her most recent being Loba *(Wingbow Press, 1978).*

I first met Diane in San Francisco in the spring of 1977 when she gave a talk and reading for Diabasis, a home for the healing of schizophrenia. She has Romanesque features, a fair complexion, and thick red hair. Her voice is delicate and feminine though strong and self-assured. I noticed that she was very quick to articulate what she thinks or feels. In her talk she discussed the origin of an ongoing group of poems which she calls the "Loba" poems (Loba is a wolf). She had been ill; during the period of recovery, she dreamed of a wolf, an image which she recorded in her journal. One year later, the image reappeared in a poem.

Some of the Loba poems I consider to be very different from Diane's other work and I was intrigued by this phenomenon. She said that "when Loba comes," it comes with a particular intensity of voice, a voice that keeps returning.

Diane di Prima: The Loba poems don't happen all the time; they happen in spurts, a couple of times a year. So I write them when they happen. Poems have different voices; this is a very insistent one. It has a self that took a long time to get acknowledged. It's like a primitive self.

Although Diane told me she felt the Loba poems are a natural development of all her work, some of them, in my opinion, have a strong archetypal quality which suggests an openness to the deeper layers of the unconscious than I would have expected from her other work. I was curious about her attitude toward "Loba" and the process of writing the Loba poems. She had also said she lived "where Loba could come" and I wanted to know where or how that was. Her authority and confidence also interested me because she seemed in many ways "an outsider." She is not an academic poet and she does not lead a conventional life.

Several months after the Diabasis talk, Diane and I and two of her five children, Rudy and Tara, had lunch in a coffee shop in Berkeley. While we were eating omelets and trying not to hear the fifteenth-century counterpoint on the loudspeaker, Diane told me that she had been writing with "the consciousness that she was a poet," since she was fourteen. She talked of her parents who were "into making it" and her grandfather who was into changing it.

di Prima: I believe if I had any obstacles when I was young, it was my family. They gave a lot of lip service to how wonderful they thought I was, but they really didn't approve of the arts at all. They were first generation born in America, Italian family. My father was a lawyer, my mother a teacher. College was the most important thing in the world.

When I was at home, I was taught that everything else came first and only when you had everything else taken care of, did you write—you know, the dishes, everything in order, the money situation.

Phyllis Stowell: That could mean the writing never would begin! I recall the piece you wrote, a monologue about the dishes . . .

di Prima: "The Quarrel"—that was written in one of my early apartments.

It was only recently that I could really let the house go, and write. I tend to like to be in order anyway. These last couple years I have a real urgency about getting my own stuff done and it took a lot of being sick, physically, to teach me. I get sick if I don't write. It's not just the writing, but if I don't have time to sit, don't have time to study, I get neuritis all over my back.

Diane seems very quiet, very poised. She cultivates this by where and how she lives, and by meditation. In a steady, quiet voice she began discussing women as poets and writers. She said she felt drawn to people like Mary Shelley, Emma Goldman, etc.

di Prima: They were enormously strong, self-creating women! Their problem was to invent a whole life rather than just simply a writing technique. They had to invent a life and live it.

Stowell: Do you feel that way about your own experience?

di Prima: Yes, but I feel it's not so difficult now.

Diane attributed her independence to the relationship she had with her grandfather.

di Prima: He was an atheist and anarchist from Southern Italy. I felt very close to him. He and I were like allies against all the grownups in terms of what we did and how we did it. He wasn't allowed to listen to operas because they were bad for his heart because he got so emotional about them, so he and I would sneak off and listen to operas, and he would tell me the stories of them. I wasn't allowed to drink espresso coffee—to this day drinking espresso is a big treat because we used to drink it and hear operas, and I liked that.

He had tons of information. He showed me a copy of Dante and he said this book had gone around the world, and it was a battered old copy and I thought that particular volume—well, I was six years old—I had a picture of housewives in the Bronx leaning out of their windows and passing it down to the next apartment—so the book could go around the world.

Stowell: There seems to be a connection between him and your willingness to be on the outside.

di Prima: There really is no place else to be. Where's the inside?

Stowell: You said your family was very conventional and conservative.

di Prima: Yes, they wanted me to be a doctor or something.

Stowell: That's what I would call the inside. I'm contrasting the way you live and what you think to that.

di Prima: Finally, I had no choice because my sanity was at stake. It's not a choice I made, like I think I'll do this or I think I'll do that. I had to do what I had to do in order to remain whole. I've got no choices there. I don't feel any outsideness.

A month later I visited Diane at the house where she was then living, a frame house in Marshall. Marshall edges between Route One, a coastal two-lane highway, and Tomales Bay, a village of boatkeepers and fishermen, with a population of fifty.

The house was a shaky green structure hanging onto the bank by rotted supports and tilting with a nervous shape over the water on pilings infested with powder post beetles. Diane, with a mixture of forbearance, annoyance, and amused acceptance, showed me where the termites entered and left above the windows, windows that looked out to the gently drifting water, ducks, gulls, and, across the bay, green hills. To the right lay a small island of rock and guano. The steady motion of the water reminded me of the comment she had made at Diabasis, "I live where Loba can come to me!"

We began discussing Loba, when she told me the following dream: First she had made love to women; then she made love to a male wolf.

di Prima: The sense of it all is enormous spaciousness, spaciousness like huge deserts; then an Indian man was showing me a book about sea otters, called *Grey Waters.*

She didn't analyze the dream. Instead it was kept in her awareness to be mused about, to be included as part of her experience just as one might include having visited Muir Woods or having seen a coyote.

Our conversation floated from the dream into a discussion of the relationship she felt between the place where she lived and Indian culture. She felt, she said, that the Indian sensibility was closer to the frame of reference around her.

Besides books on Indian literature, I noticed books on mysticism, tarot, Madame Blavatsky, who, Diane said, "was the grandmother of us all." We both agreed, however, that she was almost impossible to read. In discussing her reading choices, she said, "There's no other reason to read except for my work." She had spent years reading other poets, not reading by plan but by whatever "seems to be a necessary ingredient" at the time.

She talked about her need to teach herself, a realization that followed a year at Swarthmore, during which time she was unable to write. She quit the college because she felt very stifled.

di Prima: They were rigid but at the same time didn't allow me to go deeply into anything—even on the academic level. I know my first-year English course raced through several centuries and everybody was I don't know where, but I was still reading books on Chaucer.

After leaving school, she lived with three friends and began to teach herself Greek so she could read Homer. She picked as teachers those whom she thought "were the best poets around," selecting especially Ezra Pound.

di Prima: I corresponded with him and visited him in the madhouse. I worked with his ideas—the precise word, precise description, eliminating the extra word.

She used Pound's ABC of Reading *as a guide. During this period she shared a house with another writer, a dancer, and a painter.*

During these years she cared for her children, supported herself and responded to her need to write. The difficulties of doing this in her own way instead of a more conventional style, were evidently natural and necessary conditions of her life.

di Prima: My work is my work.

She might just as energetically have added: My life is my life.

I asked her about periods of change in her work. Besides the beginning of the Loba poems, she mentioned several other dramatic changes that occurred around 1959 and 1960. There was, she said, an opening up that reflected a change from her earlier style. Three things happened:

di Prima: I first took peyote; I began to study under James Waring, a choreographer for the Living Theater; and I fell in love.

There's a point where the poems just suddenly, completely change. It's like accepting this other layer of being when I don't shape the poem, control the lines, shape my life. It's not that I'm at the beck and call of every wind that blows, but that suddenly the area that I know about myself and the area that I know about the poem, both, seem to be very small. It's like a recognition of the certain inevitability of the shape of my life and the shape of things that happen to me.

Stowell: Which you don't control?

di Prima: Which I don't control, which I never did control. The early poems have a controlled line. But then what happens is like recognizing the inevitable shape of what's happening. In one sense, you're spinning it out of your head but in another sense you're completely at its mercy.

When I ate peyote, I found other levels in my head. Later I wanted to get to the same places without the peyote.

We discussed peyote, mysticism, and the interaction of "other levels" with poetry. We discussed women with psychic powers and how frightening this can be to some of them.

di Prima: There's the question of how you're used and how you allow yourself to be used and when you should allow yourself to be used as a medium. Of course, you are a medium if you write a poem.

James Waring, the choreographer, was also important for her growth as a poet at this time.

di Prima: Jimmy taught techniques of turning off the critic in your head. We did moving pieces and sound pieces. We learned a lot of random techniques. He was teaching us to work spontaneously and trust what you, Phyllis, would call the unconscious, I guess. I remember one lesson he gave—we all came to the Living Theater for our class and Jimmy said, "Tonight we're going to talk about form. Everything has a form." That's all he said. We sat and sat and waited and waited. And we got up and went away and I was really looking. I was suddenly aware I didn't have to make form and force a piece into it. Now Pound never says make a form and force a piece into it. It wasn't at odds with everything I'd been learning but it was additional.

We don't have any real rules about how a poem is supposed to work. You wouldn't know from talking to some people though. One teacher used to tell people in her writing class that they shouldn't use the word "I" but that's clearly just cheating because you're still going to write about yourself until you transcend "I" anyway. You're not transcending it by leaving out the word "I." It's deceiving yourself and trying to trick your audience. When you have people who are just beginning to write, what's the good of telling them to leave out "I"? You know you can't. I mean what they are completely engaged in is writing their emotions, or what they consider is theirs, what they think they own.

Stowell: Do you think they eventually transcend it?

di Prima: I think you do it until it doesn't happen anymore. I think it reaches a point where if you're writing a lot or if you're practicing anything steadily, whether it's art or meditation or whatever, you begin to see yourself against the background of the whole human tapestry and then more and more, you fade into it. But I don't think it is a thing that can be legislated.

Stowell: Then form, as you see it, is whatever feels right, like the fit of a shoe?

di Prima: I think you can't just decide anything at all except that you are going to stay open to seeing what happens. You probably have a pretty good instinct as to whether or not the thing works and whether or not you're being honest. You can work with your ear. You can work with sound and rhythm.

Those who are beginning need to write first and for a few years. When they feel a little confidence about being able to reach the places where the work comes from for them, then they can start working on technique. I've seen too many damaged people who wanted to write but got a teacher right away who began to tell them how to write it. I think the problem, especially in our culture, is getting to the place where the thing happens. If they can get to that place often enough so they know the pathways for themselves, so they feel confident those doors aren't going to slam shut eternally (You know how people who have even been writing for a long time say, "My God! I haven't written in three months! I guess I'm never going to write again!") if they get the confidence that all the doors always open again and you know how to find your way there, then it's time to start working on technique. Also until you've done that a whole lot, in whatever blundering way, you have no idea what your particular context is. You have a whole nexus of image and emotional complexity that's only yours. You have to make acquaintance with that. It's like playing solitaire; there are only certain images that are really yours. You juxtapose them in different patterns, patternings, as you work with your particular life, shaping (individuating or whatever you want to call it) as you make your own mandala.

Stowell: You mentioned the experience of falling in love was the third event that affected your poetry.

di Prima: It was never a happy "ho ho ho" experience. From the first love poem I wrote about it and the first time we spent together, the sense of it was that it was going to be very hard—not tragic especially—but difficult.

Stowell: Painful?

di Prima: Painful, and a forced series of recognitions. You get picked up by the scruff of your neck by things that say: "Okay, now you've played awhile, now get down to looking more at who you really are." It was like that kind of calling out of your original face and your innate nature.

Stowell: Were you conscious at the time, though, of what you just said about it?

di Prima: I was conscious of a sense of recognition. There was no surprise. It was, "Oh, now this starts"—which was pending forever. It wasn't pending for a few weeks or months, it was a recognition of something that was pending from the very beginning.

Stowell: Did you fight it?

di Prima: For about twenty minutes. I said, "Look, this is going to be very difficult. I mean, this isn't going to be fun." [The man is a Black poet who was married at the time—P.S.]

Stowell: Some people I think would walk away.

di Prima: I don't think people value the wholeness of their sanity very much if they can walk away from all those things because what else is there but to fill out your whole shape?

One of the reasons Diane eventually left this relationship was that she found she no longer had the resources to maintain it. This led to another change. She said her body told her that for her survival, she needed to go away.

di Prima: Survival information can come in a dream. It can also come to me in my body. I just get sick. Or it can just be a signal that just bursts out from my subconscious level: I can't do it this way anymore. I have to go another way.

When I left New York, it was because the only way to live there comfortably would have been to become a social figure. A poet as a social figure is one who is invited to the right evenings and the right dinners and all that. Some people, I think, write because they want those things. I tend not to enjoy it. I don't like the public that much. I don't mind meeting the public sometimes, but it's got to be pretty well on my terms and not on anybody else's.

Diane told me she had five children with four different men and raised them, for the most part, alone, though she was married twice. I asked her if a lot of her stresses were economic—as a result of being a poet and a woman with five children.

di Prima: I'm rich or I'm poor. It's a constant juggling act.

Stowell: How does it affect your poetry when your financial position gets risky?

di Prima: That doesn't make it harder to write. Right now, in my present financial situation, I could go on here forever because I'm working and there's the bay and there's the ocean and I can run, and we don't care very much what we live on in the way of food and all that. Brown rice is our favorite food. But there's a level where it's beginning to take a little more time than I like to keep the refrigerator and hot water heater running, and all that junk. The people who are buying this place have no money, so they're not going to fix it. It's going to fall into the bay.

Stowell: I guess the romantic idea that the poet enjoys suffering and needs to be—

di Prima: I don't think that's a romantic idea. It's just like the idea that women enjoy being subjugated, that the artist enjoys suffering. I don't think it's a romantic idea at all!

Stowell: Do you think you've written just as much poetry that's valuable out of feeling good and being—

di Prima: I think finally I can write very valuable stuff out of a classically feeling good place. I think that I have to report on, of course, what's going on in the way of struggle but that the writing, finally, is valuable as writing when it reports on breaking through that or being beyond it in some way. I don't think struggle is the most interesting thing in the world.

Stowell: Can you define what writing does for you or what role it plays in your life?

di Prima: No. My work is my life. It's not a separate piece.

Interview with Diane di Prima

Raul Santiago Sebazco / 1982

From *New Blood* 6 (April 1982): 27–29, 104–9.

Diane di Prima: The earliest episode I can think of was when I was four years old. My grandfather, an anarchist on my mother's side, and I found ourselves one night in this park in the Bronx. We had sneaked out without the rest of the family knowing because he was going to make a political speech to the people in the park. I don't know if it was a scheduled rally or whether he was just going to talk to the people who were around. Anyway, I was so small I wouldn't have known the difference. All I remember was he was talking about love—how if we don't all love each other we are all going to die. Everyone will die if we don't learn to love. To me he was very tall. He was taller than most of the Italians I knew at the time. He had very white hair and blue eyes, burning blue eyes. He was an old anarchist and had been a friend of Emma Goldman, and as well, a friend of Carlo Tresca before he got killed by the Mafia. So I went with him to this park, and I am listening to him make a speech about love and above the stars were shining. You never went out when you were a child back then, they didn't let you. I remember I idly pulled some leaves off a tree. He then came up to me, pulled my hair, saying, "That's what it feels like when you do that to the tree. That's what the tree feels like." Also, another time he told me, "When you get older you're going to look at the sky and you're going to wonder how everything got here, and then you will study like I studied, and you'll suffer like I suffered— and at the end you'll have nothing." I remember I felt very sorry for him, and I wanted to tell him to be happy, that I was going to be okay! And he showed me a copy of Dante. It was very worn out. He said that it had travelled all around the world, and in my mind I saw the housewives in the Bronx leaning out of these tall buildings, and passing it to the next window. This one copy had gone around the world that way.

Raul Santiago Sebazco: What year was this?

DdP: This was in 1938. Another incident very vivid is my eleventh birthday, which was also Hiroshima day. We were all waiting for my father to come home so we could have our candy and cake. We didn't know anything about what had happened. In my family we never talked about the war, because half the family lived in Italy and half lived in America. We never listened to the news. So, this night my father comes home late, and we have our party hats on. He throws the paper on the table and we see a very big headline on it. He was a very bitter, conservative man who never said anything against the government or against anything. He had his own ideas, but he was very frightened. He throws the paper down in the midst of this supposed party and says, "We lost today!" And everyone gets up, "We lost the war, how can that be?! We were winning!" He said, "Whatever we do now, we already lost!" That was my eleventh birthday. That was 1945.

Another incident I remember previous to that was just before the war came to America. I remember going down to the docks in New York to see my grandfather's brother and his whole part of the tribe, who were going to get on a boat to go back to Italy for World War II, and my other grandfather and his part of the tribe decided to stay in America. I was so young and the boat was so big that I was sure that by the time it left New York the other side would already be touching Italy. That's how big it looked to me.

RSS: After the bomb, do you think a lot of people realized what it was that happened?

DdP: I think at that point a few did. I think it took a couple of years to really begin to realize the immorality, the wrongness of having killed these people in this way. We had lost—and we had lost morally. It would take a few years for this to be felt. Also, other effects would unfold in the next few years following.

In 1948 I began to be involved with a group of people in my high school in telepathy, healing, and séances to talk to the dead. We were interested in talking to the Romantic poets—Keats and Shelley especially. The group was composed of eight women who were going to high school together. We would gather in my room in Brooklyn. It was a brownstone with shiny clean linoleum floors. It was my mother's Italian house that my childhood friends were always welcomed to. After family supper we would all go upstairs and shut the door—and all of a suddenly it was another world, telepathy, séances, Italian opera, mysticism, Nietzsche, Schopenhauer, and doing this healing work. We had quill pens to write things down with, we had crystal ink wells, and in the dark would materialize these glowing forms . . . through them we'd have mental conversations with Keats and Shelley.

RSS: I heard around 1948 there was a powerful psychic changeover.

DdP: Yes, well that's what they do say. Astrologers say that, and for me that's true. It was in '48 that I began to meet this group of people while I was in my second year of high school. Also, '48 was the year I accepted the idea that I was going to be a poet. That was a very important step. I was standing in the backyard one day and I had been reading Keats's letters for days. I looked up at the sky and all of a sudden I realized that I had to be a poet in the same serious way that this person was one. Also in the same moment I realized everything I had to give up to do it, and that made me begin to cry. I realized the, how can I say it, that this would remove me from regular human life.

RSS: What did you consider regular human life?

DdP: The way it was regularly lived by the people I mostly knew. This made me very sad because I thought of all the difficulties and all the things I couldn't have. But at the same time it was very exciting. I wrote a poem about it right there.

RSS: Do you have the poem?

DdP: I doubt it.

RSS: How old were you?

DdP: I was fourteen. After that I began the psychic healing group. Then came college, and there was nothing interesting there. I couldn't write there. I wasn't learning anything. . . . So in Christmas of '52 I decided to split, and this girl named Lori, whom I was in love with, helped me decide. She was in love with my best friend Joan O'Malley, who is mentioned in *Spring and Autumn Annals*. She is also in *Memoirs of a Beatnik* under the name O'Reilly. So, it's Christmas time and I am in a gay bar named Arthur's Tavern, which is still there. . . . We are sitting at a table together, and by this time they both had dropped out of school. They tell me they wanted to get an apartment in the city but they were afraid to do it alone, and they wanted me to come too. They wanted me to be a part of it. So, I made the commitment to leave school and take this apartment with these two friends and accept our gay triangle relationship. I just turned eighteen.

RSS: What did your parents say?

DdP: Well, I came back home with O'Malley and in the same room that we used to have our séances and psychic readings, I packed my stuff. I sent her my things down the back way. I then went downstairs to the living room and told my parents that I was not going back to school and that I was getting my own apartment. There was this whole Italian scene. My father throws me on the floor at my mother's feet and yells I am breaking my mother's heart and destroying everybody's life. . . . Meanwhile, O'Malley is waiting for me in the Village with my possessions. Later we met at this crazy busy gay women's bar, the Swing Rendezvous, which doesn't exist anymore. It used to be on MacDougal Street. When I walked in, the bar was full of people and music. Joni James was on the jukebox, a lot of Dinah Washington, rhythm and blues records and people dancing the twist and all these dykes with their hair slicked back wearing white men's shirts and jeans.

RSS: The twist in '52?

DdP: Oh, wait, it was called the fish. It was an earlier version of the twist. It was slower but the same dance. You put your knee up into the other person's crotch and you rubbed. It was like for slow rhythm and blues, like Nat King Cole singing "Lush Life," that kind of music. We ended up sleeping in the hallway that week because we had no place to go. Finally, these two people never joined me. Lori's mother was a very powerful international lawyer and threatened us with a mental hospital for being gay, unless we left her daughter alone. In those days between eighteen and twenty-one you had no rights at all. You weren't a minor and you weren't a grownup. Lori, though, had this psychological attachment to her mother. Eventually, she went back to her family home and went back to school. So I found myself eighteen years old on the Lower East Side with an apartment—521 East 5th Street, Apt. 4C was my home and I paid forty-five dollars a month. There I had my first love affairs. It was February '53. In those days there was no scene or freaks on the Lower East Side, just Polish and Jewish housewives. It was very, very straight lower class. But anyway, I lived there and wrote poems. I had a full-time job and I gave a lot of my money to Lori, who was back at school.

After I got my place nothing much was happening. I worked in an office downtown and then got a part-time job in an electronics laboratory at Columbia. I was taking classes all over town. I didn't care whether I got a degree. I was studying what I wanted to learn. I studied ancient Greek at Hunter, math at Brooklyn College. I remember one night while I was going to class I heard on the radio the news that Dylan Thomas had died. I cut my classes and I sat on the grass at Brooklyn College and looked up at the night sky. It was the first moment since I had left school, which had been eight months earlier, that I just completely stopped to think. By the next day I got sick. Dylan Thomas used to hang out at the White Horse Tavern and I had seen him in passing a few times, but I had never talked to him. I used to listen to his records all the time. They were an important soundtrack to the fifties. His death was like a stop-action moment for me. There I was pushing so hard, studying, working a full-time job, writing—and then death, mortality. He was only thirty-nine.

I would go to dance classes almost every night. I took ballet for years. I would study piano. I would go to Village coffee shops that were just opening, especially one called Rienzi's. It was on MacDougal Street. The coffee shop scene included a lot of folk singers that hung out in Washington Square Park, like a guy called Eric Darling who later became famous on the banjo; also the guy I had an affair with who is mentioned in *Memoirs of a Beatnik* called Johnny Gavin. He never made it, but he was a beautiful singer and person. Folk song was the protest song, and this was before the Gaslight and Dylan. There were at that time a couple of places for folk song, but most of it was being down in the park. A lot of the information was exchanged in the park, like how to do this riff and that riff, how to play this song and how to play that. In '53 I was also hanging out with the jazz scene. Most of the people I was hanging out with were musicians, jazz artists, folk singers, not too many writers, a lot of painters. There was a café called Montmartre. Sometimes there was calypso, sometimes there was jazz, and we would go there and hang out. There was a period between '53 and '54 that I was into making it with everybody. I would just go to the bar and go home with somebody. Sometimes I'd go back to the bar and make it with somebody else the same night. I was experimenting, finding out what was going on, checking out everybody's pad, their scene, their whole universe.

I already had met Freddie Herko and I knew the dance scene. I met Bret Rohmer and I became interested in the painters' scene at the Art Students' League. O'Malley and I are by then living in the front. Bret Rohmer, the painter, Freddie Herko, the dancer, are living there, and later Ben Carruthers, the actor, and the whole Actors' Studio scene came in. You see how it all centered on schools. There was, who did you study with at Art Students' League? Did you go to Ballet Theater? Or study with Anthony Tudor? Or, were you doing modern à la Graham tradition or the Hania Holmes tradition? At that point it was very school-oriented. Only later did it begin to break up. That was '55.

I started modeling in '54 for Raphael Soyer. I had just gotten sick of those full-time jobs and I realized I could make enough money modeling. I met Raphael Soyer, Moses Soyer, and that whole tribe. Between '55 and '57 they were working in a building called the Lincoln Arcade that was in the sixties in the West Side. The buildings were later torn down for Lincoln Center. All this is in one section of my book *The Calculus of Variation*. It describes the different painters and their studios.

One incident that happened to me by chance and was very important was when one day I was walking down the street looking for a job and a car packed with people stopped alongside of me on the sidewalk. The driver of the car said, "Hey, you want to go to the country for the weekend?" I thought about it for a second and sure, "Sure, why not!" I climbed in with my office clothes and high-heeled shoes. A little while later I found myself in the country with campfires, people sleeping out and a whole hill covered with folk. It was almost like a be-in, except there was no acid or pot. All these people had been invited by Jimmy Gavin's father, who was a friend of Pete Seeger and these socialists. All these young Village people came up for the weekend and were all covering the hillside—campfires, fucking, beer, and folk songs. After the end of the weekend I decided to stay. I immediately sawed off the heels of my high-heeled city shoes so that I would be more comfortable. This incident was important because it was for me the first be-in, the first gathering of people under the sky. Country people did this all the time, but they called it a hootenanny.

RSS: How did you meet Pound?

DdP: Well, in '55 I had already been corresponding with him. When I dropped out of school, one of the things I did was take his *ABC of Reading*, which tells you what to study to find out what already was going on in poetry. I began studying what he was saying in the book and following his directions. I taught myself a little Greek, just enough to read a little bit of Homer and get the feeling of the sound. I read things in Latin, things in Italian. I did the whole thing in his *ABC of Reading*. Meanwhile, I was writing poems. So finally I sent him a couple of poems in a letter. He was in the madhouse in Washington, DC, at that point. I don't have any of his notes anymore. I had sold them years ago when I was broke. He wrote back about my poems. Then he wrote a couple of more times and told me if I wanted to I could visit him. So O'Malley and I saved twenty-five dollars, which was a lot of money then, and got on a bus to Washington, DC. We already knew Sheri Martinelli, who was Pound's mistress of sorts. She was a painter and she had been gay at one point; also I believe she had been a junkie. We stayed at her house, where she was living with a Chinese modern classical composer named Gilbert Lee, who Pound decided should take care of her and marry her. Amongst the Poundians, Pound is telling everyone, "You take care of this one, you marry that one's who's pregnant, you go through the Library of Congress and copy down all the music of Thomas Campion, because it's going to be lost if we don't publish it. Yes, I want you to pursue how this happened in the Middle Ages." He told me to get all these things on the media. He wanted to get all sorts of things on television, things I couldn't possibly do in 1955 because I didn't have any contacts. He had this confidence that we could do anything. He was directing his little band of followers to be active. I remember when I first visited Pound there was this big kind of day room for all the mad people. Off to the side there was this little alcove where Dorothy Pound is cutting cake and serving tea as if it were somebody's living room. Pound is looking gorgeous in shorts, he had muscular legs and he was looking healthy and handsome. It was about springtime. Pound greets us, kisses our hand, bows, a very Victorian gentleman. We, the mistress is there, the wife is there, the tea is there, and meanwhile as we are having this cultured conversation these madmen are literally dribbling by as Pound tells us anecdotes and encourages us in our work. We stayed about a week and visited him every day.

RSS: Wasn't it "un-American" or politically suspicious to be visiting a figure such as Pound?

DdP: Well, there was nothing particularly in our lives that was American. The only thing was that we were being very quiet about it, not about Pound, but our un-American-ness. Everybody was totally paranoid at that time. I remember the day the Rosenbergs were executed. I was sitting on this stoop on 12th Street. It was one of those moments of being completely stunned. It was suddenly a real sense, a real paranoia that political assassination was part of daily life. I also remember the day Wilhelm Reich died in prison. Between the Rosenbergs' death, which was '53, and Reich's, which was '57, in that whole period, there was a prevailing sense that being there was nothing we could do about it, that we were very much in the minority, we better keep our opinions to ourselves and be very, very careful.

RSS: McCarthyism?

DdP: McCarthyism and just about everything else. I think that whatever energies and hopes were generated after the end of World War II were completely cut off by the Korean War and did not return for that period at all—at least in my circles.

Somewhere along the line, I made an important decision. I decided to have a baby. I didn't want to live with any man. I didn't want a one-to-one relationship, but my body wanted a baby. I was twenty-two. I asked Freddie Herko if he wanted a baby; he didn't want a baby. He was my first choice. I had six or seven lovers, and what happened then was I made a semiconscious choice. The man I chose was a man I had been in love with six years before. He was in town only occasionally, and studying at Johns Hopkins at

the time. He was still an exciting person to me. I didn't intend to get preg-
nant that day, but I did. I didn't tell him I was pregnant until the baby was
three months old. I then wrote him a Christmas card that said, "By the way
you have a daughter in New York, come and see us some time." We were all
into being very cool back then, you know.

RSS: That is cool! [*laughter*] The concept, "cool," what did that actually
mean?

DdP: Well, cool was when you understood your feelings.

RSS: Then, to be cool was to be frigid?

DdP: No, no, not to be frigid. You had a lot of feeling but you just didn't
state it, and nobody stated theirs. Thus you built up this tension of all the
unstated. It wasn't anger, but a web of interplay. Things that you would say
full out now, would then be stated in a small gesture. A little phrase or act
would say the whole thing.

RSS: Why?

DdP: Why what?

RSS: Why did cool come about?

DdP: Oh, why? Good question. I don't know! [*laughter*] I guess it was
the fashion. It was, though, a reaction to the oversentimentality of the gen-
eration of our parents—the soap operas, Frank Sinatra, the blah, blah, blah
feelings. So the jazz was cool, we were cool, everybody was cool. And, if
you were cool that meant that you gave everybody more space, sort of, but
come to think of it, you didn't really—because no one knew for sure where
they stood, so finally they didn't have any space at all. We just thought we
were giving each other more space. For example, Roi [Amiri Baraka] and I
were together for three years, and I think we used the word "love" only once
or twice. You see, there was a depth of passion to the not stating it that was
very intense.

RSS: How did you come upon the writing and the writers that about that
time were about to happen?

DdP: Well, a friend brought *Howl* when it came out. It wasn't yet in New
York. He had brought it out from the West Coast. I remember I was cook-
ing and someone handed it to me and I started reading. I had to give the
spoon to somebody else to stir the soup. I got so excited that I went out-
side and walked for blocks. I was laughing and crying throughout. Here was
somebody doing what I was doing, in that they were using the slang of the
streets. Previously, I felt so isolated doing my kind of writing. There were
people speaking that slang talk all around me at jam sessions and cafes, but
my friends kept telling me that in ten years no one would understand my

writing because the slang would change. Then appeared Allen's book, and here was somebody doing this and getting it out. The next day I went down to the 8th Street Bookstore and said I wanted to buy *Howl* by Allen Ginsberg. They said, "What by whom?" They told me they never had heard of it. I said, "Well, you're going to hear of it again. I think you better get some copies." It was 1956.

Interview with Diane di Prima

Mary Zeppa / 1985

From *Poet News* (May 1985): 1, 5–6, 8. Reprinted by permission of Mary Zeppa.

Diane di Prima has been writing and publishing poetry, first on the East Coast then on the West, for thirty years. She has more than twenty books to her credit, among them *Dinners and Nightmares, The New Handbook of Heaven, Seven Love Poems from the Middle Latin, Memoirs of a Beatnik,* and *Loba.*

Di Prima has also run both Poets Press and the New York Poets Theater and edited (with LeRoi Jones—Amiri Baraka) *The Floating Bear: A Newsletter.* Currently, she teaches at both the San Francisco Institute of Magical and Healing Arts and the New College of California.

This interview is the result of a wonderful and wide-ranging telephone conversation. I hope you enjoy it as much as we did.

Mary Zeppa: You've been writing a long time and you've been publishing a long time. How do you feel about all the things you have in print? Are you ever sorry you published so much?

Diane di Prima: No, no. I like everything I've done. I like the stuff from the fifties. I like it as much as what I'm doing now—in its own way. I did a reading about three or four years ago where I did fifties stuff and then sixties stuff and then we took a break (I did a four-hour reading) and I changed clothes and then did seventies and eighties stuff.

It was very nice for me and people loved it. It revealed to me something of the underlying unity that we have, that anyone has. Essentially what you're after is the same stuff you were after when you were young. It's just you have different tools and different experiences that enrich how you say it. Our essence is something we come into the world with and what we try to do is probably there from the time we were little babies.

MZ: I've been reading both *Selected Poems* and *Loba* and I'm interested in the evolution of your style. In many of your earlier poems, you wrote very directly about your life, you often called people by name. But there are other poems in which you are much less direct, much more universal.

In "For Frank O'Hara: An Elegy," for instance, the first section talks directly about your experiences, your memories. But then in the second section, you imagine that he is sand now: "I take you up by the handful, I watch you run through my fingers / I see you disperse on the North American coast."

DdP: Actually, that's just as direct, I was sitting on the beach when I was writing it.

MZ: Sure, that's direct but it's also much more universal than your specific memories. How did that work for you? Do you still write poems as direct as those early ones?

DdP: I got very uninterested in my personal life at some point, maybe in the early seventies. It wasn't where my attention was anymore.

And also, when I'm talking directly in a poem to Jimmy or Freddie there's always a sense that these are not only people but also metaphors in themselves, symbols or possibility of people or a kind of soul. There's both at once.

I don't think about metaphor. I think a lot about correspondences. I think that there's a kind of soul or being or group of beings (I wouldn't have been able to say this then, but I would have felt it) that I addressed when I addressed, for instance, Jimmy.

But as time went on, my attention became more and more inner. That began, really in the sixties. But by the seventies that was the main thrust. In the sixties, it comes out in *The New Handbook of Heaven* poems like "The Party" or "The Ballroom." They seem indirect and yet they're very personal. Written to a lover, actually.

I would never say that I had written in metaphor. If that's what I was after, I would have tried to have a consistency and a wholeness that doesn't happen there. What is happening there is the experience of certain images coming up with the pressure of the emotion, sort of like an earthquake.

That's very, very different. And I've had trouble with that. With, especially, male interpreters of my work, not understanding why the metaphors aren't consistent. Well, first, to me they weren't metaphors. They were like a direct experience before my eyes. Sometimes the way the sand (in the O'Hara poem) was: that I was literally sitting on it. And sometimes in terms of the inner experience becoming bigger and bigger so that more and more of the time when I'm writing I'm in a state close to what I guess people would call hallucination.

So it's just using what comes to hand, or what comes to eye, or what comes to me at that point, rather than seeking to craft or structure a way of writing where metaphor says: a ship is a horse riding the hills of the sea. I'm not ever consciously looking for metaphor. I accept whatever the mind or the consciousness or the imagination brings forward at that moment under that pressure.

MZ: Don't you think that's the way most metaphor or image or whatever phrase we use to describe it, that really works come about?

DdP: I don't really know. I know there's a lot of interest in the kind of thing where the image is consistent and holds throughout at all points, blah, blah, blah. The world shifts too much for me for that. The inner world especially. It has that kaleidoscopic quality like dream . . .

The personal stuff just seems to more and more have dropped away. I have a very rich personal life but it's not where my focus is. I think as our kids grow up and we get older, that gets to be more and more the case. Maybe it's a bad generalization, but I think women's tendency is to live with a much larger and more mythic view of the world. It includes the personal but it doesn't limit itself there.

MZ: I read an essay recently by Alicia Ostriker called "In Mind: The Divided Self in Women's Poetry." Among other things, she asks the question: Is there women's poetry? Do you think there is?

DdP: Maybe, it's soon to say. But there is a way of coming at the world that bypasses a lot of the restrictions and strictures that analytic mind lays on us, that women feel free to use . . . I'm not sure if it's because we're women or because we've been an oppressed group. Black people and other oppressed people also use these nonlinear, nonstructured, nonlimiting ways of seeing the world. I'm not sure if it's a sex thing or a class thing.

But I do think that women's writing has that quality of no holds barred. Which is in itself a huge step at this point.

MZ: Ostriker describes four key elements in women's poetry: 1) the quest for the autonomous self-definition (no more masks), 2) the intimate treatment of the body, 3) the release of anger (sexual politics), and 4) the contact imperative (the intense craving for unity and relationships).

DdP: I would tend to say that she's underselling us right down the line. We've had our autonomy always. What we've been looking for is a language to express it in. A lot of the other stuff—intimate treatment of the body. Contact imperative—is important but it's only the groundwork, the launching pad.

The release of anger . . . well, it's everybody's business but it's like what I said about the personal becoming less and less interesting. It's everybody's private business too. I don't mean we should go home and do it in a closet. But after a certain point, it's not really an interesting source of the work unless it touches real mythological, common roots.

Most rage is . . . it's part of our human process to have to process that stuff and it doesn't only happen to women. But past a certain point, it's boring to see it in print unless you get it to a place where you're really throwing new light on it as cosmic process. As part of the warp and woof of how your universe gets made. Poiesis.

I think we undersell ourselves if we get stuck in those things as a definition of what we're doing instead of a way of clearing the ground for what we want to do. I won't want to read in another fifty years the poetry of the rage of the sexual politics of the moment.

We have to realize that a lot of personal stuff is just that and unless we see it against the tapestry of all human condition, there's no point in writing 20,000 more poems on why I'm mad at my father. I'm not at all saying there's no point in being mad at your father. You absolutely have to be. Hit the bastard on the head with a cast iron frying pan all you want [*laughter*], but unless you can bring it to a new place in consciousness . . .

One thing we need right now is to see rage as a really legitimate, glorious part of the human condition. Not something we have to eliminate and express and get out of our systems. Jacob Boehme talks about the wrath and the love, the fire and the light that make a cosmos.

I do think that as women we are in the forefront of figuring out what it is to be human. Because I don't think the guys have got the slightest handle on it yet. I'm not mad at them for that. I just think they are kind of slow [*laughter*]. They've been caught by these structures, they've been caught by all the things that make their little male, white, supremacist world work on a temporary basis. They're in love with those things. So they're too slow to realize that there's endless potential to the imagination, to the human emotions.

And art is only interesting when it's pushing at those boundaries.

MZ: I think that *Loba* is very mythical. There's a grandeur to it. And it encompasses a lot: both personal myth and traditional myth—Lilith, the Virgin Mary. I'm curious about how it got started for you.

DdP: The name Loba came out of one of Pound's troubadour poems. The troubadour Vidal is running wild in the woods as a wolf and calls his mistress Loba.

The book *Loba* started for me in two ways. There was a dream [which is partly described in the poem called "Dream: The Loba Reveals Herself"]. And then, a year after the dream, I was teaching one day when—and this happens not infrequently with me—I'll just hear a voice. And the voice will be very insistent and not mine. Insistent in that it won't go away and will keep repeating the same phrase until I start writing and then it will go on to the next phrases.

Anyway, I was teaching in Watsonville in Poetry in the Schools with another poet and I just sort of dropped back from the class and let the other poet carry on and wrote this stuff down. That was the first part: "If he did not come apart in her hands, he fell / like flint on her ribs . . ."

The "Ave" poem that opens the book had happened about a month before but I didn't know that it was a prelude to anything else at the time. And the first sections came like that. Over a period of a few days, they were sort of dictated.

And then somewhere in Part 1 of the book, I started to set time aside to work on this piece. I had a five-month-old baby at that time and I had somebody come certain mornings. A man who was a fellow Sanskrit student and impoverished yogi came to answer the doorbell, do the grocery shopping, and hold the baby for two or three hours a morning, two or three mornings a week.

I found that the mind could be conditioned so that if it knew it had that time coming, the stuff would wait and happen at that time. I had to set a ritual: throw I Ching and work on a collage and then the stuff would start coming. So although it was like dictated material, it kept itself confined within time bounds so I could handle it—being the mother of five kids at that point. And then parts came like that for several more months and then later, the material became more irregular and came whenever it wanted to.

Loba had a very particular different feeling than other poems I was writing. Internally, so I would know: Oh, that's a piece of *Loba*.

I've had the experience twice during *Loba* of having a conversation with someone in a car, and, at the same time, another piece of my mind splitting off. So that I kept on writing. One was the part that begins "The day lay like a pearl in her lap" and one was that whole piece "The Loba Recovers the Memory of a Mare," where I talk about all these women that I've known who've been destroyed. I wrote that whole thing with somebody else's kid climbing on me and I was talking with the guy. We were driving to the airport to pick up somebody. And it just wrote. I was writing, talking, and being climbed on, all at once. And there was almost nothing that needed to be changed. My attention didn't break. It's odd. The experience of having your mind break off and be two minds at once.

MZ: Do you think that happens more to women than to men because it has to?

DdP: I don't know that. What I do know that happens more to me and most of the women I know than it does to men is that we write short pieces or we write long pieces in short chunks or we write series pieces or we learn to work a lot of sketches into a main piece. Because people were always wanting something else from you. Up to a certain point. Then your kids start to grow up and they defend you. "Mom can't talk to you now!" They get very fierce.

MZ: How have you managed with all those children? You've had a very active life and a very active writing life.

DdP: People ask me that constantly. And I'm really at a loss because it wasn't really a problem. I had my first child on my own when I was twenty-three in New York back in the fifties because I wanted a baby. By the time she was two, she was painting all the time and when she was littler, she'd lie across my lap face down and drool on the floor while I typed. And usually we were both very happy [*laughter*].

And then when there's more than one, they help with each other and they amuse each other. I've had my kids mostly on my own. I mean there's been guys around but it's been my trip.

The thing was, you just really know that the most important thing in the world, on one level, is getting the writing done. On another level, everything feels equal. It's just as interesting to make the bread as to make the poem. And that used to make me think I wasn't a writer. Because all the guys I knew would never find it as interesting to grow their herbs or build their houses as to make a poem. To me, a poem was part of your life like everything else.

Now, as I move out toward the second half of my life—toward menopause and all that, I'm fifty years old—the family starts to move out, which is very nice, and the fact of the work gets to be more and more central all the time and yet I still need those other things. I'm doing hands-on healing work, I'm teaching magic, I'm gardening. For me the work always needs the texture and context of a whole life situation. I could never be one of those New York artists who lives in a two-room apartment, rises up, writes all day, watches television, and goes to sleep at night. You need the garden and the hands-on work and the going out to the ocean.

That seems to me to be something that women know more than men now. Very often we undersell ourselves and think, I'm not a serious artist. I used to think that all the time: I can't be serious because all the men I know have moved on to writing critical articles as well as poetry and I can't write a critical article.

Back in '62, in New York, they first asked me would I write a retrospective of Denise Levertov. And I couldn't do it. They were all mostly writing these literary magazine critical articles and I thought, Wow. Maybe I'm just not real. 'Cause I can't do this stuff.

So I went away to Stinson Beach with a lover and thought about it. And I found that every morning I was waking up and going to the window where I could look out on the road and the garden and writing—I was working on a five-act play on the death of Shelley—and finally it occurred to me: Oh, I must be a writer because I'm writing every day. That's what a writer is. Somebody who gets up and automatically writes.

MZ: I think tasks that are essentially mindless and mechanical—baking bread, planting the garden—free your mind. So that you can think about a poem or a painting while you're doing them.

DdP: Yeah. I think they free your mind from the analytic, rigid structured base that we've all been locked into in this culture so that the mind it frees is closer to body-mind, closer to instinct and intuition. It frees the unlogical and inconsistent part that really makes the poem happen.

MZ: That reminds me of something else I wanted to ask about *Loba*. Did you feel freed by writing, in a sense, through a persona? Freed to break out in different ways that you wouldn't have . . .

DdP: I really don't know. I think personae are very interesting and I think we're almost always writing through a persona. Even when we say "I" to a lover, we're talking through one mask or one part of the I. The "I" in a love poem is still a persona.

In '61 with *The New Handbook of Heaven*, I began to write more without the critical mind. I had learned some techniques, some ways of turning off the part of the head that gets in the way when you're writing. So that sense that the material you're writing down might have nothing to do with anything expected or intended had already been happening for a long time.

I think that the expression of one particular kind of feral side of my nature, the experience of *Loba* did free. But every persona frees some aspect. Every mask you put on allows you to speak in one particular way and they're all really true, they're all really there. *Loba* was wonderful for what I sometimes think of as the "wild woman" part of myself. That wasn't all of it.

She certainly has her intellectual side. But there's also—and strongly—the feral side.

But then other masks have done other things. The three masks of Shelley, Byron, and Mary in that play I mentioned freed other things ten years earlier.

MZ: I see what you mean. To jump to something completely other: you edited *The Floating Bear: A Newsletter* with LeRoi Jones in the sixties. How did that get started? How did you decide to do it?

DdP: I did *The Bear* with Roi for three years and without him for about six more. There had been a plan I had with another poet and friend of Roi's named A. B. Spellman. He and I were going to do a magazine. Just a regular literary magazine and again, it had an animal name: *The Horse at the Window*. We got ready to do our first issue and A. B. chickened out at the point where he was going to have to reject some manuscripts. He didn't really want to reject anyone, anywhere, ever. So he decided he couldn't be an editor and he quit. Which was very endearing in a way.

And, at that point, I still had a bunch of stuff and Roi and I knew each other. And the idea came up of doing it as a newsletter and mailing it out every two weeks and using some of the stuff from *The Horse at the Window*. So *The Horse at the Window* became *The Floating Bear*—a simple Ovid-like metamorphosis.

It was mimeographed sheets at first, twelve pages at first, every two weeks at first, going out to maybe 150 people at first. And then it increased and increased and grew to be farther apart in time, especially after I left New York but those first few years, which were perhaps the most exciting, the most seminal time, Roi and I worked together. With very different editorial points of view but no particular editorial conflicts. We both made room for work that the other one liked. We trusted that the other one's instinct was good.

He liked work that was more sinewy at an intellectual level. And I was really looking for another kind of work. But neither of us had any problem about that. Sometimes we'd say, "Okay if you're putting that in, then I'm putting this in. I mean if you're taking two pages for that, which I'm not very interested in, but I will type, then I'll take two pages for this." And it always worked out.

And then, when I left New York, and was with someone else—I had been lovers with Roi for a few years and have a child of his, Dominique di Prima Baraka . . . When I went to California to live, soon after that, Roi wrote me and said that he didn't want to go on being the editor. And I continued the

Bear on a much more casual basis, but it still was coming out fairly regularly for a long time. Then the issues got bigger and more magazine-like. The list got to be 1,200 people and the thing came out more like a few times a year. Till finally in '69 we did the last issue.

MZ: You published some amazing people. [Gregory Corso, Edward Field, Gilbert Sorrentino, Robert Creeley, Jack Kerouac, John Wieners, William Burroughs, Denise Levertov, John Ashbery, Allen Ginsberg, Robert Duncan, Gary Snyder, Diane Wakoski, among others.]

DdP: Yeah, we published most of the people who were doing writing that was interesting (to us anyway) at that time. When I first came out West, people asked me how did I manage to publish people from the different schools of writing without more conflict? I had no idea what the schools were! [*laughter*]

I was just totally insensitive. Apparently at some point, Spicer and Duncan were not agreeing—or maybe they were. I can never remember which years they did or didn't. Everybody also was in their own turmoil. And I know George Stanley who was a writer from the West Coast was ostracized by his old mentor Jack Spicer when he came back to this coast because he had published on the East Coast and that was considered prostitution . . .

And, God, I don't know. How was I supposed to know all that stuff! [*laughter*] We just published what we liked! [*laughter*]

MZ: That's wonderful. So you were trying to publish new work and you were trying to get it out fast but there was no system about it. It was just things that came to you . . .

DdP: That were really innovative. Either in terms of language and syntax or line or subject . . . Stuff that showed you new things you could do with the medium.

MZ: So it was a good experience for you, but would you want to do it again?

DdP: Oh, no. None of the things you do when you're young you do later. At least I don't think so. I would certainly not want to run Poets Press again or the New York Poets Theater again. That's the work for the young and I don't see the young doin' it right now, so this is a call to them to come forward! [*laughter*]

MZ: Tell me about the New York Poets Theater.

DdP: The New York Poets Theater went on for, I think four seasons, 1961, '63, '64, '65, in New York in various small theater locations. The first season was in a tiny theater behind an art gallery on East 10th Street which was the avant-garde street of art galleries at that moment and we did one-act plays mostly and we did plays by poets exclusively. Well, we did a play by a chore-ographer once, and a kind of poem-opera by an avant-garde composer once.

And we always had painters do the sets. We had people like Alex Katz and Red Grooms doing sets. We usually didn't use regular theater people for directors either. We tended to use choreographers and people like that.

We did Wallace Stevens, we did Frank O'Hara. We did the first staged piece of LeRoi Jones that happened—before *The Dutchman* or anything. And the performers tended to be not actors but poets, dancers, painters. So it really was—I don't know any other word for it—art theater. The kind of art theater that might happen in Europe where say, Cocteau was playing the horse in his own play. Everybody performed.

We did the last act of Robert Duncan's *Faust Foutu*. We did one by Bar-bara Guest. George Herms came out to do the sets for Michael McClure's play *The Blossom*.

That went on for several seasons. We would run about a four-month sea-son and then close down, exhausted, raise money, and do it again. What we did most years, when we did a real theater instead of the back of a gal-lery, was plays three days a week (Friday, Saturday, Sunday). And one night we turned it over to something else. Usually the Cinematheque would also show experimental movies on our dark night. And then during the week we'd have a jazz night, a dance night, and so on. So there was an event every night of the week and the plays on the weekends.

We spent what we considered great fortunes. We'd put on a four-month season for $15,000. Some of the things we were doing that we were get-ting a lot of shit for were done a few years later for grants. Like we got the neighborhood gang kids in to help us build sets. Because it was either that or they were going to vandalize us. So we were teaching them set-building. And our Ukrainian neighbors threatened to call the police because we were using child labor.

We didn't get any of the money from grants. There were no grants for that kind of thing then. It was almost all personal money—from painters, a few art patrons, people that ran the galleries. And we had volunteer help working in the theater that all slept in my house and ate stew. And we'd send one of the volunteer people off to say, Billy Rose's house to get cash. Or Richard Lippold who was a sculptor would say, "Have so and so on such a corner at such and such a time." And he'd come by in a cab and stick his hand out the window and hand you an envelope with money in it.

And, there were the usual problems. We got arrested for Jean Genet's movie, *Le Chant d'Amour*, and the landlady locked us out of the theater, because the movie was obscene. All that kind of garbage that used to go on when you did things. [*laughter*]

MZ: I'm told you're interested in alchemy now and you mentioned a little while ago that you were teaching magic. Can you say more about that?

DdP: Well, here in the Bay Area, even in the Poetics Program at the New College at which I'm part of the core faculty, a lot of what we teach is the Hermetic tradition. And privately I teach the Western magical tradition. They are not exactly the same, but they are related. And the notion of poetics at New College includes that sense of the Mysteries and the mystery schools of the West.

In teaching magic more specifically, we have a small group called the San Francisco Institute of Magical and Healing Arts. There are four core teachers. And what we teach is rather simple, unglamorous, and grounded. One of my main courses is called "The Structures of Magic." And it really literally sticks to the algebras, the geometries behind various systems and how they fit together.

What I've been working on since '78 is getting down to the bare bones of the different branches of the Western tradition. We're skipping all the blathering theologies and moralizing and purple prose of the different schools and pulling out the hard information for people to play with on their own.

I do other things. I teach various breathings. Learning to use your body as an instrument where breathing into different parts of it will give you different results. There's an impersonal—to come back to that personal/impersonal—aspect to how you use yourself. You begin to understand that compassion itself, or connection with others, is an impersonal experience in some ways. Your energy connects with their energy and you work.

I'm teaching a course at New College called "Hidden Religions in the Literature of Europe" which goes from prehistory to twentieth-century magical groups and tries to trace what people used to call the secret tradition. And it's interesting because the secret tradition tends also to be the tradition of anarchism, and the tradition of equality between women and men and the tradition of sexual freedom. And it's often a tradition of property held in common, also. Tribalism. These things are linked all through European history. So it's a nice, interesting, and slightly revolutionary course to teach.

MZ: Well, does this all connect into what you're writing now? Are you focused more on things like alchemy?

DdP: I have been for a long time. It's definitely all through *Loba*. Moving out West in '68 made a lot more room for all that in my life but it was there from the beginning for me. It became more of a study as time went on. And by the seventies, a major part of what I read and study.

The book I'm writing right now, or that is writing itself when it feels like it, seems to be a book called *Alchemical Studies*. It's a book of poems, and poem fragments sometimes—just like the texts, they don't always complete themselves—that are based on images from alchemical material that just seem to come forward for me. And *Loba*'s continuing too.

MZ: I was going to ask you how it felt to be teaching in a college. I couldn't help but remember . . . I think it was again in that poem for Frank O'Hara where you talked about how you and he and Roi "read aloud at Rutgers 3 different poems at the same time / confounding the students" . . . [*laughter*]

DdP: Well, nobody wanted to be the last reader!

MZ: I never thought of that solution before! [*laughter*] But it sounds like the kinds of teaching that you're doing are not exactly standard academic teaching.

DdP: No. New College has an incredible master's program in poetics. Robert Duncan, and myself and David Meltzer and Duncan McNaughton and Louis Patler, two poets from Bolinas, are the core faculty.

It is poetics rather than a poetry writing program. And it really concentrates on areas that have been ignored in modern times. David usually teaches a course on the Kabbalah. Right now, he's teaching a study course called "In Beginning" which is a course in Genesis, using all the various interpretations. Everybody is studying one person's system of working with Genesis, like Blake's or Boehme's.

And I teach "Hidden Religions" every other year and in between things like a course in John Dee, Paracelsus, and Giordano Bruno, three magicians from the early Renaissance. And this year, I'm teaching the "Poetics of the Romantic Movement," which is just heaven. Because when I went to high school and I loved those guys (like Shelley and Keats), it was really bad and naughty to like them. The New Critics were prevalent and you were supposed to like, I forget who you were supposed to like! But I didn't like it, whoever it was!

It's a very, very rich program at New College. You can really make great strides in your own work while you're teaching. I don't know how I would do in a regular university.

MZ: I was curious. [*laughter*]

DdP: I don't think they're curious—they've never invited me! [*laughter*]

The *Gnosis* Interview: Diane di Prima on Magic, Healing, and the Western Esoteric Tradition

Jay Kinney and Hal Hughes / 1985

From *Gnosis Magazine* no. 2 (spring/summer 1986): 12–21. Reprinted by permission of *Gnosis* and Jay Kinney.

Diane di Prima is a poet, teacher, and healer. Her many books of poetry included the well-known *Revolutionary Letters* and *Loba*. In recent years she has been active as a core member of the poetics faculty at New College of California as well as a founder and teacher with SIMHA (the San Francisco Institute of Magical and Healing Arts).

This interview was conducted on January 15, 1985, by Jay Kinney and Hal Hughes, at the SIMHA house. It was transcribed and edited by Jay Kinney. This final version incorporates further editing and revisions by Diane di Prima.

SIMHA can be reached at Suite 103, PO Box 15068, San Francisco, CA 94115. New College is at 777 Valencia St., San Francisco, CA 94110.

Jay Kinney: I thought we could start with your describing the nature of your current work with the New College and SIMHA [San Francisco Institute of Magical & Healing Arts]—the courses you've been teaching and your reasons for focusing on these subjects.

Diane di Prima: From the sixties on, involving myself as I did in the West Coast revolution out here, I had a really strong sense that there had to be our own European traditions to turn to. I saw so many people turning to Black tradition or Latino tradition—which wasn't theirs—just to have a sense of a root somewhere. It occurred to me one day that Europe was once a forest filled with hairy medicine women and men in furs rattling their little gourds too, and that it was just that we had been so completely cut off from that and completely brainwashed about it. So I began to take what turned out to be a twenty-year detour trying to find out who we were and what was ours, and that led me straight into Western occult traditions.

So that in the *Revolutionary Letters* and other poems I was writing at that time, and in talking to young people around the country, which I was doing endlessly for ten years or so, I could tell them something solid that they could turn to and go back to and find out about themselves. This is a bit simplistic—there's also the fact that my family is southern Italian, so there's always been that pagan root, and my grandfather was also an anarchist.

Then, when I was fifteen and in high school, I was involved with a group of eight young women who were all writers and were all experimenting with telepathy and trance. So there was that instinctive or intuitive playing with the occult stuff, but that went away for a while because I was so completely a writer—by the time I was eighteen I was completely committed to a life of poetry. The occult, or whatever, returned via this search through the revolution for what are the European roots, how do we begin to find who we are. That led me to a lot of reading and other work, and via all of that to the course that I now teach at New College. It's called "Hidden Religions in the Literature of Europe."

It begins with Gertrude Levy's book *The Gate of Horn*, and carries on from guesses at prehistory like John Michell and *Hamlet's Mill* through the Paleolith and Neolith as constructed in various intuitive ways by people like Gimbutas. Then we spend a month or so on the Gnostics, move on to the heresies of the Christian tradition, and then on to a long view of alchemy, backwards and forwards from that Middle Ages point, and what the Renaissance was about in terms of the Magus as cocreator with God, and then on to the early Rosicrucians and the splintering off of the continuity of the tradition in the seventeenth century, where one part of it becomes revolutionary thought and one part becomes what we now called holistic medicine—Hahnemann [father of homeopathy] inherits the traditions of alchemy via Paracelsus. So that whole course is trying to make a continuity of our tradition and our lives, out of the fragments that we've got left.

That's the main thing I'm particularly contributing to the poetics program at New College, and the poetics program as a whole tends to be a looking at the traditions from many people's personal search. Like David Meltzer is teaching from his own tradition and many years of study of the Kabbalah. Robert Duncan's bringing his unique point of view about Western tradition in relation to other kinds of search, like linguistics, into the program. It's definitely a program where poetics is a form of Hermetic work, in some sense. Every other year I teach a different kind of course—I don't always teach "Hidden Religions." Next year, for instance, I'll be teaching Pound.

A couple of years ago I did a lecture course on "Paracelsus, Dee, and Bruno" there. I met a little opposition from some folks who wanted to know how that related to poetics, but it was quickly resolved that it did indeed relate to poetics, so that was okay.

As for SIMHA, that grew out of the fact that there were—again, this all comes to me from writing. It's all a gift of poetry to me; poetry gives it all to me. At one point early in the seventies I began to teach writing. I waited 'til then—I was born in '34—because I thought and still think that you need to know a hell of a lot before you start teaching, especially in the creative arts. I found out that most people who wanted to write out here at this point in history weren't reading very much. So the work had a certain thinness that was very unappealing—it didn't have more than their own lives in it. I wasn't going to be able to force a million books down their throats, so I began to invent a lot of visualizing techniques to get them to go deep into themselves, because as we all know (who have read Jung—or who haven't for that matter), if you go back there you are going to find all the same stuff you're going to find in books. It's all there: the richness of symbolism . . .

Kinney: In the unconscious . . .

di Prima: How do we know it's the unconscious? Maybe it isn't! [*laughter*] I hadn't studied any kind of visualizing, I just invented techniques that would get people deep and get them far, and did a lot of work like that. I did one dream-writing workshop where people used each others' dreams to write with: the dreams belonged to the whole group. We met for over a year, so everybody's symbols got mixed up with everybody else's and that was very wonderful. Out of all that came more and more interest in visualization.

Then a friend who had been with the Diggers gave me a system of visualizing. She came up to my house in Marshall [California] and did a weekend workshop for six of us. Part of it was material that people had adapted from Silva Mind Control and added to over the years—all kinds of eclectic other stuff. So it was kind of a Digger hodgepodge that included a real simple technique for going very deep very fast on a countdown basis—which is more or less common knowledge now, but this was about '75. And then I taught a few people myself about three years later, and at that point the people I taught it to and myself decided that we wanted to use these techniques to investigate magical stuff.

Our first idea was to investigate alchemy, but we decided that we were not very prepared, so we would just start with the four elements. We made tattvas of the elements and the subelements, and we spent something like three and a half years meeting once a week at first and then every two weeks, and going deep and using the old Golden Dawn technique of parting the curtain, entering the tattva, and recording the material. We have about two hundred tapes of elements and subelements information. We learned quickly how to separate the personal garbage that you come up with nearly every time you visualize—because there's always something on your mind: your sex life, or stuffed-up nose, or your kid, or whatever—from the kind of more hard information, that is, information about what Water or Ether might really be about.

So we did that—we completed that work, and then we began working with the Major Arcana. We only meet every few months now because out of this group which met so long and so often we began to form SIMHA, and now we have tons of work to do as a group in the world, and much less time for the inner stuff. One of our sessions usually takes us eight to ten hours, say from seven p.m. to four in the morning. Through the work of those years I began to understand what a magical group is about: it's about making the circle around someone going into a deep place where they'll need protection. So that one or another of us—it might only be a deep place where we find our own stupidity or vulnerability, but when somebody would be starting to come up against their stuff you could hear it in the visualizations several weeks or maybe several months before they heard it. And we'd even talk and say, "So-and-so is going to need a hand on this when s/he comes up against it."

We got to know each other that well, and there was a period of years when the group worked for all of us in that way. Some people dropped out and four of us remained, who had been doing the work from the beginning. SIMHA grew out of the fact that slowly the four of us got to the point where there was stuff we needed to teach, and we began to reach out. The two core things that had been there for some time were the visualization work and the "Structures of Magic" class.

Now, I'd been teaching "Structures of Magic" since 1978—the same year that I began the visualization work. For me, the idea of it was to make a way of presenting the actual bare bones of Western tradition without so much of the theologies or the purple prose of various occultists—without anybody's moralizing or any particular person's point of view.

You can take certain things as if they were fact—as if it was fact that once things come into manifestation they polarize: there's immediately good/

bad, light/dark, etc. We can take that as core. And then take other things off of that: like out of this polarization the Western world has grown the four, which are the elements. And then working that slowly and consistently and without too much worrying about "is yin bad or good?" and trying to circumvent all the feminist questions that come up at about this point from the I Ching and everything else, to just work the three, and the three in the four (the Zodiac), the ten on the Tree [of Life], and the twenty-two, and how the whole thing interlocks, so that there is a relationship between the Kabbalistic, alchemical, and other traditions, a relationship based simply on number.

I keep it simple; it is a beginning course. It's a course for people to begin to see how that stuff might be there as reference: so you can use the Tree— like they used to say—as a filing system or however you need it to work that material for your own purposes. So that things have a coherence in the world for you again: your dreams, what you see, and so on. What happens as a bonus is that there seems to be a coherence and a co-inherence of a group of people who have worked with these various materials and have each other to refer to. Various other work is going on around that: a loose network of people consciously working in a tradition: the deep visioning work. Sheppard Powell's ritual and Talismanic classes, the more intellectual stuff of "Structures of Magic," and the rest. It's very exciting.

Hal Hughes: About how many people have been through the program?

di Prima: Counting the people who came for the course, and those who I've worked privately with doing visualization, I'd say over three hundred people in the Bay Area have been somehow touched by this whole process.

Kinney: Do you have a working definition of magic that you employ in class? A lot of people's notions of magic are toned by projections of "black magic" or "white magic."

di Prima: You know, I don't. I couldn't be as simplistic, as to say, like Crowley, it's "change in accordance with will" . . . that would take in too much, though on some level I do agree with that. For me it has to do with pushing people to look at the forces behind the things rather than just at the object or event. If I have a working definition of magic, it's that behind every single thing in the world an infinite tunnel opens of reference, cross-reference, and forces, and how these things interlock in nets. What I would basically say is, yeah, learning to see force . . . learning to see the etheric and the astral, etc., and the thinner and thinner layers of stuff. And learning to work off those layers rather than . . . if you want to push that rock you don't necessarily have to go out there and put your shoulder to it.

And that came to me from poetry too, because what happened to me was: I wrote the *Revolutionary Letters* in the sixties, working with the Diggers out here. I was living in San Francisco and delivering the food, free food. That was our gig, our commune "did the food," and from June of '68 until I left the city in the Fall of '69, I wrote the *Letters* and did a lot of readings and performances with the various folks who were working here then. And at some point I decided, well, if I'm going to do this, if I'm going to write about going back to this more primitive way of seeing the world and living in it, I should really do it! I was reinforced in that idea by the fact that there wasn't a day of my life that the FBI wasn't at my door, so it was a very good time to go away to the backwoods. [*laughter*] Everyone who had been through my house was either a White Panther or a this or a that, so it was time to go away.

So I went and lived in the north woods at Black Bear commune in late '69 and early '70, and at one point things got very clear to me. I did a lot of sitting that winter—I'd been studying Zen with Suzuki Roshi while I had been working with the Diggers. He saw no contradiction between revolution and Zen, and neither did I! [*laughter*] It got clear to me that writing that stuff [*Revolutionary Letters*] and reading it at rallies and all, what I was doing was kind of like an ego trip, because who was going to pay for it was my Black neighbor down the block. I was going to be home writing these *Revolutionary Letters*, you know. And I ain't no Marxist. I can't live that way. I know that there are people who sincerely believe that the intellectuals should go home and think it and write it and the other people should fight it. But my grandfather was an anarchist and so am I. I can't buy that.

So thinking about that, and thinking wait a minute, you know, a lot of what I'm saying is real, but is this the right means?—made me start to wonder how do you outflank the situation because clearly on any material confrontation we lose. There's no way we win, because the ghettos can be napalmed as easily as Vietnam can be napalmed, that's clear to me, they're out there where nobody else sees them. So then it became: how do you deal with it without a head-on confrontation? And it began to be clearer and clearer that you really have to understand the forces behind stuff rather than blindly react to stuff. What I said one day was, "Actually, none of it's important except poetry, magic and Zazen." [*laughter*] I know there's still a big ballyhoo amongst the political folks in town that those of us who went into these other disciplines abandoned the revolution, but from my own point of view there was no abandoning. It was a question of: do I really want Mrs. Casey to get hit on the head for me 'cause I have a belief that she should have more food! [*laughter*] This kind of came up again this summer [1984] at Naropa Institute. Amiri Baraka was there, and we had a very interesting symposium in which, for him, Buddhism and in fact any form of "mysticism" were absolutely abandoning the revolution. From my point of view, intellectuals putting their neighbors' lives on the line is mad egoism. [*laughter*] It was an impasse! A rather loud impasse!

So, if there's a working definition of magic it would just be that: learning to work with the forces rather than the physical manifestations. So that makes all kinds of healing work—that isn't allopathic medicine—magic, too.

Hughes: Do you feel like you can communicate those methods or concerns to your students as well as the techniques?

di Prima: Yes. You see, "Structures of Magic" is the only course that we do that is mostly intellectual. Most of the courses involve a lot of hands-on work. In Janet Carter's workshop on the planets, for instance, you're actually handling the metals for each one; Carl Grundberg's approach to Hebrew Kabbalah is through calligraphy; Sheppard Powell has everyone working with oils, incenses, stones, herbs, etc. In "Beginning Healing" I'm really basically teaching ways to breathe and open up so that you can let energy through to the point where you can lay your hands on a client and let that healing energy in so they can feel it. Most of the work is experiential. Even in "Structures" we do a lot of visualization. Or I'll spill out a huge box of semi-precious stones on the floor and people will clearly begin to see that some of them have strong energy and some of them don't. I'll ask people to build a Tree of Life with them, using the qualities of the stones, not just the color—the quality of the stone that makes it more like Geburah or more like Hod, and so on. . . . The course looks like kindergarten in a lot of ways, but it has enough hands-on so that people begin to actually experience the energies. People know this stuff anyway, they just don't cop to it, because we've been so completely trained out of these perceptions. What's important is that they can admit they're perceiving with other than the five senses. That they realize that's even going on for them. Because when we start to learn to speak, all the perceptions that are very subtle are ruled out because we have no words for them.

Hughes: What I was really wondering was if you feel like your students see these things in a political context. In my own experience, that has been hard for me to communicate.

di Prima: I think that it's a very subtle process where what happens for people is that they start to get more and more "in touch with themselves"—as we say on this coast in our New Age language. As that happens there are certain things that get ruled out in their lives, and certain things that get more important. Sometimes inadvertently the simplest thing in a SIMHA class will put somebody's life into a chaos, and in the process of that, it they start to realize what their real needs are, it begins to extend out from there to other people and things. Another simple and subtle process is that nearly every class begins with ten minutes of silent sitting, and ends that way if possible, so that there's that time where you're just there as a group of people and just silent together—just breathing.

For people to consciously, intellectually begin to know that what they're working on is political, happens more for me in the poetics program, in the "Hidden Religions" class. Nobody's taken that course and not said they've been changed by it. Mainly they'll say things like, "Well, I've learned that I have to read between the lines of everything I read." Stuff like that. And people will have more of a sense of the whole sweep of European history.

In the magic classes, a lot of it is what happens to them turns the whole thing upside down. The most dramatic changes happen in the "Deep Visioning" class, which is a two-weekend intensive, where everybody lives here the whole time and we do twenty-five hours a weekend of visualization. Visualizing, sitting up, writing it down, sharing what we've got, going down again. So by the end of the two weekends people have come up against some of their garbage that they had no idea was there, or had no intention of dealing with in this life. And the work gives us tools to deal with it. That's the beginning, you know, because the ground for real political action seems to be that you have to feel compassionate towards yourself—and that includes towards your own garbage—out of which grows the sense of connection with other people.

I'll get people in the magic classes who are very politicized, women who have studied Wicca, or been feminists, or whatever, who will object to the work for not being more stridently feminist per se, and the interesting thing there is to try to bring that stuff in them also into touch with what their own real needs are. Because very often, just like me in the sixties writing *Revolutionary Letters*, the feminism is very important, but at the same time it can be a way of not looking at how you are handling *your* life—just like any other political platform. Then bringing those two together so that you don't have to throw out the one to do the other starts to be a dance. So the work is political in a lot of funny ways—for instance, people stop believing their doctors—that's important! [*laughter*] If you don't believe your doctor or your newspaper you've made a start!

Kinney: How do you view the Western hermetic tradition in relation to some of the new alternative spirituality that people have been evolving or rediscovering, such as Wicca or neo-pagan groups, and Women's Spirituality?

di Prima: About Women's Spirituality, I just saw that every woman comes so much more often face-to-face with death, in having children, just the possibility of having children. And we come face-to-face with the literal insides of our bodies at least once a moon—there is a spirituality that is inevitable. It has nothing to do with feminism, or Wicca, or the New Age, per se. It's always been there.

I remember when I was a youngster running around New York making love a lot and really not bothering with birth control from the age of eighteen to twenty-two—I never did get pregnant—but my feeling was I just won't lie with anyone whose child I wouldn't be happy to carry. Not that I'd necessarily ever want to see the man again—but to be happy to bear the child. I lay with a lot of people, but you know—it gave a really core feeling to going to bed with people, it wasn't casual, but it was impersonal. It stayed real.

And I'm not saying we should do this now, but there is always that edge in women's lives, no matter how much we talk about how wonderfully we've been liberated by the Pill, it's still there: we face death when we bear a child, we see our blood every month, and we can never get completely out of tune with the seasons or the Earth because of that.

I also think that for me there's some way that—I was going to say that Wicca was the root, but it's more like *a* root. For me paganism would never be satisfying by itself simply because there's too much of me that it doesn't take into account. But it's very much part of the ways that we're returning to, and those for whom it is a full path do very well with it. But for me, since I'm not inclined to view the Earth as my home, I have to say that rituals that are exclusively devoted to that are not satisfying. It's like Taoism as opposed to, say, Buddhism or Hinduism, which have a view that goes beyond what simply fits.

Ever since I was very young I always kept the equinoxes and solstices and all that was important to me, and yet it isn't the whole thing, the whole picture for me. It simply wouldn't be enough to celebrate fertility and the sun and the moon and the seasons and the Mother and the Earth itself, because if that's all there is I'd rather be dead. To that extent I guess I'm a gnostic. I don't feel like this world is bad and evil per se. It's just a not very interesting way station on the journey; it's certainly not the most enthralling of possibilities that I can imagine. If my imagination can go that much farther, surely the imaginations of those I can imagine can go even farther! [*laughter*]

I think paganism is a root and it's an important part of the work. We have to be on the Earth as well as off it. We have to work with the body as part of the thing—and the Earth is in some way analogous to the body—it's the ground you have to push against when you take off. But even as far as material worlds go, it's only one of them, you know. It's where we have to start from, but it's not by any means the whole picture. I need Kabbalah, I need alchemy more than anything. I need that sense of a) transformation; b) worlds beyond worlds, and world inside of worlds, or else I would just as soon lie down and forget it. Because this is nice but it's not that interesting. [*laughter*]

Kinney: There's a political critique that goes along with a lot of Wiccan thought that a spirituality that is immanent is somehow preferable and more benevolent than one that's transcendent.

di Prima: Well, I don't think any of it's transcendent. I don't think there's any Trees out there. They're here, they're in me, but I've got to know that there's more than the game that we can see here, what we perceive. More than the two hundred billion galaxies. It's such a silly thing of "the in and the out" anyway—what's inside, what's outside—obviously we're all moebius strips, or Klein bottles or something. [*laughter*] There is a sense that we are it while we're here in this form, and also that we make it, create the worlds, but definitely "it" has to be more than is offered in the celebration of so-called life: fertility, joy, death, the Triple Goddess, the green forest—that's not enough. I don't think it ever was.

So, when I started to say that it was the root at one point, I was going to say that I once believed that there was a long period of time when we were pagan—"we" meaning humans—and that then there came the point when we said "Eeek! This is a horrible yukky trap" and we became to some extent, in different ways and different cultures, what we think of as gnostics, or as Hans Jonas used to call "pessimistic gnostics": "Let's-get-out-of-here people!" [*laughter*] And then at some point alchemy's answer to that was instead of "Let's get out of here," let's trans-mute it, instead of just let's transcend it, let's transmute it and take it with us (or stay with it). The Earth can be this thing that it isn't, which is everything, not just matter, and not just full moon, but all these levels, these boxes within boxes, all these dimensions, these worlds within worlds at once.

But now I think that probably from the very earliest I have read about or found any traces of, we always knew that it wasn't just this. It was never just that the seasons, and so on, were enough. I think that from as early as we can read about—possibly into the Paleolith—there was this piece of a tradition from before the Ice Age that talked about other worlds. So I can't be so sure that paganism was the one root that all the rest grew out of. I don't sense that, just like I don't sense that my soul grew out of my body, although the Reichians would have it so.

Hughes: And there are enough other cultures that, for example, think that the dream reality is the real thing . . .

di Prima: Of course. Way back to the first caves that we supposedly came out of we were dreaming, so there were always those other worlds.

The one thing I find not so good in modern Wicca is that I think it should take a leaf out of the book of the other Western traditions to the point of making some consistency of correspondence. I read these books of witchcraft, and you're burning a gold candle for this and a red candle for that, and in the next book you're burning a blue candle for what you used to burn a red candle for. And those are minor things, but they're not. In the long run, that Mandala that is the directions and the elements, the colors and the forces, whatever system you evolve—that Mandala is your *topos.* You should spin a system out of your center and stay with that, so that there's a consistency in the workings that you're doing, and I don't see that. I also find that a lot of people I work with who had worked in Wicca don't know enough about making strong protections of a strong circle when they're working, so often they're drawing down more force than they probably thought about in the first place. Because they're calling on protections like "Oh, Forces of the Western direction, give me a little help here" instead of really going out there and seeking what that force is. And, by the way, there's all kind of forces in the Western direction! There's not enough sense of awe, of how real all that stuff is that they're dealing in, and sometimes, because the workings are appropriate, there's some influx of force that is more than they bargained for. I've worked healing folks who have gotten into this bind. So those two things: that they should get their correspondences straight, and learn to protect themselves, to take the stuff seriously.

Hughes: Part of that comes out of trying to recreate or cobble together a tradition that feels right for you at the moment.

di Prima: I respect that everybody in the group would have some say in what the ritual is, but then it should form itself within that group into a consistency. On the other hand, perhaps the laxity of protections comes out of a sense that nature is in fact "good," which I won't question, but we're dealing with more than nature as soon as we begin to pass this cup around in a ritualized manner. Those are the worlds behind the worlds that I think Wicca doesn't deal with seriously enough, and yet calls on, but without a real sense of how much power they can bring in.

Hughes: Even if you manage to define nature as good, it's hard for most people to see the good side of earthquakes and tornadoes . . .

di Prima: Or even getting emotionally turned inside out because you put on this funny-looking mask and talked through it at the Circle and didn't realize it was the Demon of Chaos. [*laughter*] "Whoops!" Yeah, just a little more sense that you're really playing with fire when you're playing with fire.

Kinney: I was wondering if you'd say a little more about the forces you were discussing. How would you characterize those forces? As basically neutral?

di Prima: Yeah, I would. I would say it's just like electricity or fire. It just is. It's just stuff. I think that our tendency with anything that's too much bigger than us we tend to see it as bad, you know—threatening. So part of it is, like, not to blow your cool, is partly to stretch your mind or your imagination at that point so that you can encompass the bigness. I think that's especially our thing as Americans and probably our contribution in both the arts and magic—the bigness. Do you know the story of what Bodhidharma said to the Emperor of China? The Emperor said to him "Give me the Word of the Holy Truth!" and Bodhidharma answered, "Vastness, no Holiness."

And I think that because this thing, this continent that we really don't belong on, is so big and so alien (in both the "alien" sense that the gnostics once had and vastness sense that you really need if you're going to go far in magic, art, or space travel—and they're really different forms of the same thing) *is* America and is in everybody's consciousness here. But people a lot don't let themselves feel that awe.

Kinney: The price of trying to be hip or sophisticated at all moments is having to reduce everything that might induce awe into something you can talk cleverly about.

di Prima: Well, see, that will create demons the same way that Western magic as practiced during the Christian era was so demon-ridden, like Faust and all those guys. That was because they were always constantly trying to conquer the beasts. They would call up a force, but instead of it just being— "oh, there's the electricity, now how do I use it if I want to use it?"—it was like "I am your Master, O Force! And you should bow down to the One Living God!" or whatever bullshit we came up with. And since we weren't cooperating—*that's* where you can cooperate more than in the Wiccan Circle with everybody trying to make up their ritual as if there was no hierarchy or tradition—you can cooperate *with* the things you call down. So like, "Hi, Force!" or "Hi, Talking Triangle, or Insect in the form of a I-don't-know-what!" [*laughter*] "Now that I've called you up, what I thought I wanted was *this*, now what do *you* want?"—or whatever. And how does this thing work? How do I make the electricity go through this wire? If it becomes a thing that you're going to meet and conquer and prove yourself Lord over, inevitably that thing is your adversary and Adversaries always win, that is the Law.

So in the same way, if you're always cool in the face of awe, it's the same hubris. Stretching your imagination enough to meet the vastness of a force or of the world or whatever, is very different from pretending to be bigger than we are. "This doesn't faze me in the least!" we say, walking into the Pacific Ocean. [*laughter*] That's the opposite of stretching to meet it. Stretching to meet it is kind of like cooperating.

Kinney: In working with the magical tradition, how have you distinguished between what medieval magic called demons and archangelic forces? To what degree do you still find some of that symbolism useful? Or have you evolved new symbolism for those forces?

di Prima: It's useful insofar as it shows up! That is, I'm working not so much from theory as from practice, like this trance visualization stuff, and ritual. So if things choose to show up in the form of angels or demons, that's how they're going to show up, that's what we work with, because you don't spend time saying, "Would you please change your form? I really don't believe in angels!" [*laughter*] All those forms have been given shape through so many imaginations for so long, but just because it shows up looking like a demon doesn't mean you have to freak out. That is the shape it might have been given by the imagination of all of us for five hundred years. Nevertheless, you still have to find out what the nature of it is, what it requires of you, what you require of it, whether this is an agreeable situation or one that you can banish or get out of in some way and go on to something else.

Mostly, I have to say, about our group—we might be very naïve or something, but we've been working since '78 and nobody's really run into like black magical forces out there trying to take them over. I've definitely run into things that completely, totally shook me to the bottom of my soul—I don't say that lightly—but simply out of the awesomeness, the largeness, the power of things, you know, which I mean, it's there. There are 200 billion galaxies, you know—according to the *National Geographic*! [*laughter*] So there's nothing metaphysical or mystical about getting shook if you let yourself, but nothing seemed it was there for the express purpose of harming. Or, a lot of it isn't there for the express purpose of helping. It just is.

Hughes: Your expectations and intentions determine how you respond to that, do you think?

di Prima: That could be. I think it's partly because we didn't ever go out expecting, like the magician with the circle and the triangle, expecting to get the Demon X to tell us where the treasure was, so we didn't have that kind of relation to it all. We just went out to learn, to know more. But then Faust claims that's all he wanted. But I wonder what would've occurred if he had simply invited Mephistopheles to sit down and share some bread with him and said, "This is what's on my mind: I want knowledge. What's on your mind, Meph?" [*laughter*] "What do you need?"

Hughes: I think along with that idea of conquering or of mastering the demons or the forces or whatever you call them, a lot of the mindset that goes along with that then carries over into how those things are used. That's where you run into all those stories of the black rays of the Dark Lodge and all.

di Prima: I'm sure, I have not investigated it, that there is the world of the Qliphoth. I have not gone dancing there. I know from experience that the Lower Astral is not a very pleasant place because it's just full of old garbage, but actually you don't ever have to wind up there. It's a question of *directio voluntatis*: direction of the will. For instance, if you know that you want to go to Water or Ether, you set a course before you begin.

And this is something that I learned before conscious magical work, when I was working with acid [LSD]. Most of my early acid was taken at Millbrook, with Timothy Leary and the community there, and I learned that if I set my course before I got high, I could learn those irregular Sanskrit verbs in fifteen minutes when I was on the reentry part of the trip, or I could use the peaking time to investigate this or that about the space between the worlds, or wherever I wanted to go.

Some of it, of course, was always unpredictable—and some of it in visualizing is totally unpredictable—but there is that sense of shooting yourself, your mind or spirit or whatever you want to call it, as a trajectory toward a particular plane or a particular area, or a particular question. So that you pretty much bypass the lower astral garbage. I've almost never gotten stuck there, though I've worked with clients who have. For them the issue almost always is: they had just wanted to open up and let anything in. And you have to really teach them that the will is a muscle that it's okay to use. You set a course.

It's like your body and your breath is a bow and you're just shooting your spirit out from it as if it was an arrow. You set a course and you go toward it.

So, it's possible that because we were always after some very specific thing like this tattva or this card or a question that the group would pose, and we didn't just go down to see what was going on in the worlds—that we didn't get caught in too much dark stuff.

I know that a friend of mine I taught this deep visioning work to, a Cuban poet from New York, was very afraid at first because of having been at a lot of voodoo gatherings and especially talking in tongues, Santeria-type events. And he was very mediumistic, but he'd never learned that he could organize the actual outer form of the spirit so that only certain things could come through it. And actually the deep visioning work for him was a chance to learn that there were ways to use that mediumship where you wouldn't waste it—and it wouldn't take you where you didn't want to go.

A lot of my work with clients is dealing with folks who either inadvertently or through some interesting quest have gotten into spaces where they don't know how to navigate, or they're reticent to use the will.

Kinney: This may be a good point to talk about the secrecy that seems to be part and parcel of Western esoteric tradition and the way that many groups have been organized in terms of graded orders, on a certain "need to know" basis. Where, until you've reached a certain level you're not going to get this scroll handed to you. I was wondering what your feelings were about that because politically you seem to have a more anarchist, non-hierarchical position.

di Prima: Well, this has been raging as an open war since the Golden Dawn, right? My sense is that at this point in history there's very little that we couldn't find out if we knew how to read. I mean there's a hell of a lot I still don't know about alchemy, that's because I don't know how to read yet . . .

Kinney: Read the symbols or read the languages?

di Prima: No, not the languages. [*laughter*] The languages are the easy part! And every time I learn another piece about how to read, like when all the color thing fell into place, so that it became clear to me that—this is just an example—although they might mix up endlessly the order of the processes in the alchemical texts, which is their favorite trick, that endlessly they provided you with the clues because they would say green or they would say black—and only at certain points in the process did each of these colors actually come up. So that you could immediately begin to sort out the tangled skein by color—and that's just one of many levels of learning to read. When they use "our mercury" as opposed to when they just say "mercury"—that's another level of learning to read. And so on.

So I don't think there's anything we couldn't find out by now that's been worked on on this planet. However, there's the secrecy implicit in the fact that we don't understand it—it goes right by us. Everybody reads Fulcanelli, right? Fulcanelli's a very popular guy, but it takes something else to read Fulcanelli.

I think that there was also a secrecy that we got into because of the Church of course, and that it became a habit.

There's also the fact that simply certain people shouldn't be doing certain operations. I'm an anarchist and I still say that. Like my students of "Structures of Magic I" should not go out and try to visualize the realms of the Qliphoth. However, Kenneth Grant's book *Nightside of Eden* is out there and if they want to I'm not their mother—even if I *was* their mother I couldn't stop them, right? [*laughter*] People are not ready to do certain things at certain points, but the only protection I know there for people is to ground them a lot and make them sit and watch their breath as much as possible—the glamor goes out of magic, finally—so that they begin to have a very down-to-earth practical sense of "this much I can handle, this much I can't." That's not going to be gotten by secrecy. So those kind of books and materials I do bring in at the last class and say "All this is there."

"Oh, I think I'd love to go into the Tunnels of Set!" says one of my little feminist students. [*laughter*] "Irma," I say, "I'd like to know you in five years—whole in mind and body! But if you've got to do that, girl, let me know how it goes." [*laughter*]

And then there's another thing there, which is the same as you not showing me the [interview] questions ahead of time. I use a certain amount of secrecy with the people who are going to take the Deep Visioning work in that I don't tell them ahead of time what they're going to come up against as I read them through the visualizations, because it wouldn't have the power and freshness. That kind of secrecy is something else again and that's involved, I suspect, in a lot of the secrecy that evolves around some Eastern visualization disciplines, like the Vajrayana work. The point is that that stuff has to hit you with its power at the moment you're open for it. Like if I tell my visualization students, "Well, now you're going to get two guides," right?—they'll think about it with their thinking minds and they're going to lie down and they're going to get two Egyptian priests! But if they don't know ahead of time, then they're in that open space. So we all need that, and to some extent that's a certain voluntary acceptance of secrecy: "You keep this until I'm ready to hear it."

Hughes: That's not so much a question of getting new information as of not knowing what's going to come next.

di Prima: Right. So that your thinking mind doesn't build all these armorings against hearing it and opening to it. So that's the secrecy that would be a part of the dance within any particular group and in that sense there would be bound to be the hierarchy of the one who's already done that bunch of work or that process, and the one that's being led through it. It's very natural for us in this country not to get heavily into secrecy or hierarchy. We have a built-in suspicion of those things. We all know that as soon as we've let her through the process she's as likely to be further along in it that I am. Ten minutes after she's done the work she may know more about it than I do and I should just shut up and listen. That's temporary secrecy for a reason.

Then, there's also the likelihood that alchemists knew enough to blow up the world all the way back then. So a little more secrecy might be nice! [*laughter*] It would have been nice if Einstein had kept his mouth shut. I know that that's nostalgia on my part . . . but I wish that we weren't sitting on that dilemma right now: it's distracting, it's not very interesting, and it gets in the way of work. It gives us very unruly children who say, "We're not going to live to grow up anyway, so what do we care?"

Kinney: Still speaking of hierarchy . . . I recall a remark that Gary Snyder made about six months ago putting down popular notions of higher consciousness. The point was: "There is no higher consciousness—there is just consciousness."

di Prima: That's a Zen point of view.

Kinney: That was how I took it, but it sort of pushed me up against my own categories and preoccupations because I tend to hierarchize the Planes and one's consciousness of them.

di Prima: Well, I think that you're having a little semantical problem there, Jay. When Gary says, "There's no higher consciousness, there's just consciousness," you're talking that core—it's hard to find the words to use—that core consciousness where the rose, the roach, and you share a sense of being, or beingness, or is-ness, or suchness or—this is not the language for this but . . . When you're saying higher consciousness, you're talking about something else. It's almost like higher intelligence or imagination or higher creativeness. That's the ground—what he says is "just consciousness"—that's the ground that we all live in. Or that's the stuff that we all mold, however you want to see that. But then there's a process of how do you mold it? And I'm sure that there are many kinds of beings with many kinds of intelligence molding away at it, not just humans.

The problem is that we don't have the words in English. When you say "higher consciousness" and talk about that sense of the old angelic hierarchies or however we might see them now, that's not the same as what Gary's saying when he says there's only one consciousness. And he may have the same semantical problem with it. It sounds like he does. 'Cause however dumb the comic book notions of higher intelligences are, there is some real core understanding behind it. And Gary tends to write things off too fast. They're two different things . . .

There's a consciousness that's only ground—that's Hinayana understanding, to go back to Buddhism. That's Hinayana experience: that's where we all connect. Then out of that understanding evolves the sense of Mahayana, where, okay, we're going to do it, become enlightened, whatever, for everybody, not just for ourselves. By the way, there's no magic that's safe unless you do it with the Bodhisattva vow in mind—no matter what tradition you come from, whatever your game is, the gains you make are for all being, they're not for you. It all gets composted back. Anything becomes a demon if you don't have that point of view.

Then, after Mahayana, comes the question—whether it's Renaissance magic or Vajrayana—of us as creative, where the ground is itself there simply to mold into the shapes it will take, so that we are both ground and we're the molders. That's where you start to talk about hierarchies of consciousness: that level where it's creativity that's involved, or imagination or intelligence—the words are all not quite right. That kind of consciousness could be way higher than ours, but the basic ground is just consciousness. So they're not contradictory.

Kinney: Terminology can be a problem.

di Prima: It's impossible! [*laughter*] We drag in Sanskrit, Tibetan, Japanese, Celtic . . . and we still can't do it.

Kinney: One of the challenges in reading somebody like Meister Eckhart is that he'll use the term "intellect" and his use of that term is for something quite different from what I'm used to thinking of as the word "intellect."

di Prima: Absolutely. In the "Hidden Religions" class we run into that with Dante: *Intellectus* is the light of the mind, it has nothing to do with the thinking, calculating part of the mind. It's the actual light of consciousness.

Hughes: So many of those terms have changed do many times . . .

di Prima: "Reason" had a whole other meaning. It had several . . . dozens, probably. Going back from the Greeks to the Age of Reason to Kant's Reason.

Kinney: That in itself would make a good article: the current understanding of those terms and their traditional uses. It's a real stumbling block for people in reading old texts . . .

di Prima: It's interesting, too, if we look at the current understanding we'd probably notice that each term has been narrowed and narrowed so that our whole concept of what we are, of what the pieces are: Intellect, Reason, Spirit, and so on, have kind of been boxed in, reduced. It's a very claustrophobic situation.

Kinney: I was wondering whether you've found that your teaching work and your magical work have been using the energies that would have otherwise have gone into public literary activity.

di Prima: You know, public literary activity is something I was never much into, though I did a lot of poetry readings and all that. But I mean being a literary person is not fun. The thing that finally catapulted me out of New York was a literary party that I went to on Sutton Place where Marianne Moore was guest of honor. W. H. Auden was drawing the name of a publisher out of a hat for the National Endowment for some annual anthology. George Plimpton was serving the punch, and the whole thing was in an apartment full of Bonnards and Legers—and they were all bad ones. It was 1968, and that night I just knew that if I didn't get out of New York and away from the literary world, some day I was going to wind up on that couch like Marianne Moore in a little black silk hat, kind of doddering with a cane, while W. H. Auden or somebody did his thing. [*laughter*]

If you mean, does the work take away from the energy for writing, that's another matter. I don't really know. But I do know that it was inevitable that where the writing was going was towards the visualizing. The stuff that I needed to go after had to come from those inner places. And so the techniques, and the conquering of at least the bare bones of what that's about, seems like it was a necessary step—whether it was a detour or just the next step. I've always had to operate a lot on blind faith in my relation to my work because there was always the question of whether having five kids on my own was going to take away from the work, but I did get written what I got written and I got twenty-one books out.

For me now there's a big question mark—and I have no idea how this is going to come down—and that is, how do you begin to bring all the material which has begun to come in visualization back into the poem? That's something that Yeats never solved, and he's the only one I know of who came up against it so hugely, from *The Vision* on. There weren't so many poems toward the end of his life, and not so many of them brought in that information.

I notice now that some of it is starting to just seep into the poem, and the poem is starting to open out again, but aside from those two hundred tapes, there's an awful lot of amazing writing that I and the others did with this work, and yet it's not anything I can recognize or figure out what to do with. It's not poems, it's not a nonfiction work on the subelements—whatever that might mean. Whether I start to embrace it and say, "okay, this is it, this is its form," or what I do with it, I don't know. And I've sort of let that lie for the last few years since *Loba*. Actually, *Loba* was published the same year we began the group visualizations, spring of 1978.

A lot of the poetry I'm writing now is stuff that at one point I once thought I'd go back and finish and then I realized that its nature is fragmentary—a lot of alchemical poems that are fragments, and they stop where they stop because I can't write the part I don't know—they just stop. The book is called *Alchemical Studies*. But then, the question is, how do you bring this other stuff in? It's so thick and rich. Either it's going to just seep into the poem of itself, or there's going to have to be some kind of wedding, some conscious working of the images from visualizing in poem form—which doesn't seem likely. I don't work like that. Or the stuff as it is—what I jot down directly after a visualizing session—is already finished and I just haven't recognized its shape yet. Which often happens to me. I don't make sense of it, and I don't throw it out, and some ten years later, I pick the thing up and say, "Oh, this is *this*."

In terms of energy for writing, the teaching is another thing. I'd like to stop long enough to write the material in the "Hidden Religions" course. There's really only one other course of that sort that I want to do—and I'd have to do years of study for it. I'd like to cover theories of the imagination in the Western world from Heraclitus to the present. Just basically what have we as a culture—what have we thought this thing is.

Sometimes it seems to me that there's less writing—less poems. But then other times there've been incredible bursts of poetry during this teaching and visualizing, so it's hard to say. It's definitely completely taken my attention away from getting the work published and having it out in the world. No books have happened since *Loba*. All my books have gone out of print, and I haven't made any attempt to—now I'm just beginning to—it's like I'm waking up and saying, "hey, gee, wow, I've got to get these books back in print, and send these ones out" . . . that's just beginning to stir for me. There's also a part of you when you reach a certain point—I'm fifty years old and twice a grandma—there's a certain part of me that knows that if I didn't publish anything for the rest of my life, at some point somebody would dig up those notebooks, and publish stuff. So the priority becomes more to get the goodies and to get them written down. To travel—I don't mean on Earth—to travel and get the goodies.

For us at New College, the whole exploration is not only of the Western tradition, hermetics and so on, but is an exploration of the imagination.

Poetics becomes for us very literally *poiesis*: the imagination as the creative force that makes the universe. So we're back to the old thing of Magus as co-creator with God. So *poiesis* and magic are not two realms for me really but one.

There was a very wonderful moment the first year of the program when Robert Duncan had come to my class and it was the end of the class and he was saying that he didn't want to know what the whole picture was—he just wanted to work on his part of it. And it was very clear to me that what I wanted was to know, even if it was at the expense of doing any more work. He said that in his one and only mescaline trip he was beginning to see the whole Tree of the universe, and he said, "Stop! I don't want to see the whole Tree. I just want to see the branch that I am to work on." And I said, "No man. I want to see that Tree!" [*laughter*] But I'm not sure it has to be at the expense of . . .

These are two points of view about the process, about *poiesis* and about imagination. Within that dialogue the whole thing is encompassed, both magic and poetry. And they're not different. And for me, healing is part of the same work. Transmutation. It's all dealing with the energy which both we are subject and we spin out—shape and spend.

Kinney: I think it would go without saying that with magical work and with work of the imagination, one can't really know the effect of what one does. Like the ripples on the pond, it just goes out there. Do you think that the effects of a poem and a magical act are identical?

di Prima: I think, yes, really, finally. Though in another sense the effects of no two things are ever identical, but that isn't what you mean, is it?

A hard lesson to learn is that you have no control over how anyone's going to use your work after it's published. Or use you or your life. The moment of the creating and the moment of the launching are what we've got in our hands—the rest of it we don't got. You can heal somebody and he can grow up to be Hitler, right? [*laughter*] That's not really your business. Your business is if he comes in sick, you're supposed to heal him.

That's important and interesting in magical work too, because when you're working for a client who thinks they're "invaded," a point comes where you're doing not only the astral work to cut their connection with this bad force or whatever, but you can see the forces behind that, and the forces behind that, and the hubris thing is to say, "Oh, I can take these on too!" The actual process is that the only part that's your job is with this client. You can throw up a crystal wall and tell Michael [Archangel] to take care of the rest, or whatever you want to call him . . . and just say "Goodbye" and get out of there, because otherwise you will get eaten alive. Sooner or later. Same with the writing, if you start to get really taken up with what the reviewers say, and with what New York thinks, and how the reactionaries are misusing your third "Revolutionary Letter" in their magazine or whatever . . . it's really the end. You can't do that. All you can do is your part of the stuff. I'm not talking about "art for art's sake" or the amorality of art or science or that bullshit. It's keeping a certain humility: that you don't have control.

Kinney: What are your feelings about the Judaeo-Christian tradition, considering that things like the Kabbalah derive at least from the Jewish tradition. I recall a couple of years ago at a public lecture at New College you had little good to say about Christianity. Yet dealing with Alchemy, you're plunged into people who were devout Christians.

di Prima: In some really wild sense . . . [*laughter*] I would love to see the Christ of Paracelsus side-by-side with the Christ of Jerry Falwell! [*laughter*] In that wild sense—which is why we spend a lot of time with the heresies in my class. It took me a long time to be able to get into and read and love the Christian stuff that is important to me, like Eckhart, Boehme, and so on, because the metaphor of Christianity was unpleasant to me for years.

My sense of the Kabbalah is that it's both inside and outside of the Judaic tradition the same way that esoteric Christianity—the Christ of Paracelsus, or however you paraphrase that—is both inside and outside of orthodox Christianity. And probably we'd find if we scratched the surface of the Sufis, that they were there before Muhammad.

Kinney: They say as much . . .

di Prima: I don't know whether Kabbalah begins in the Judaic tradition or begins with the Chaldeans for that matter. Nobody does. It was given to Abraham and he came from up there. The thing that I have endless trouble with is any moral system that sets up our possibilities and our acts as essentially evil. That sets us up for guilt. And there I am a Crowleyite: "The word of sin is Restriction." Or a Blakean for that matter—same thing.

The Christian metaphor was soured for me by being around so much and so unpleasantly when I was little, but in returning to it I find in Boehme and Eckhart and Paracelsus the same stuff that I'm after. I'm not uncomfortable with Kabbalah—the Judaic thing was never around for me, so I have no problem there. With the issues that sometimes come up in magic class about the Names of God on the Tree, and so forth—"These Names of God are Names of God the Father"—I'm not uncomfortable with that because they're not. Tetragrammaton is equally male and female. Elohim is ambiguously male and female, singular and plural. And so on. If you scratch the surface you get somewhere else.

Did you know that the ancient Chinese bone oracles they've found—that some of them have fragments of the I Ching on them—all have the radical for woman? So "The Superior Man does such and such" came from the matriarchal period and said "The Superior Person comma Female does such and such." And so the I Ching, or the Judgements, which are the oldest part, stems from the matriarchy. Joan Sutherland, a friend of mine in Los Angeles, who is a Chinese scholar, was telling me that stuff. So again, this stuff gets bent to political use, but it's just like Buddhism gets bent to the use of the Emperor, but it doesn't belong to the Emperor.

But I do object to any religion that tells anyone where, how, and when to make love and with whom, what to eat, and so on. [*laughter*]

Kinney: I've been involved in this ongoing debate with a resolutely atheist anarchist who maintains that the original oppressive act of religion is the dividing of reality into Sacred and Profane. That this division sets up the Sacred over the Profane and defines the Earth, Humanity, etc., as beneath this Sacred realm.

di Prima: Never tell him a secret, and I would hate to ever make love to him. Because if you don't establish a *temenos*—the sacred space in which what occurs is other than the rest of your life—there's no way to keep a secret. Making love, seeing a client—you cannot have any human relation that's finally trustworthy without making a distinction between sacred and profane. Or sacred and more scared, you could put it that way. Maybe he would like that better. Profane and less profane? [*laughter*]

I mean, there are certain points on Earth that are fiercer than others. There are certain moments that exist outside of the rest of our lives . . . Maybe he's never been in love.

Kinney: I can't speak for him on that. [*laughter*]

di Prima: See, girls play dirty when they have intellectual arguments. [*laughter*] But you see what I'm saying: there's always the sacred. There's always the event out of time, or the dream so numinous that you can't refuse it. Or you can refuse it, but . . .

Kinney: He's taking this sort of neo-Zen viewpoint that any characterization of that which is is reification and therefore religion is the original reification because it's trading an abstraction for . . .

di Prima: You know, there's a real threatening aspect to the New Age which is that it could be very boring. It could be very boring if we get down to every consciousness is the same consciousness, or there's no sacred or profane. It could be so boring that we would all just want to kill ourselves. I see a lot of New Age in California—amongst even my friends—that I would want no part of, because it has the flavor of a sophisticated neo-paganism with a lot of good art collections on the side. It's difficult because that's all right and true enough, then there's the Other too, and if the Other isn't there casting a shadow, all that stuff is one-dimensional. There is that danger. Luckily we're in a tight enough spot on the planet that we won't just glide into a boring New Age! [*laughter*]

Art, Magic, and the Dharma: An Interview with Diane di Prima

Tim Hulihan / 1988

From *Half Pint: A Newsletter of the Naropa Community* 1, no. 1 (November 7, 1988): 1, 7, 9. Reprinted by permission of the Jack Kerouac School of Disembodied Poetics, Naropa and Anne Waldman, founder, core faculty, professor.

Half Pint: My question concerns the relation of art, meditation, and magical practices. Are they different, or all part of one spectrum? How are they related for you?

Diane di Prima: When I started to sit in 1962–64, it took a long time to bring that into my writing. When I started to sit a lot, when I came out to the Bay area to study with Suzuki, there was a period of time when I wrote very little. And then it slowly came back in. In my last interview with Suzuki in 1971, I brought him the question, "How does Zen, which seems to be the emptying of the mind, and poetry, which is full of images (I told him my life is image)—how do those two fit together, I mean am I doing the wrong practice? What is happening here?" And he talked about them as being two sides of the same coin, that I should think of going to meditation as I would go to rest, and that by resting more fully, I could also be more fully open to the image.

And I would say also that being able to be empty is primary to any occult work, to healing or magical work. You cannot do it through your personality, your persona. First of all it's very dangerous, and secondly, it's very ineffective. The first thing I teach in all my classes at the San Francisco Institute of Magical and Healing Arts are practices that will empty you, at least for a brief time, of your self, of your opinion—you can't heal without that—I do laying on of hands work, where I am actually just bringing energy down into me and through me and into the person I'm working on.

In the same way, even Aleister Crowley will point out that in order to do magical work you have to start with a good sitting practice. His understanding of sitting was completely Hinayana, it came through Allan Bennett, who was one of the first British people to study Buddhism, who finally wound up living as a monk in Ceylon for the rest of his life—Theravadin Buddhism. But Crowley did at least have the basic understanding, although he didn't always convey it to his students, which is why people burned out.

There is a valid, important, and incredibly rich tradition, in the Near East and Europe, which is my tradition. That lineage was, we used to say broken, but I think more that it was hidden from time to time. I'll give you an example: in the story about Trithemius, who was the teacher of Paracelsus and Agrippa, there was a man, an unknown stranger, who was the teacher of Trithemius—hidden in that there were probably people who just showed up, and it still happens, people who instruct you and go away. . . .

HP: Have you found people like that?

DdP: I myself, no, I have not. One of the people I work with has a teacher like that. He was taught an infinite amount of stuff in one night by this person who promised to come back and teach him more and was never seen again, who gave a false name and couldn't be found. And it was real, the teachings were real, they were solid. But, because the lineage in the occult tradition is incomplete in the West, I found that as I was doing work on deeper and deeper levels—trance work for people who were in danger to themselves—I encountered energies that were more than I knew how to handle. I felt the importance of seeking teachings in a lineage that was unbroken. I had known Chögyam Trungpa since 1970 when he came to Tassajara, and I had been sitting on my own in the Zen style since Suzuki died. I had had many interviews with Trungpa Rinpoche about meditation practice, but I still kept with Suzuki's teachings and he respected that. In '83 I came to him and told him my dilemma, that I had been working with Western stuff all these years and I felt the need of more teachings now, and I felt the need of a sangha, because you can't process this stuff alone when you're encountering heavy forces in your life, but that I wasn't really willing to give up. . . . In my mind I put it that I wasn't ready to give up Paracelsus for Padmasambhava—I wasn't willing to give up the Western teaching for the Eastern, but I felt the need for the Eastern. He told me there was absolutely no problem, that, in fact, it could be a fantastic help, for having these two points of view. The only instruction he gave was to my friend Sheppard, which was to keep them separate.

HP: Keep them separate?

DdP: Yeah, separate altars, separate practices. He didn't tell me that but I assume that that's the basic rule altogether.

HP: So they are not at all the same tradition.

DdP: No, and yet they have so many things in common that one can't help playing with the idea that there might have once been a world culture. The mandala of the four directions that we use in the banishing ritual in the Western tradition, which I spoke about a little, with the angels and the colors and the elements, is not that different, with switched directions on certain elements, from the Tibetan tradition, with the Buddhas of the directions and the Buddha families in that mandala, and it's not so different from the Navajo tradition, which has four colors, four directions and forces which are, you'd say, four dakinis, four goddesses, or women, and it has a central mountain, like Tibet does. So it's tempting to say that there was one point of view in common, but who knows. They aren't the same tradition, when you're working Western magic, almost all the time you are working in the sambhogakaya, you're working with the world of form.

HP: Yes.

DdP: But going to the sitting practice in its simplest form, as in Shamatha or Zen practice, is to touch in with the formless, the world of formlessness. I find a need to do that both beginning and end, just as you would in any Vajrayana visualization. To clear yourself, and remember that all these things arise and disappear.

HP: So you find them complementary then?

DdP: They are very helpful to each other and to me. And I think that for us in the West there is a lot that speaks to us in our own tradition, and we need to not abandon that, we need to stay with that.

HP: And art?

DdP: I don't know, when I work . . .

HP: Well, for instance art is often involved with a persona, or personality, a presentation of yourself in a definite form in the world, it's not an emptiness practice.

DdP: That got to be uninteresting to me very early, even before I met Suzuki and began sitting in '62, but by '59 (I was about twenty-four or so) I was already working with people who had learned how to let go of the personality-cult of art. I was studying with James Waring at the time, who is a dance choreographer in New York. He had gotten it from his predecessor John Cage, and all of that group; Merce, Jimmy, and so on, were reading D. T. Suzuki. And although they didn't sit, the ideas of Zen—it seems strange but Alan Watts worked that way too—were penetrating their world. I took classes with James Waring that showed me, through very simple exercises, ways to just drop the personality for a brief period of time and allow the poem to come through. And though I use the experiences of my life in my work and did for many years, there was a way in which it was no longer my life—it wasn't personal to me. And as I got older that got to be more and more the case.

HP: So art in a personality-cult way, or expression of personality, could actually be an obstruction to the artist?

DdP: I think it is, and I think it's been an obstruction to how we see art in America. Because many artists will drop that as they work, and yet the critic looks for that, they seek that personality-cult.

HP: So it's more how art is perceived, rather than how it is made?

DdP: In many cases. And then of course there are people who build their whole work on their persona, it's similar to me, although I don't want to condemn the artists, it's similar in a sense to black magic, in the sense of doing magic to gain power for yourself.

HP: Egohood.

DdP: Rudra-hood, exactly. That sense of accumulating and consolidating your own person.

HP: A lot of new-age things tend to seem like that to me, and also some of the involvement with magic I've seen.

DdP: Uh-huh, Uh-huh, well I think everything is based on what your motive, what your intent is, what you are doing it for.

But, finally, when the work comes through you, I don't want to be adamant, and say, like Spicer (Jack Spicer), "Dictation," and yet something like that happens, you're not really deciding and writing, it's just happening. Suzuki used to say that the work that you decided you wanted to write and you just made it up and wrote it, that that was okay, but you had to remember it wasn't really writing. It was okay to do it as long as you didn't mix it up with the real writing.

HP: When you speak of the Dharmic tradition, the Western Occult tradition, and art, from what I've been hearing, it sounds like you are talking in terms of different functions, with the emptying, or egolessness as some kind of ground and the magical practices more as an interactive thing, a healing or helping, moving things around—and art, what would you say is the function of that?

DdP: Art is its own thing for me. Art is a place where we are continually recreating the world, recreating consciousness. I think that finally, especially from the non-theistic point of view, we are the constant creators of our world. The excitement for me in art is that the actual shape of consciousness, and how we see the world, is changed by it. I can see from the changes that have happened in my lifetime, from becoming a young writer in the early fifties, right through now, not merely changes in the consciousness of artists, but in people who are never going to read any of us. I think in that way we are, as Pound said, "the antennae of the race," which means that we report back the changes, but I also think we make the changes.

HP: It sounds like art is a different kind of tradition, not so much a tradition where you enter into defined terms, but a tradition that is constantly being created, a tradition of re-creation.

DdP: I would imagine that in the higher forms of meditation you get to the point where you are actually recreating the forms of the deities you are working with, and I know that there is some element of that creativity in the healing work, because each person you are treating is completely different, and you can't use formula—but with art that is really the primary condition, that's the whole essence. And I think that the faith there is that simply by doing it you are benefitting other beings. Simply by doing it you are enabling consciousness to remain flexible and not solid, to keep changing and evolving. For me, I don't have to know that this piece is going to reach so and so many people, or that I'm going to tell everybody to dismantle their plutonium plant, although I might write that kind of thing, like the *Revolutionary Letters* I wrote with a street theatre group—but it's not the primary thing. It's simply to allow that thing to move in you that's more than you understand. And the ground for accepting that you don't have to understand, don't have to be in control, is meditation. The ground for just allowing the work to be itself, beyond anything you already understand, and just trusting in the process, comes from meditation. And the work itself is its own end, and my feeling is that in just existing, just allowing that to come through and be there, you begin to benefit others.

My sense too, is that all three things we are talking about have that sense of what I keep calling "allowing something through." Whether you are sitting and emptying, or doing magical or healing work, and the same way in art. And every time we do that the persona also learns and grows, but I'm not sure how that happens—we become more flexible and more open, more experience has occurred for us, because we haven't fenced it in to our personalities.

HP: It sounds to me like these practices don't have any definite goal, in terms of getting somewhere or achieving something, but perhaps have more to do with simply learning to be more fully as you already are, more completely what you are . . .

DdP: And to respond immediately to what immediately is at hand, whether it's a person come for healing work, or the meditation cushion that you're sitting on.

HP: Or the mind that's making itself up at the moment.

DdP: Exactly, or the one word or one image that triggers ten hours of writing and you don't know why. To use Buddhist terminology, there's something of surrender in all of it.

The Beatnik and the Rapper: Hipster Poet, Hip-Hop Daughter Ride the Same Wavelengths

Alice Kahn / 1992

From the *San Francisco Chronicle*, July 17, 1992: E3, 5. © 1992 by San Francisco Chronicle. Reprinted by permission of Hearst Communications, Inc.

The scene: Hip women talking.

The place: Dining room of an immaculate San Francisco townhouse, a room dominated by a conga drum, a framed photo of Billie Holiday, and an enormous microwave oven.

The players: Dominique DiPrima, twenty-seven, tough and sexy rap artist and MC of the many-Emmyed TV show *Home Turf*, which features the hottest hip-hop stars and youth trends in a format that reflects the social concerns and creative spirit of the MC. Daughter of Italian American poet Diane di Prima (who spells it that way) and the African American playwright LeRoi Jones (Amiri Baraka). It is her clean house and her microwave.

Diane di Prima, fifty-eight, calm and cerebral onetime beatnik madonna, mother of five, author of twenty books. When asked by a Berkeley coed in 1968, "What ever happened to the beatniks?" she answered, "Well, sweetie, some of us sold out and became hippies."

Di Prima teaches and writes in San Francisco while striving for nirvana in Point Reyes. The Brooklyn-born grandmother, who has been on an Ezra and Allen basis with every poet from Pound to Ginsberg, has never owned or operated a microwave.

The reason we're here: 1) This madonna and child will perform together tonight in a program called "Spoken Word Meets Rap—At Last" sponsored by Wordland, "The Anti-Fascist Spoken Word Ballroom." And: 2) They are two cool women.

Action:

"People think of poetry as something on paper, a dead form. All rap is a form of poetry," says the daughter, Dominique.

"It's related to the blues and the African oral tradition," says the mother, Diane.

"The beat stuff is more related to blues and jazz," says Dominique.

"Well, some Sicilian sneaks into my work, too," says Diane. "My work's gotten more esoteric, but it still dips down into idiom or slang."

Voice-over: These two women have forty years of counterculture between them. They respond to a question about whether rap hasn't gone mainstream. Neither is shy of opinion.

"This country will mainstream anything if it has commercial value," Dominique says with disdain. "But the fact that they come down hard on it—Sister Souljah is under attack, Ice-T and Paris are under attack—compared to the mainstream it's still counterculture."

"To young people across the country, it's mainstream. It's a young people's cult," says Diane.

"Most people only know the mainstream artists," says Dominique. "They think rap is Vanilla Ice or Hammer."

Diane comes in on the upbeat: "Cocteau says that not to be co-opted, an artist has to be an acrobat. You have to stay three somersaults ahead."

Ginsberg's Breakfast

Wait a minute!

Do these women always talk this way? Has their life together been one long PBS series: "Today on 'Art, Woman, Culture,' Mama di Prima talks Cocteau with Kid DiPrima"?

Oh, no, the two insist, their time together consists of family gossip, rap gossip, and poet gossip—in-between discussions of art, meaning and politics. Like, what's an example of poet and rap gossip, anyway? "Oh, I might tell her what Allen Ginsberg was eating for breakfast when I saw him last year," says Diane. "It was oatmeal with shitake mushrooms and tamari over it. I thought it was going to be awful, but it tasted great."

And an example of rap gossip? Something juicy perhaps, like Latifah sleeping with one of the Ice Men—Cube or T or Vanilla?

"I might tell my mother that during the Rodney King rebellion, it was X-Clan who organized the march by telling their concert audience to walk out," says Dominique. "That's the kind of thing she'd be interested in. She's more interested in that than in who's sleeping with whom."

"Everybody will be sleeping with everyone else," says Diane. "That's the law of the arts."

Okay but *wait a minute!* Don't they ever do mundane mother-and-daughter things . . . like fight?

How did Dominique rebel against a mother who at fifty-eight talks about her current "lover," against a mother who lists the following item on her published resume: 1967—*Twenty-thousand-mile trip around USA in VW bus, read at discotheques, bars, storefronts, universities, galleries. Birth of third daughter, Tara.*

This trip occurred when little Dominique was five, her big sister Jeanne was ten, her little brother, Alex, was four, and her brother Rudi—well, Rudi would not arrive until three years later, when the family settled down for a spell at the Tassajara Zen Mountain Center near Big Sur.

Material Girl

Sure, the kids have rebelled.

"I have a couch," says Dominique, looking at her mother, who realized she's never even had a living room. "I have a new car. I like clothes. I put more emphasis on external things . . ."

And here the ubiquitous microwave seems to light up and glow red-hot with generational defiance.

"But I still eat brown rice, I still know not to believe what I read, I still have a left-progressive world view," says Dominique, who never knew that parental threat "I'll wash your mouth out with soap."

How could she go to her room? She didn't have one until she went away to boarding school.

"I'll say anything to people," Dominique says. "Someone had to teach me that women shouldn't be all in people's faces. I had to learn that. I've got my mother and father's rocky temper. They taught me to be opinionated and independent. Now she has to deal with that."

Diane has no regrets. When she made a commitment to poetry in 1948— as the fourteen-year-old daughter of conventional parents—she never turned back. Her anger at her strict upbringing—"It was almost Arabic"— gave her the courage to do things few women were willing to take on, from moving to her own place on the lower East Side of New York in 1952, to having a baby out of wedlock in 1957, to being busted with Jean Genet for obscenity in 1961, to teaching poetry to psychiatric patients at Napa State Hospital in 1976.

"Once I started, once I decided to do it, I did it," says Diane. "I always knew I didn't want a husband, even when I was married.

"I also knew I wanted a baby, but I didn't know if I could and still be a writer. I didn't want to be an artist at the cost of being a human being. So we just lived our lives.

"I haven't compromised my belief system or, as the Sicilians say, I haven't gotten my hands dirty. But the kids got teased for having miso and rice crackers in their lunch."

"None of the other kids wanted to steal our lunch," says Dominique. "My mom broke the mold. I think people don't give mom enough credit 'cause she's got kids—she's fine and we're fine. There's no *People* cover story here—no junkie, no Betty Ford clinic."

The two have grown closer in the last few years. Dominique has even influenced Diane to finally get a TV set for the first time in her life. She bought one last year but only watches *The Simpsons* and *Star Trek* and her favorite show, *Home Turf.*

And when Dominique says she has to leave, her mold-breaking mother says, "Come here and give me a kiss."

The fundamental things survive.

Diane di Prima: Memoirs of a Beatnik

Ron Whitehead, Sharon Gibson, and Kent Fielding / 1992

From *Beat Scene* no. 27 (1997): 7–17. Interview conducted in 1992. Reprinted by permission of Ron Whitehead.

Possibly overshadowed by the men who rose to become the Beat Generation, Diane di Prima is at once part of that generation and a completely individual writer in her own right. The racy novel *Memoirs of a Beatnik* in no way represented who di Prima was at that point. Her writings before and since have shown a poet who feels the world's ills and reflects them in her output. Like Ginsberg and Snyder she is not an ivory tower poet, some might term her an activist, certainly she's ruffled a few feathers in her time.

Recent books like *Dinners and Nightmares* have demonstrated well her current inspirations. In a recent interview with Ron Whitehead, Sharon Gibson, and Kent Fielding, Diane di Prima reveals the state of play for her after forty years as a major American poet.

Sharon Gibson: You have received a lot of recognition as a Beat poet but much of your most interesting work was written later in your career. Does that sometimes annoy you?

Diane di Prima: I don't know if it annoys me. It's very usual for people to want a label or handle. I have never thought of myself as a Beat poet even when there were Beats around. The idea of Beat got invented sometime after I was doing what I was doing. That was a label and it was okay as a label, and then in what seemed like two minutes all these people were imitating— becoming imitation Beats. So, you never really had time to think of yourself as a Beat. Movements are like that. Especially in America. Because of the media, they come and they go like that. It is odd. I think the thing that does to some degree bother me is that in using that label people block out the variety of work that was going on at that point in history. Because there wasn't only Ginsberg, Corso, Kerouac, and people like me but there were also people like Olson and Duncan. There was being a surrealist like Philip Lamantia. And some of these people sometimes get lumped in with the Beats. But what does that mean—because they were not doing any of the things that were the Beat poetic, really. You can hardly say that Duncan used the vernacular of the streets in his work. Everyone was doing something different, and the variety gets lost. But that's what happens when you stereotype or label anything. So, I feel partly I'm seen in the context of Allen and Jack and Corso and their friends whereas in fact I met them rather late after I'd been doing this kind of thing for several years and my own group of friends just happened to be people who didn't get very famous for the most part. My own early friends, when I was first writing from '53 to, say, '57 were people like Fred Herko, the dancer, Bret Rohmer, a painter, and so on. As well as actors and painters that got well known. But in general the circle of people I knew wasn't seen as a circle so the tendency is to lump me with the Beat circle, though actually I was in New York and that circle was mostly on the West Coast. We met in early '57 for the first time and a lot of water was under the bridge by then. It was the non-academic literature of the time, but it wasn't all Beat—that's the thing. There were a lot of groups and it's more interesting if you see it that way.

Gibson: Ann Charters asked in her letter of January 23, 1984, "What gave you the courage to live as you pleased in the mid 1950's?"

di Prima: I used to think it was kind of simple. I got certain kinds of ideas and values from my grandparents, especially my anarchist grandfather, who besides being an anarchist, put six girls through college in the 1920s on the salary of a custom tailor. He backed it up. He didn't just talk it. My mother and all her sisters got degrees then. I thought it was kind of simple that I just got certain values and it was easy to go ahead with them. But as I've gotten older and more in touch with what went on at home when I was young— part of it was just pure rage on my part, and a real need to get away from the home environment. 'Cause there were my grandparents with their values and all that, and then there was within my immediate family my father who was very repressive. He was born in America but raised in Sicily. And he was a batterer, he was a rage-aholic. He never touched my mother, only the children. And since I was the oldest of the children I was always coming between him and my brothers. All that kind of stuff was going on. I was oldest of all the cousins. Now in an Italian family it's very close, so your first cousins are practically your brothers and sisters. I basically took care of everybody. I remember I was changing diapers when I was four. I think that something about the dysfunction of the situation made me who I was.

For a long time I didn't know this and so I didn't say that. And I would tell women, well, you know it's easy, if you feel independent just go do it. And I think I was doing a disservice to a lot of people who would think, "Oh God, why aren't I as strong as her?" But a lot of it was pure rage and it took a toll in other ways in terms of tension-related health problems and this and that, but it still got me out of there, and rather than going crazy, I became a writer. It was the mix of values from my grandparents and whatever sturdiness I had in myself with the dysfunction and the craziness of my family. My mother was a hysteric. She would have nervous "fits" when things didn't go her way. That and my dad being the way he was. Then all the craziness of trying to transfer the Italian culture to the American situation. Girls weren't supposed to go out at night. You could be sixteen and they still wouldn't let you go to the opera, much less a date. No dates. No. That was for later. I never went out on a date till college, and then only twice. I probably didn't have a lot of distractions. By the time I was fourteen I knew I was going to write. So, by the time I left home I'd been writing every day for four years.

Gibson: Why did you leave school and go to Greenwich Village?

di Prima: Hunter College High School was a very unusual place when I was there from 1948 to 1951. It was an all-women's school. You got in by test. It was at that point supposedly for the brightest women in the city, whatever that means. What it meant was that you had a group of really wild young women. They were really nuts. And it was a very free environment. The teachers were all women, and there were some very smart women teachers. It was an environment where you really couldn't go too far in your mind. All kinds of things were accepted. One day we were walking out the door to play hooky and go down to the bookstores on Fourth Avenue. As we were going out the door our English teacher stopped us and said, "What are you guys doing?" We said, "Well, we're leaving!" She said, "Be careful—don't get caught!" It was like that. There were seven or eight of us who were writing (one of my classmates was Audre Lorde) and we'd come in every morning early to read our poems to each other. That kind of thing. So from that kind of freedom—one of my friends left when she was fourteen to go form a kibbutz and be with her lover—from that kind of thing—to suddenly find yourself at Swarthmore! And then when I was in high school the Korean War broke out, which for me and my generation destroyed any faith we had in the system. Because it happened so fast after World War II. We had been promised peace. It sounds naïve, but we were fourteen, remember. All of a sudden this other thing happens and it's the boyfriends of your girlfriends who are going to war. Cynicism was rampant at that point. The Korean

War created a generation of immense skepticism. Anyway, all that and then suddenly you find yourself in suburban Pennsylvania, where everyone is mostly from the upper class, all dressed in their little cashmere sweaters and a strand of pearls. There was this whole "everything-is-all-right" veneer about their world. And being who I was I tended to see through that even at my age. All the time. Everything is all right? For instance I would be the only one who would know that this particular guy, although he was dating the right girl and all that, was really gay, because my way of seeing through things was such that people would also confide in me. So, this whole charade that was going on that was called "college" was ridiculous. I was running around in cut-off jeans with a red sash because I wanted to be a pirate, and hair down to my ass, running through the woods and reading poetry and I wasn't wearing cashmere sweaters. And they didn't know what to do with me and I didn't know what to do with them. Then, most of all the interesting women in my class all quit at the same time. And two of them, who were lovers, asked me to quit with them. I was actually sort of in love with one of those two. We were going to set up house with three people. So, in the middle of my sophomore year I decided to do that. To the credit of the school, they weren't objecting to the red sashes or red satin ballet slippers. They really wanted me to stay. But when the woman who was the dean at the time realized that I was intent on going, she mediated with my family for me and told them to step back and leave me alone because I was the most creative person she had known and they'd better give me some room. They didn't, but it was nice of her to say that.

Gibson: Did you begin your real study at that time?

di Prima: Actually before that. When I was eleven I read my way through the philosophers that were in the Brooklyn Public Library, Carroll Street Branch. Starting with Plato and just reading my way. I couldn't understand Kant but most of the rest of them I got pretty well. And then I moved on to the novels. And when I was reading Somerset Maugham I found a quote by Keats and that led me to the poets. Once I found the poets I didn't understand why the philosophers bothered because they had to come up with one idea, one position, and stick with it. But if you were a poet you didn't have to. And since obviously no one position is true, poetry gave me the flexibility to really explore the world. You can't enclose reality in one position. Obviously. That was when I was fourteen. So I was reading at that point the Romantics a lot and what I found in college—I found Pound and Cummings and Auden. But mostly Pound, that was a big next step. They weren't in the Brooklyn Public Library.

Gibson: With the resurgence of interest in the Beats, do you think your time is come?

di Prima: Well there is some level where I think the time has come to get it all out there. A couple of years ago I started really using the Buddhist idea of death to look at my work and say it's time to put it in order. I'd wake up and I'd say to myself okay, probably you don't have more than twenty active years to get this together. I was fifty-five at the time, and I've got shelf upon shelf of manuscripts. I've got two four-foot shelves of spring binders and I've got seventy bound journals with collages and writings that I want to place somewhere. But I haven't even typed most of the stuff in them, much less put them in volumes. So now, instead of being an unpleasant thing to think about, it's just a matter-of-fact thing to think about, in terms of, okay, how do I make these collections happen? How do I make the work get out there? My feeling is if the work gets out there, it will find its own way. Whether I get famous or not in my lifetime or not, is not an issue. If it's out there, sooner or later it's going to find its way.

Gibson: A lot has been written about the double vision mystics have of being in time yet timeless.

di Prima: Blake said it has to be fourfold.

Gibson: Fourfold! Okay—but much of your earlier work was in time, of the moment and a very fresh response to the moment. Was "Canticle of Saint Joan" a turning point?

di Prima: No, what about *The New Handbook of Heaven*? That goes back to 1960 and it already has that double vision. My first book came out in 1958 with stuff from '54 on—it's only a few years before it's both. And then it stays both. *The Calculus of Variation* was written in 1961–1964. It's kind of interesting: This morning I was writing this little poem about Louisville. It's about the weather and walking to the river and a guy in a top hat that was the bellman who did a pirouette when I asked him where to get the trolley. And he really did. He spun around. So that thing you mentioned about my work being very immediate is still around.

Gibson: For instance, your poem "Rant" is a wonderful mix of both. When did you write "Rant"?

di Prima: I wrote "Rant" I think in 1986. Did you recognize how many quotes were in it? There are quotes from Olson and quotes from Keats and other people. Paracelsus. They're not in quote marks—they're just adapted to the poem.

Gibson: What about the line "The war against the imagination."

di Prima: That's mine. "Every man and woman carries a firmament inside" is Paracelsus. The world as a vale of soul-making is Keats' phrase. History is to see for yourself, is Olson, from *Causal Mythology*. And so on. I was in a hotel room, which is a good place for a lot of stuff to come together. I was in Buffalo. I just wrote it in one sitting.

Gibson: What about "Canticle of Saint Joan"? Did you have any particular inspiration for writing that?

di Prima: Well, sure.

Gibson: It seems to be very much like *Loba*. Did you write it in preparation for *Loba*?

di Prima: No.

Gibson: Or was that where you were heading?

di Prima: "The Canticle of Saint Joan" is a monologue spoken by Saint Joan at four different periods of her life. The first part of it is spoken before she decides to go into battle: "How can I decide France will be free," and then the next two are spoken while she is burning. And what's involved in it is seeing St. Joan as a continuum of the natural magical religions of Europe and as a practitioner of the same and therefore someone who heard voices, and so on. Had trances. And someone for whom there wasn't necessarily a devil but a horned god. And someone for whom the woods themselves were the temple. That's why she says, "the cross was ours before you holy men." It's like the whole process of deciding you're going to engage politically, the various processes of what happens to you once you are trapped, incarcerated—in hands of the others, and the actual process of transcendence, because fire— death by fire—my own sense of it that it's terrible but it's not terrible at all, it's quite amazing. That's all. I can't say there was an inspiration. I wrote it in the 1960s in San Francisco during the time I was working with the Diggers, and we were doing a lot of revolutionary stuff, a lot of all kinds of stuff and so, it came out of my own sense of how do I decide, how do I make a decision. I don't make a decision but I've been put in this position. So, like my flirtation with fame in other ways, I left there and pulled out of that, because I didn't want to be a "leader" of other people. I left San Francisco and went away to just meditate and write. Because it got to the point where maybe I was going to be saying these fiery things, but it was Black Mrs. Casey and her three kids in the next building who were going to meet the cops on the corner. I mean, even if I met them too, if this thing was continuing the way it was going right then, the burden would be on them. And I didn't feel like I wanted to pull anybody else into a direct confrontation with any authorities because that wasn't the way we were going to make it happen.

I didn't want to see anyone get hurt because of my writing or ideas. And because also my anarchist background does not permit me to want to be a leader, in the sense of I tell you, you know. In the 1960s I would go to read my *Revolutionary Letters* someplace and people would say to me, "What is your plan for the people of San Francisco?" I didn't have any plan. These groups would be very Marxist and very ready to tell others what to do, but I didn't have any plan for the people of San Francisco. Our plan is that the people on every block will make their own plan. I am an anarchist. So, Saint Joan is about the first stage of that, when you're engaging and where it could go to. And whether it happens with prisons and fires or whether it happens in other ways, you still go there. Because once you're committed to an engagement, whether it's with poetry or politically, there is no place to go but the fire. That's not sad or tragic and it's not somebody else's doing even if—in the case of Joan—they put you in there. It's still not their doing. It's your decision.

Ron Whitehead: I recently read a critic who said that in the 1960s the United States was comparable culturally to the Renaissance or the Romantic movement. Do you have any thoughts on that?

di Prima: Well . . . no. But when you read about any particular period of the Renaissance or any particular period where there was a big cultural flowering, you always have the potential to be amazed by how short it was. The flowering of the Heian culture in Japan. Poof! Gone in fifty-odd years. The important part of the Medici court one generation really. So, in that sense it could well be if we look back later—I wouldn't say the sixties—I'd say probably from the late forties through the sixties—so you'd have Poof! twenty years. Because you got to figure it going further back than the writing or the rock and roll. You got to figure in Charlie Parker and early De Kooning and Dinah Washington. And then you've got a flowering that lasts twenty years. And Poof! Yeah, it's gone that fast. So in that sense it's possibly so, but I don't think we're in a position to know that and also—if we did know that, what good would it do us? We still have to keep working. The ladies who came after the great Japanese writers still did pretty good writing. Maybe they didn't know they were past the flowering.

Gibson: Allen Ginsberg said at Camp Kerouac that the legacy of the Beats was literary liberation and a catalyst for gay liberation and Black liberation and women's liberation. I'm paraphrasing, but do you agree with him?

di Prima: I think Allen was claiming a little bit there. Well . . . but what brought the Beats into being? And then you go back to bebop. You go back to that cynicism I was talking about after the Korean War started. So it's not like we did this single-handed. I remember Ginsberg saying to Leslie Fiedler during the Vietnam War, "I, Allen Ginsberg, single-handed, will stop it." I said, "Allen, watch out! That's a little bit of hubris there." Yeah, I think the Beats had something to do with all that but I don't think it was a cause-and-effect relationship, so simply.

Gibson: What are some of your own favorite poems?

di Prima: That changes. Very often it's what is useful at a given moment when you're doing readings. Right now "Rant" is wonderful to me. But in the terms of work I love to do, *Loba* is the work I love to do. Any poems for me happen when they want to happen. I can't make them happen.

Whitehead: Many people think that inspiration comes easy. And that the way out is working over something by doing twenty or thirty drafts. But you've made it clear in your writing and in interviews that it takes a lot of work to prepare yourself for inspiration.

di Prima: Yeah, well, you have to work all the time. And part of it is writing a lot of the time. Even if there isn't any particular thing coming through. Some of that can be working on pieces, some of it can be doing some translating. Some of it can be journals. Right now I'm teaching a few women on the West Coast and I gave them an assignment to imitate the Japanese Court ladies' journals called Haibun. They write this prose and then right in the middle of it there will be a tiny poem. Sort of like they're making a setting and putting a jewel in. over and over again. And I told them they should write this journal about one particular theme in their lives. You can write about an affair. You can write about your struggle to write. You can write about poverty or riches or whatever is on your mind. But one theme throughout. That's like a contrived exercise, but at the same time it's a way of keeping your hand in between inspirations, so-called. Now of course I'm engaged on at least two large prose works that I can always fall back on and work on. I find that I don't need that kind of inspiration for them. But when the poem comes, most of the time, especially if it's a powerful poem like "Saint Joan," there are almost no changes to be made. The thing you work on—and I think part of the work for me has been done through meditation— you work on holding your concentration so that you're willing to stay with it. For instance, "Saint Joan" is long. I wrote that all in one sitting. I didn't go back and say, "Oh gee I think I'll write stanza 4 of Saint Joan now." No. I sat down on the bed. I remember the room I was in, and it just all came out. Sometimes I've done that with *Loba* at the same time that I'm carrying on a conversation in a car with the person who's driving and I'm writing "The day lay like a pearl on her lap." I remember my friend was driving to go buy a boat and I'm writing that one. Another time somebody's kid was climbing over me and I'm writing "The Loba Recovers the Memory of a Mare." Because the voice, when it comes in, is clear. Those hardly have any changes to be made. It's almost like taking dictation. But it's not quite like that. There's some sense especially of what Spicer talks about of what Robert Duncan calls "obedience." You just put yourself in the hands of the thing. You have no idea why it's going that way and you let it say what it says. But everything you've done before that, all the reading and studying, all the things you've thrashed out, all the sitting, all the languages you've played with and learned a few words of, every time you've read the Sanskrit roots in the dictionary, all that's there. That is part of the instrument that can be played. And if you have an instrument with less strings, then the song comes out, not necessarily worse, but certainly a lot simpler. In *Loba* I'm always fondest of the part I'm working on. Right now there are many Psyche and Eros poems.

Gibson: What about your life in California sometime after the Diggers when you moved off by yourself? You spent a lot of time studying Zen.

di Prima: When I came out to the West Coast I came out for two things. One was to study at the Zen Center. So, I did that at the same time that I was being political with the Diggers. Then I moved up to northern California for a while to a commune called Black Bear for six or seven months. I just did a lot of sitting and writing there. And then came back to the city and continued to study at the Zen Center until Suzuki died in 1971. At that point the organization itself [Zen Center] was not enough to hold me. They were too bureaucratic. So I started to sit on my own. By 1973 I moved out of San Francisco up to the north coast, to Marshall, which is a town of fifty people. The house was slowly falling down, but it was beautiful. I lived up there for five years. While I was up there I did a lot of writing on *Loba*, a lot of collaging, kept these journals I was talking about and it was very quiet but very intense. I would go out on the road to get money and then come back and work. But it was also very hard, because it was a long way from anything and I was up there with four kids. So, it was a 125 miles a day drive on the average here and there—picking this one up at painting class and taking that one to the movie in Petaluma. So, I was wearing out cars faster than I could afford to buy them. And I was dealing with powder post beetles, termites, and a broken water heater. And when the rainy season came: no lights, no phone half of the time. And when the rainy season didn't come you were hauling water from people's houses in Point Reyes, because the spring box went dry in the summer. So, by 1978 after five years of it, though it was very great, I moved back to San Francisco. I had a choice: I could have moved to Wyoming. They offered me a Poet-in-Residence there. But I looked at it, and I realized I was going to be in a place where I would be solely a teacher. I wouldn't also be much involved with people who would be teaching me. So I opted to go to San Francisco and be a student as well as a teacher. And then in 1980, I began teaching in the Masters in Poetics Program at New College, which I started with David Meltzer and Robert Duncan, and which lasted six years. It was a highly evolved program which had to do with the hermetic and the occult in poetry. In 1983 I helped found the San Francisco Institute of Magical and Healing Arts. So they overlapped for a while and that one we kept going until 1990.

However, what I am doing now is working on books from the tapes from the classes taught at San Francisco Institute. A book called the *Language of Alchemy*, which is a four-lecture course that I gave. It's about the language that's used in alchemy texts and the kind of coding that went on and why and how you can find your way somewhat through an alchemy text. So those kinds of books will be probably showing themselves. *Structures of Magic* was a course that started with the basic polarity, the basic dualism, yin/yang or whatever, and the four elements that evolve from that, then shows how the three fit with the four and creates the Zodiac. And works with the numbers up to ten and the Tree of Life and shows how the Tarot cards fit on the Tree. This is a course I gave many times and people really learned a lot. Working with all those things and then looking at the Hebrew letters and how they relate to the Tree and the cards. Then looking at how different people have tried to put the Eastern systems, especially the I Ching, on the Tree and how that works and doesn't work and various correspondences of that sort. What I decided when I started to try to do this book is that it has to be a text with a workbook. Because a lot of the work we did was hands on: people making diagrams of the elements and so on. I'm not going to work on that till I finish *Language of Alchemy*, because it's long, but what I wanted to do was strip magic down to an algebra of what the forces were and how they interrelate.

Whitehead: In relation to all that, could you comment on the act of visualization as it relates to the act of creativity from a poet's perspective?

di Prima: They are the same and they're not the same. We tend to think that no ordinary mind is going to be one kind of non-ordinary mind and that's it. But there are many kinds of non-ordinary mind. For a technical example, if you are doing a psychic reading you're going to get your information—this has been true of myself and the people that I've checked it out with—in a much more simplified, almost cartoon-like way—symbolic—than if you go into a trance and do a visualization and you want to read the same person or situation. Where you'll maybe get more dream-like, rich kind of imagery. That's just a really superficial example but it's one example. There are a lot of different minds. Meditative mind is an old one: Zazen mind is not the same as Vajrayana mind. And then beyond the meditation stuff, there's putting yourself into what we could call a hypnosis or a trance, and having a plan ahead of time of where you're "going" in trance—doing a particular visualization and working that way. And then, as I said there is the altered state you put yourself in if you just want to do a quick reading for somebody. Hands-on healing work works that way, too. You're in a trancelike state, but you're also transferring energy. And creativity, when you're just sitting up there and the poem is coming through and someone's kid is climbing over you, is its own state. However there are times when in visualization you discover a very interesting, wonderful, or strange place and you could call it a state of mind or you could call it a place and you want to pursue that further and write about it, in which case you would use visualization to keep going back there. Try to use the same kind of suggestion or the same kind of technique to get back to the same place and finding out more about it and writing. I'm convinced a lot of good fantasy books are written this way. Also, if you're stuck creatively for any reason, you can visualize. Physical and mental relaxation. Getting into a familiar deep place and the trick is to make it familiar, to go there a lot. Just like I'm sure a good athlete has a conditioned reflex to hit the home run. The way some of them move sometimes tells you they are in a particular state of mind. I had a book half-finished on Shelley, and somewhere along the life of Shelley I reached a point where I really didn't have the words for where they were at. I could tell I was coming at it too much from my head, from what the biographies said, and I just went into a visualizing state at that point and tried to see the Shelley family—okay, what was going on? And what comes in then, isn't just what you're seeing. But the seeing in that state isn't just visual, it comes at the same time with an emotional tone. It's like a wedding of those two things together, so I could get a real feeling tone of that. And that's what I rode when I came back up, it isn't so much that I described what I'd seen in the visioning, but I rode that feeling tone, which was really actually a very desolate and difficult one. Those are some different ways—there are other ways, I'm sure many—to use visualization. But those are some ways to use visualization in your writing.

Whitehead: Through visualization we enter the door and can enter the shadow and communicate with that subconscious self, and then, our poetry truly becomes creative. That's the way I interpreted a lot of what you were saying.

di Prima: If you make a relationship with what you are calling your subconscious self, you are making a relationship with all the material in you that you have kept at a distance and that you fear. That relationship carries over into the waking state. Those voices will speak in your poem when you're not in visualization, too. They feel rapprochement, some place to come to, some area they can speak from that is not going to be denied, and then they start to speak. And sometimes you can be very surprised by some of the dark parts of yourself that are okay. They're just there.

Whitehead: I think it's a part of the alchemy. Then you begin to be transformed and are transmuted by the poetry and you become a different person.

di Prima: Yes, for instance, rage can become a simple kind of cutting through, once you've let it into your world.

Gibson: Because you write the way you do, you probably don't consider your audience at all. And in the Waldman interview you talked about some of your audiences getting frustrated. Do you consider audiences at all?

di Prima: No. But I don't ignore them on purpose. I don't say "Oh fuck the audience." That's not what I'm doing. I'm just putting down whatever I'm being told to put down. But what's happening is—I don't find that audiences are so frustrated now. I think it's the changing consciousness, because people are more willing to allow some uncertainties. Like when we read a poem, we don't understand everything in it. Like a brand-new poem from Charles Olson or somebody. But that's okay because we get the thrust of it. People are becoming more willing to do that.

Also I think I've learned how to read more clearly than I used to. I take my time with images and words, so people have a chance to really get into the space. But no, I don't think about the audience except to have a belief that if you're going someplace in your mind, and writing about it, especially, hopefully if it's a place that hasn't been written about before, other people are going to find an echo of that. It's something that you're not the only one who's feeling, you know.

Gibson: You must think there is an audience out there to make the effort of writing and publishing.

di Prima: Well, no, I would write just to write. If this were 1600 and I was Giordano Bruno, I'd probably write, even though it was all going to be burned when I was burned. Because the act of it—the doing of it—is the thing itself. But then you have to believe that all humans or maybe all beings—all sentient beings, like the Buddhists say—have some common

ground. That consciousness has some characteristics in common every-
where. And that these characteristics will hear what you're saying, what
you're talking about. When it gets scary, especially when you're a younger
writer, is when you are writing about something that nobody has written
about before. Do you remember that little poem in 1964 called "I Get My
Period"? When I'm talking to my husband and saying I'm menstruating and
I can't forgive you. Because I'm menstruating and I want a child and we
hadn't been making love. That felt scary to write because nobody had been
writing about that stuff in 1964. It probably wouldn't seem scary now. But
at the same time I had to believe I wasn't the only one who felt that, so that
if I spoke it then that much more ground has been made for what can be
spoken, and then people go further after that. So in that sense an audience,
but not in the usual sense. You know what, I think that whatever act of con-
sciousness is accomplished by a being isn't lost. So I don't think it matters
if somebody else reads it or even that it's articulated. Some of our acts of
consciousness might only be accomplished in a remote place in meditation
or in visualization and yet they are part of the whole schmear. They are just
there and we draw on them. I think there's a level where we all know that we
are in one soup together. We all know that. So that from that place anything
that you can share around makes it better. It just makes it more livable in
the world if more people have acknowledged their pain, or disappointment.
Or anything. Especially anything from the shadow. I, one time, realized that
there have been billions and billions of anonymous artists of all sorts. They
make statues. They make pots. They make quilts. They are like the leaven-
ing. They are the yeast. Without those billions of people making it a little
more bearable to be on the planet it really wouldn't have been tenable to
continue as a race. There's so much that's hard, you know. And imperma-
nence and death and all that are not things we take very easily as a species.
We're not comfortable with all of that. So, if it weren't for that constant leav-
ening of beauty in the world, how could we survive? And I realized that this
was the big deal, was to be part of that proletariat of billions of anonymous
artists. This is where I put a lot of pride. That's what I'm proud of. I'm really
grateful. I'm really proud to be part of that. In terms of me, and my work,
and an audience—it's hard to think about that. But it's not hard to think
about, well, if somebody reads a poem of mine and it gives them courage,
hey, that's my job, what I was put here for.

An Interview with Diane di Prima

Joseph Matheny / 1993

From Literary Kicks, litkicks.com/Di Prima Interview. Reprinted by permission of Joseph Matheny.

Since I was young I've admired beat literature and its developers. My young mind was taken with the romantic image of Kerouac roaming the interior of the body politic, a mad sweating virus on the loose in the highwayvein of Amerika, Ginsberg holy maniac, chanting, praying, exorcising a generation ruined by madness, Burroughs and Gysin, pushing the envelope, rubbing out the word, and di Prima, conjuring, straddling the magick/dream line, throwing us bits of tasty metamorsels and sumptuous subconscious feasts.

If you're saying to yourself, "di Prima?" you are one of the main reasons I wrote this article. Even if you have heard of Diane's work you have to admit, in a field that already has an amazing paucity of women, to overlook even one seems like a capital crime, especially this one. Diane di Prima is a San Francisco writer and poet who works in healing, magick, and alchemy. Her more recent books are: *Pieces of a Song: Selected Poems*, City Lights, 1990, *Zip Code*, Coffee House Press,1992, and *Seminary Poems*, Floating Press, 1991.

I spoke to Diane on September 22, 1993, in her cozy booklined SF apartment. We spoke of rebellion, liberty, conditioning, and on being a woman in the beat generation.

Joseph Matheny: When you started out as a writer in the fifties, were there a lot of control systems set up to punish anyone who tried to break out of the consensus mold?

Diane di Prima: It was a weird time. Especially for women. Rebellion was kind of expected of men.

JM: When men rebelled they were romantic, free. Women who rebelled were categorized as being nuts.

DdP: Yes. Nuts or a whore, or something. Yes.

JM: Do you feel it's any different now?

DdP: Not much. I think there's been a lot of lip service paid to how much women have managed to advance. The younger women that I know are behaving pretty much like women have always behaved. Maybe they don't have so much the middle-class housewife dream, but they'll still be the one to get a job, while the man does the writing or the painting or whatever. I can think of example after example of this. I think that the internal control systems that have been put in place for women haven't been dented. It's such a big step forward to single mom, but so much more could be going on besides that.

JM: That's where the most effective censorship and control systems reside, inside ourselves, our head!

DdP: Yes! How it gets there is interesting too.

JM: How do you think they get there?

DdP: I would guess that it starts in the womb. Getting imprinted with the language pattern that's around you. The way people move, the way they hold themselves. To break it you'd have to do some really deliberate debriefing, on every level. The place where I was lucky in my own life was that I had a grandfather who was an anarchist. I didn't see much of him after I was seven because my parents thought he was bad for me, but from three to seven I saw a lot of him. I was still malleable enough so some debriefing occurred there. He would tell me these really weird fables about the world. He would read Dante to me and take me to the old people's anarchist rallies, and all this showed me these other possibilities . . .

JM: So you had an early imprint of a kind of . . . anti-authority, authority figure. [*laughs*]

DdP: [*laughing*] Yes! Aside from being an anti-authority authority figure, the imprint I got from him and my grandmother as well, was of two people who weren't afraid, at least from my child's point of perspective. They would just go ahead and do what they believed in. In all the other years of my early life I never encountered anyone else who wasn't afraid. I think kids today may be a little better off in that they encounter a few people who either aren't afraid, or who will go ahead and try something anyway, whatever it is. There's a possibility of that model, but during my childhood that was a very unusual model. I was born in 1934, during the Depression, and everyone seemed to be *frozenwithterror. We . . . will . . . do . . . what . . . we . . . are . . . told!* [*laughs*] and I don't think it's changed that much. Every day people are told that they should be afraid of not having health insurance, they're going to die in the gutter and to be afraid of all these things that aren't threats at the moment. Of course there are present threats but nobody's paying attention to those.

JM: It seems to me that rebellion itself has become a commodity, the media has co-opted rebellions like rock 'n' roll, Dada, Surrealism, poetry, the rebel figure. Do you feel that this co-option has succeeded in making rebellion somewhat ineffectual?

DdP: No. What you're seeing is an old problem in the arts. Everything is always co-opted, and as soon as possible. As Cocteau used to talk about, you have to be a kind of acrobat or a tightrope walker. Stay three jumps ahead of what they can figure out about what you're doing, so by the time the media figures out what you're writing, say, women and wolves, you're on to not just a point of view of rebellion or outdoing them, or anything like that. It's more a point of view of how long can you stay with one thing, where do you want to go? You don't want to do anything you already know or that you've already figured out. So it comes naturally to the artist to keep making those jumps, that is, if they don't fall into the old "jeez, I still don't own a microwave" programs.

JM: Reminds me of a story about Aldous Huxley. When asked if he had read all the books in his quite impressive library he replied, "God no! Who would want a library full of books that they had already read?"

DdP: [*laughs*] It is true that rebellion is co-opted, but then it always gets out of their hands, it slithers in some other direction. Then they go "oh, how can we make this part of the system?" Like rap. Okay, they are co-opting all this regular rap, but now this surreal rap is starting, native tongue, surreal imagery, spiritual anarchism rap, it's not about girls or politics or race and it's starting to happen.

JM: Is this something your daughter brings to your attention?

DdP: Yes, I go over once in a while and catch up on what's going on. You see as soon as something is defined, it wiggles off in another direction. I don't think that it's such a big problem in the sense of reaching a lot of people. How does the artist reach a large audience? The people that know are always going to find the new edge, but the mainstream are not that smart or the guy making a Top 40 record is not that smart. It often takes them a long time to figure it out. Now that is a problem, because we don't have the time. We need to reach everybody, right away, because we have to stop the system dead in its tracks. It's no longer a question of dismantling the system. There isn't enough time to take it apart, we just have to stop it.

JM: Do you feel that there's a somewhat centralized or conscious attempt to defuse radical art or rebellion through co-option or is it just "the nature of the beast," so to speak?

DdP: I think it goes back and forth. There are times when it's conscious, but not a single hierarchical conspiracy but rather a hydra-headed conspiracy. Then there are other times that it doesn't need to be conscious anymore, because that's the mold, that pattern has been set, so everyone goes right on doing things that way. I'm not quite sure which point we're at right now in history. It's so transitional and crazy that I wouldn't hazard a guess. Just check your COINTELPRO history to see an example of a conscious conspiracy to stop us. Other times it was just a repetition of what has gone on before. Like the ants going back to where the garbage used to be. [*laughs*]

JM: Robotic functioning.

DdP: Yes, and it's all in place when the next so-called conspiracy comes along, which is very handy isn't it? Wonder how we've made this monster we have here?

JM: Okay. Say we stop it dead in its tracks. What then?

DdP: It would be nice to say it's unimaginable, wouldn't that be great. That would be my hope! [*laughs*] For one thing, we'd have to use the same tables, wear the same shoes longer, read a lot of the same books, maybe for the next few hundred years. Dumps would become valuable places to mine!

JM: They already are to me!

DdP: To some people, yes, but not to enough people. Screeching to a halt seems like the only possible solution and I'm not even sure how you would go about it. Of course the good old general strike would be a nice start.

JM: As long as we're on the subject of deconstructing, how do you feel about the predominant intellectual fad of postmodernism, deconstruction, and the nihilism implicit in these systems?

DdP: Well, when I read that stuff, it's so frustrating. Western thought always keeps stopping on the brink. It never really makes that extra step. It could really do with an infusion of Buddhist logic. At least fourfold logic and then what's beyond that. It seems that although it's dressed up in new language, nothing really new has happened in philosophy in the twentieth century. Well, maybe not since Wittgenstein. It seems like the same old thing. You know, sometimes when people ask me for poems now, I'll send out poems that have been lying around for years, I don't always have new poems lying around everywhere, and these things that I wrote as cut-up stuff, cutting up each others' dreams in workshops and such. I'll send these out. Everyone seems to be taking them very seriously and publishing them. They think I'm working off of some language theory when actually these are just things I did for fun.

JM: What are you doing now?

DdP: I'm working on two prose books. One is called *Recollections of My Life as a Woman*. I'm 120 pages into it and I'm still eight years old. I'm still dealing with how the conditioning happened. In my generation a lot of it happened with battering, you got hit a lot, and screaming. Your basic conditioning came through abuse, not really different from concentration camps or anything else. I think someday we're going to look back on how we're handling kids at this point in history and wonder how we could treat them such. Like when people say "how could women stand it when people did such and such?" We'll be saying that about the way children are treated.

DdP: The other prose book is called *Not Quite Buffalo Stew*. It's just a rollicking, fun, surreal novel about life in California. It's in the first person, and in the second or third chapter in I found that the "I" that was the narrator was a man, so that breaks a lot of rules already. The "I" is a drug smuggler named Lynx. There isn't a whole lot of continuity, just whatever scenes wanted to write themselves.

JM: Are you using any kind of random/divination systems, i.e., cut-ups, grab bag, I Ching, Tarot, coin tossing, etc.?

DdP: Not with this one. This one dictates itself. The system I guess I'm using is that I can't write it at home. It won't happen anywhere that's familiar turf and it likes to happen while I'm driving. So I'll probably head for Nevada at some point and finish it.

JM: What do you see in the future for poetry and literature?

DdP: I would like to see authors really use magick to reach themes. I'd like to see more work coming out of visioning and trance. I'm really tired of reading about human beings! There's all these other beings, I'd like to see a real dimensional jump and I'd like to see people working on the technical problems. Like when you come back from trance or visioning, or drugs, and what you can write down about it at that moment. What you can make into an actual piece, we haven't figured it out yet. Yeats certainly didn't figure it out. It's more than needing a new language. There are actual forms we need to find or the forms have to find us, that will hold all that material without trying to make it reductive. The attempts at visionary painting in the sixties and Yeats's last poems show how vision didn't translate into these old artistic forms. Of course taking the raw material and presenting that as a piece doesn't work either. Maybe a blending of vision, word, and sounds can achieve something. We haven't really had time to think about what the computer is. Most of us still think of it as a typewriter, or a calculator. We don't think of it as its own dimension. It has its own medium, possibilities, to bring this kind of material across. I also think about deliberate invocation to find the plane or thing you want to write about.

JM: Do you see us heading into a post-literate society?

DdP: Yes, we might be. I don't think that will stop poetry, in fact it won't stop any of the arts at all. Even if it's oral there may be a split like there was in Europe when there was the written literature in Latin and then there was the oral poems of the singers in the Vulgate. We have that to a degree already with the poetry of the great songwriters. Really, though, I don't think literate or post-literate really matters. Were cave paintings literate or pre-literate? Did they read those paintings or just look at them? [*laughs*] Of course the only reason a completely literate society was developed was for thought control, and now that thought control can be done via TV, etc., it's not really needed anymore. They don't want everyone reading Schopenhauer!

Everyone needs to remember that they can buy a small press or laser writer, or copy machine, and go home and do what the fuck they please and it will take a very long time for anyone to catch up with them all! No one seems to remember about a few years ago in Czechoslovakia, without access to all this technology like we have here, even with every one of their typewriters registered to the police, they still managed to publish their work! In order to do this they would type it with ten carbon papers to make ten copies! We are in a situation here in the US where no one can register all the computers, no one can figure out where all the copy machines are. Get one now! Remember we can do it without government money. Government money is poison, take it when you need it, but don't get hooked. We can say what we want. They can't possibly keep up with us all. Real decentralization!

JM: That's great, helping people find their true desires, but do you think that we're so full of false, spectacle manufactured desires that we can no longer identify our true desires?

DdP: I think it doesn't take that long to deprogram false desires. Anyone who knows that they have the desire to know about themselves, what their true desires are, will find the tools to do it. Drugs, autohypnosis, you could also do it by following the false desires until they lead to a dead end like Blake recommended. . . .

JM: Hmmm . . . somehow that seems . . .very American.

DdP: Hmmm. You're right . . .

A Poet's Take on Life and Learning

Stephen Schwartz / 1996

From SF Gate, 1996, online. © 1996 by SF Gate. Reprinted by permission of Hearst Communications, Inc.

Diane di Prima has been a major figure in the American poetry scene since the 1950s, when she joined the Beat writers in the New York avant-garde.

She has attracted attention as the only female writer prominent among the Beats, who are now gaining a wider audience among young readers.

Among her books are *This Kind of Bird Flies Backward*, *Dinners and Nightmares*, *The New Handbook of Heaven*, *Memoirs of a Beatnik*, *Revolutionary Letters*, and *Seminary Poems*.

Di Prima recently completed her autobiography, which is scheduled for publication next year.

In this interview, di Prima recalls some of the literary examples, acquaintances, and political ideas that marked her career.

Stephen Schwartz: If I had a fifteen-year-old and said, "I'm going to send you to Diane di Prima and she's going to give you a reading list," what would be on your list?

Diane di Prima: At the risk of sounding trendy—because multiculturalism is trendy right now—we have to understand Western culture starts relatively late—what we call Western culture. I had a wonderful dream recently in which the *Iliad* was cast, in the dream, as gangster rap, which is precisely what it is. These guys and those guys you dissed my chick and blah blah blah.

All is relevant. I Ching is relevant, some knowledge of astrology would be important as well as modern astronomy. All of these things are relevant and the youngsters know it and they want it. What we tend to box off as the occult or the hermetic, they want as much as they want the rest.

So, to list my whole curriculum would be impossible, but these are the things that come to mind first: Enheduanna, the Sumerian priestess poet, which is the earliest writing we have in the West; the I Ching; oral traditions and native American and African, Australian, whatever we could grab that's still left. I cried when I first read in Kroeber's *Handbook of California Indians* that the song cycles of the North California Coast Miwok Indians were all lost—because imagine what those might be like.

And with that, if they're European kids, give them a strong grounding in Western culture. By that I mean, from the Near East on over through America, starting as far back as possible, making them understand the parts that people leave out, like the Kabbalah (the mystical lore of Judaism) in Shakespeare. The root of it is magical and magical isn't different from religious, and magic and religion aren't different from poetry or song, or the practice of all the arts. So, giving them that as a background they go into the world curious and excited.

Schwartz: Would you say there is a very intellectual, spiritual, scholarly multiculturalism that you have been doing since you were a young person, that does not fit any of the clichés from either left or right, but that is in the mainstream of modern and postmodern literary work?

di Prima: I think that's true. There's this unity of concern throughout the world; we have the same concerns, and they are not mostly materialistic. They are mostly about where we're going, what we are, and so on. These are the threads of mystery that run through all cultures and have tempted many people to say that once there was one culture. When you appeal to young people or anyone on the basis of those kinds of questions, you can take them very far. And they'll take you very far, you know, it's a mutual process.

But it's not divisive, it's not about my people only did this and your people only did that. It's about what the human quest is about. I think that's really what poetry is about, what that human quest is. And the excitement of language, the excitement of all languages, is that they, in their own way, embody a piece of that by embodying a world view.

Schwartz: Is that parallel to Noam Chomsky's argument that language is a universal innate capacity?

di Prima: We all have these wondrous differences. But we are on a journey. The mystery of existence itself is the same for all people.

Schwartz: Were you influenced by the poet Ezra Pound?

di Prima: Well, I went to college in 1951, to Swarthmore [in Pennsylvania]. I only went for a year and a half because it was not a good place to write. But while I was there, the bookstore had many things that I hadn't really seen because although I was in a very good high school in New York, Pound and even e. e. cummings weren't part of what I knew about.

What I knew about was the Manhattan bookstores, on Fourth Avenue, and all the old stuff, books of engravings and early Aubrey Beardsley illustrations. I didn't go to uptown bookstores. Not enough Pound was in them anyway. But when I was at Swarthmore, I found all these things, in less than a year, and took with me the collected works of e. e. cummings, and [Pound's] *The Cantos*, up to whatever point they were at in early '53, in the early New Directions edition with a black cover, and I read through it, promptly, on the spot.

And I also embarked on trying the reading Pound suggested in *The ABC of Reading*, so that I found myself learning a tiny bit of Homeric Greek, and reading, sounding out, some of the *Iliad*.

I had four years of Latin in high school and it was good, I loved it, so that made it all easier. I read a little Dante, just borrowing things . . . texts with both languages. And then in '55, I went and visited Pound. I wrote about it in my autobiography *Recollections of My Life as a Woman*, which will be out in 1997.

Schwartz: Pound had been locked up in jail and a mental hospital since the end of World War II, charged with treason because he supported Mussolini. What was it like to meet him?

di Prima: It was in 1956. We were very, very poor. I saved up fifty-five dollars; round-trip bus fare (from Pennsylvania to Washington, DC) was something like twenty-five dollars of that. And we got down there and we stayed with a woman that was a friend of Pound's, a kind of symbolic mistress named Sheri Martinelli. An old friend from the Village, she moved down to DC, where he was in St. Elizabeth's Hospital.

It was like the rest of him, a paradox. You walked into a day room in this madhouse and people were wandering around, men were wandering around, doing the kind of things they do in madhouses, talking to themselves. The television, which was very new in '56, was blaring. And there was one little niche, kind of like an alcove within this day room. And in this alcove, Mrs. [Dorothy] Pound was serving tea and passing out cookies and Mr. Pound was holding court.

Sheri came with me, and several other people were there. Pound was telling anecdotes, he was very strong looking, very healthy, very voluble. And conversation was very civilized. We talked a lot . . . me and a friend that came down with me.

I was twenty-one, twenty-two. We had all these earnest questions about the work we were doing as writers. He was very gracious and wonderful, you know. And when we would leave—I wrote a poem about that once—he walked me graciously to the door and waited for the warden to unlock it.

It was April or May and he was wearing shorts. He was very much into outdoors and being healthy, air and all that. He would walk us to the door and then he'd wait. And the warden would come and let us out. He got us permission to come back every day, even though there were only two of those days that were visiting days, because we were from out of town.

So, we arrived every day and spent the day. And he would give us little bags of food that he had stolen off the table in the dining room of the madhouse because he said poets have to eat. So we'd get these cold sausages and that awful kind of canned fruit salad they used to eat in those days.

I remember feeling really guilty that I was disturbing Mr. Pound from finishing his translations of the Chinese odes. And I said, "You know, really we shouldn't bother you. You're working." I didn't have any comprehension of how when people are incarcerated they like to be bothered. "Oh, no, no," he said. "I can work anytime."

Schwartz: Is Kenneth Rexroth, the San Francisco poet, an important figure?

di Prima: I knew two Rexroths. I knew the Rexroth who came to visit me on the Lower East Side when I was a dropout from Swarthmore, maybe a twenty-three-year-old writer. And I had my first child on my own, which you didn't do in 1957. And he really came on heavy to me, which we now call sexual harassment.

But then I knew also a very loyal, staunch friend in the seventies when he knew me and my work better. I remember one conference; I was giving a seminar called "History as Paranoia," in 1973. And he just came in and sat in the back and corroborated all these points I was making, and he'd put in another whole bunch of facts that I didn't have, but then proved my point. Very, very sweet and very loyal friend.

Being a girl, you got to meet both of them sometimes.

Schwartz: You developed a curriculum at New College with the poets Robert Duncan, who died in 1988, and David Meltzer. In Duncan, we have someone who was politically an anarchist, spiritually a theosophist, and, especially, long before anybody else, an out gay. Can you talk about the influence of Duncan?

di Prima: Oh, Lord. Do we miss him.

The other night I said to my partner, "San Francisco lacks something since Robert died." There's a whole part of the grace and the fun of life in San Francisco that is just not there. I was putting on my coat for some literary event and I said, "Oh, I wish I had a cape to put over it, like Robert."

The area lacks a sensibility and overview of what we were all about and what we were doing—and especially and specifically what we're all doing out here . . . on this edge of the world. He really made that a part of the whole universe of the arts.

I came out here for the first time from New York in 1961, stayed at Michael McClure's house. Michael had stayed with me on the Lower East Side the year before. And I guess Michael invited Robert to breakfast to meet me, and I don't think Robert was all that interested in meeting me. He seemed kind of offhand, and he was blabbering along.

There had been an early breakfast. I had hair that was so long that I could sit on the braid. And I really hadn't gotten myself together. So after breakfast, I wandered over to the window in the dining room and started brushing my hair. And just getting myself together and making a braid. And Robert interrupted one of his monologues which were so wonderful and so absolutely off the wall. And he said, "You have the most marvelous hair I've ever seen. Will you come to lunch?"

We became friends after that. I lived at Stinson Beach in '62 for a bunch of months and he and Jess [Collins, Duncan's partner for thirty-seven years], were some of our closest friends in the city.

We would go to Robert and Jess's and they would assure us, no matter who we were schlepping along in the way of writers and stray dykes from Stinson Beach, that everyone would be welcome. And Jess would concoct something for us all to eat. They were still relatively poor.

But that assurance that you are going to see artists that can really welcome you, it was really wonderful. And then in the seventies, Robert used to come up to Marshall. I lived on the coast, and he spent Christmas with us every year up there.

He was wonderful.

Schwartz: What about the curriculum at New College?

di Prima: There were two other poets involved: Lewis Patler and Duncan McNaughton were already teaching at New College and they conceived the idea and brought us together to do a program for a master's in poetics—not in creative writing but in poetics.

In the curriculum a lot of attention was given to stuff that we don't usually talk about in poetry and in writing. David's courses were based on Kabbalah. He brought in translations that friends of his were working on that hadn't been published. Robert was giving very brilliant and esoteric classes in things like "The King, The Sage, and The Fool."

I was giving a course in "Hidden Religions in the Literature of the World," which went from the cave times and went all the way to the magical groups of the twentieth century. I looked at nonorthodox threads that ran throughout. Certain references move us because they are in the air and in our nature, without us really knowing the hermetic or esoteric traditions.

We were looking at the sources of poetry, other than just poems alone. Robert gave a reading for us that was Baudelaire, Emily Dickinson, and Walt Whitman. He said they were the three great innovators of the nineteenth century.

It went on for almost seven years. I gave a course on the Grail, a course in [the Renaissance mystic] Paracelsus, and in Giordano Bruno. When I first proposed Paracelsus, Robert [Duncan] went away from the faculty meeting grumbling, "What does Paracelsus have to do with poetry?" Then, that night he had a dream and an angel stood in front of him and said, "You know very well what Paracelsus has to do with poetry!"

Schwartz: We have discussed classical, archaic, ancient, traditional topics that are an enormous part of your life. This clashes with the cliché view that people have of the beatniks, among whom you were the main woman writer, and the hippie era. Tell about the anarchist movement you participated in during the sixties in the Haight, the Diggers.

di Prima: Well, I came out here to live in '68 for two things. I came out to intensify my Zen study, and I came out to work with the Diggers. I had been out here briefly on a reading trip and was very taken by what was happening. Especially because I grew up under the instruction of my grandfather, an Italian anarchist and a friend of [Italian American labor leader] Carlo Tresca.

In the fifties, I kept my political stuff under wraps, I didn't do much with it in the writing. I didn't do much with it because the feeling was so back-to-the-wall paranoid that you felt it was quite pointless except among people who already understood your point of view.

I came out to work with the Diggers because it was so exciting to be able to actually put the stuff out there. That had started a little earlier for me. In '67 a poet on the East Coast named Sam Abrams had rented a flatbed truck, and we were going around with an amplifying system with radical folksingers, if you can remember such people, and poets and guerrilla theater plays.

I started my book *Revolutionary Letters* for that kind of situation because my other poems were too intellectual for that. You couldn't read them on the street and get a response.

My household was responsible for delivering free food around the city because we had a VW bus—three times a week. Two days we picked up vegetables that were given to us and one day the fish from the fish market,

Saturday morning, because it was still such a Catholic town, people ate fish on Friday night in San Francisco. There were twenty-five communes we delivered to in the city. And then we dropped food off at two free stores. One in the Haight and one called the "Black Man's Free Store."

The Diggers had a serious vision for how the city should be. And one of the things was that each neighborhood could be autonomous and run by that neighborhood. If there were abandoned or free buildings in that neighborhood, they should be turned over to the people of that neighborhood for housing or for playgrounds for the kids or whatever people wanted in that area.

These were not ideas off the top of our heads, held for a week. These were serious political experiments that went on for several years. The anarchist group out here was much more advanced than what was going on in, say, Chicago.

Contrary to the image that's projected of the sixties, this wasn't the only serious thinking that was going on, or the only political experiment, artistic experiment.

Something was different on the West Coast. I'm not talking about conscious abundance. I'm talking about a sense of ease, that life's always going to be possible somehow. There's no sense like that back east.

The Movement of the Mind: Tim Kindberg Talks to Diane di Prima in San Francisco

Tim Kindberg / 1997

From *Magma* no. 11 (Winter 1997). Reprinted by permission of *Magma*.

Diane di Prima was born in Brooklyn, New York, in 1934. She lived and wrote in Manhattan for many years, where she became known as an important writer of the Beat movement. For the past thirty years she has lived and worked in northern California, and currently lives in San Francisco. She is the author of thirty-two books of poetry and prose, including *Pieces of a Song* (City Lights, 1990) and *Seminary Poems* (Floating Island Press, 1991).

Tim Kindberg: How and when did you begin writing?

Diane di Prima: I started writing when I was seven. At fourteen I knew I was going to be a poet. I wrote every day. I always knew you just had to let the thing come through you. I went to a very intellectual school for girls in New York City, '48 to '51. About eight of us came in early each day to read to each other what we had written the night before. Reading Keats, when I was thirteen or fourteen, was the first time when the poetic came at me, it was something I could take away, a complete theory of poetics, in the letters.

I published my first book in about '58, it was called *This Kind of Bird Flies Backward*. This was during a period when I was working very much on how much you could take out and have a really clean line, a very simple poem. That was from around '53 when I dropped out of college until around '60. I was trying to find the cleanest line that retained a lyric sense. It seems to me that that was the only time that I was writing in anything similar to a Beat voice. I'm still known as a Beat writer, whatever the hell that means. After that period, in *The Calculus of Variation*, I was really trying to follow the movement of the mind. Philip Whalen, in a statement on poetics, said poetry is the graph of the moving mind. My work came through me, I didn't revise it a lot. I try to respect the original form of the poem. It can be important to leave the imperfections; they can make a way inside for the reader. As Keats said, poetry should come out as easily as leaves to the tree, or it had better not come at all.

Kindberg: It sounds like a Zen-like point of view.

di Prima: Yeah, it is. Also in Abstract Expressionism, their interest in the gestural and so on. You have at the same time this vast view and an intimacy that that poised sort of gesture makes in the piece.

Kindberg: You describe the "clean line," removing as much as you can, as in Occam's razor. Was that the influence of the Imagists?

di Prima: No, it wasn't consciously Imagist. It was more influenced by Matisse. A book of his line drawings came out around '52. And I noticed that there were very few lines in them; they even implied color, not only three-dimensional shapes. There was a feeling the eye was tricked for a moment and there was color there. I was very interested in how little you could use to imply so much. And I spent several years on that but what happens is that when you've really learned a technique you incorporate it so that later you're using it automatically. Then there were those years when I worked on what exactly is going on as the mind moves in those poems. That was a very internal exploration. After that there was a period when I was working externally. I began to write the *Revolutionary Letters* and be very active out here. The feeling was that up to that point there had been no way to be active. Because the world was too repressive. Until the late sixties. I moved out here and worked with the Diggers, and wrote the *Revolutionary Letters*, a lot to be performed on the street. In fact they were started because in New York a friend, another poet named Sam Abrams, had rented a flatbed truck and we were going out with a generator and microphone, people were singing political folk songs, people were doing guerrilla theatre. Most of my poetry was too intellectual when I tried to read it on the street. So I wrote the *Revolutionary Letters* almost as theatre, as street theatre. And that kind of worked. But it was concomitant with other things happening. When I was writing the *Revolutionary Letters* I was also beginning *Loba*. You're entering one kind of work but you're still doing another kind of work at the same time.

Kindberg: Your writing was too intellectual for the street?

di Prima: Well for instance I had a poem called "Lumumba Lives." But by '68 the people on the street didn't remember who Lumumba was. He was the Socialist head of the Belgian Congo, who was killed in, I believe, an airplane crash. There's been proof that the CIA was involved in his death. At that point we put in the guy who ran Zaire until about two months ago. And the guy who's now running Zaire was one of Lumumba's lieutenants or something. Four years after his death nobody knew what I was talking about. You had to write direct, simple poems, like my first *Revolutionary Letters*, when I had just realized the stakes are myself; I have no other ransom money, nothing to barter but my life. People can hear that, they understand that. The first couple weren't written with guerrilla theatre in mind, but by the time I had found that voice and done two, then the flatbed truck came along, the assassinations were happening, the year of Martin Luther King's death and so on, so between the opportunity to perform on the street and what was going on they just got written. I was also out there on the steps of City Hall with Peter Coyote—he was in the Diggers. They were a revolutionary political movement. They had a slogan "1 percent free: trying to get 1 percent of the profits from all the stores in town to contribute. They were occupying buildings and giving them to the neighborhoods. They were getting City Hall to turn over empty city-owned properties. Free food was distributed three times a week, which my household was in charge of. We would pick up the food that the market people wanted to give us and delivered it to twenty-five communes. This was happening around San Francisco—that's part of why I left New York.

Kindberg: So from the meditative phase, if I can call it that, to the activist phase. Was that a concomitant of the move west?

di Prima: Well moving west was for two reasons. One of them was meditative and one was active. It was to study with Suzuki, who started the Zen Center here. And the other was to work with the Diggers. So it wasn't one or the other, it was both at once.

Kindberg: Did something click: the time came to be active?

di Prima: Well it wasn't that the time came, I was always willing to be active, but there was no real way to do it more than be reactive in the fifties—not letting the FBI in when they came to your door looking for someone was as active as you could get. There was no real way to get out there with any kind of message. Then, at the same time that I was writing the *Revolutionary Letters* I began *Loba*, so it wasn't really either/or. The *Revolutionary Letters* had been going about two to three years when *Loba* began and interestingly the introductory poem to *Loba* is a kind of poem in praise of all these wandering street women in the world. And that led into the love poems, some of which are very much about political consciousness, about prostitutes in my neighborhood, and that kind of thing. This is all through *Loba*. In *Loba* both are encompassed but there isn't an either/or about meditative or not.

Kindberg: Did other poets inspire you at that time, or was it, for example, the political circumstances, or paintings?

di Prima: You have to go back and realize that my mother's father was an anarchist from southern Italy and a friend of people like Carlo Tresca, an anarchist in New York who was killed by the Mafia. He had an Italian anarchist newspaper in New York that my mother's father wrote for. So I took that in when I was between about one and six years old. I spent a lot of time with him and learned his anarchist values. So I always had a totally wild point of view, and then of course being Italian American during World War II gave you not necessarily anything specific but a general dubiousness about what was being said and whether it was true or not, about what was being said by the papers, about what history tells. Who writes the history? So I grew up in that kind of world and from the time I was eighteen and went to college there was always trouble in the world that I was face to face with, like the Cold War going crazy. A friend of mine's boyfriend had been left here by his Yugoslavian father. His father was recalled—he was a cultural emissary—recalled by Tito, and the father was afraid to bring the son back. The father was imprisoned and killed. We found ourselves in the position of having to hide his son. The FBI decided he was a Communist spy. I'm talking about being eighteen and being in this position: being on my own for the first time in an apartment and having the FBI at the door. It was a constant thing. I was very aware, I knew exactly where I was, when I got the news that the Rosenbergs had been executed. There was always the feeling, you were always doing stuff quietly. Hiding people. And everyone was using dope. The whole world was a little bit off.

Kindberg: So you were very much out away from the center of things, certainly in political terms. And was that true of the poets who inspired you?

di Prima: Well, in the early period there was Keats and then there was Pound. And I had made friends with Allen Ginsberg in '56, when his book *Howl* came out. I was writing the same kind of street language. That was the period when I was taking all the extra words out, his poems were also in the vernacular, in the hip vernacular that I was writing and I was interested in what he was doing because on the East Coast I was reaching a lot of opposition about "you can't write in the vernacular and get published." So, since I was already doing it I felt this kindred thing and I reached out and wrote him and Ferlinghetti. Ferlinghetti wrote the introduction to my first book.

Kindberg: Did you feel that certain aspects of what you were doing were also "Beat"?

di Prima: Well, there was no such thing as Beat in the fifties, in the time we're talking about; that all came later, the word came later. What I felt was: Oh, good; other people are writing in the vernacular that I knew. This was very interesting. It was very important, the language we were speaking. But we weren't calling ourselves Beats, we never heard of Beat, just like Buddha never heard of Buddhism, as somebody said. There are all these debates; John Clellon Holmes said he invented it, the guy who wrote the novel *Go*. Then Kerouac said he invented it. Who knows. It's one of those words. There are a lot of meanings to it that they've attached, like beatitude and so on. We didn't think of ourselves as a movement. We were people writing. In the rewriting of history that happens with hindsight, we became a movement. I was interested in the fact that other people were writing in what we were calling still slang and getting stuff published and I wanted to be in touch with them; so it was something I was very interested in. I was very aware of early French poetry, and people were still reading that, even though they didn't know the meaning of a lot of the words. The argument on the East Coast was: you can't write slang because in ten years nobody will know what you were talking about. Well of course it's forty years later and people are still reading it.

Kindberg: Was there a political motivation in writing with the street vernacular?

di Prima: No, it was the beauty of that language . . . and the precision. The political motivation was so ingrained in me that I wouldn't even have thought of it as being a separate step.

Kindberg: Do you think it was the same for Ginsberg and the others?

di Prima: I don't know, I don't think so. Because when Allen talked about those years, he sounded like his memory of them was more middle class and more protected than my memory was, it was only later that he became more radicalized, I think. I don't think it happened quite as early. You see, he went on to be in college and he went on to have degrees. I dropped out. In my sophomore year I got an apartment on the Lower East Side in New York, which was pretty much all really poor Eastern European people.

Kindberg: Allen Ginsberg described you as being heroic in life and politics. Is that how you feel about yourself?

di Prima: It depends on how you use the word "heroic." In terms of larger than life as life is lived in the twentieth century, yes. I have a lot of trouble with the kind of poetic that underestimates human consciousness. I don't particularly like tea-cup poetry. But it's not about ego. It's about writing poems whose subject matter and therefore forms evolve as the mind expands; but also some of my poetry, *Loba* in particular, is mythic. It's very long now, about four hundred pages. It goes all the way back in time.

Kindberg: And what are your thoughts on Robert Creeley's foreword to your selected poems, *Pieces of a Song*, in which he says, to paraphrase, "men give the world specific form, yet there is no-one there unless woman, the 'other person,' is there as well"? [Actual quote is: "We stretch out long on the earth, as men, thinking to take care of it, to give it specific form, to make manifest our experience in how we take hold. Yet there is no one there unless this other person of our reality take place too, with a generosity only possible in that act. Diane di Prima is fact of that 'female principle' whereof Williams speaks—not simply, certainly not passively, but clearly, specifically, a woman as one might hope equally to be a man."]

di Prima: I thought it was very much how Robert always saw me, what I was to him; and I was glad to be of use to him! I love him, you know, he's a very deep man with, to me, a lot of sorrow. That maybe he wasn't conscious of. We had a lovely relationship. I haven't seen him much in ten, fifteen years. So, yes, that's what he saw. But what he said was nonsense: the world gives the world specific form, which changes every minute, and we will always make of it what we will, what we can, men and women.

Kindberg: Do you feel part of any strand of women poets?

di Prima: I think of myself more as an artist and secondarily a woman's voice—which made it possible to hang out with the guys, because it was mostly guys who were writing. Some women were writing that had a lot harder a time—I don't mean in terms of getting published, but a lot of them had the belief that they should keep it all together for the men, keep the house. I never wanted to live with a man in those days. I wanted a child and I had one in '57, my first child, but I didn't want a man. I don't think I even fell in love until I had the affair with Amiri Baraka, which was in the sixties. That obviously was not going to work as a way of life so I went on to other things. Now I have five children. But I was never looking for, nor was I looking to keep the world together for a man. I had kids, I had a very strong ethical feeling that I should try to keep it together for them.

Kindberg: These other—largely male—poets: did they respect your independent spirit?

di Prima: I think so because I never got much shit from any of them. There were few that even tried to come on. It was very much my choice when I had an affair. I rarely slept with writers. Too intellectual! Painters, musicians, dancers, but not writers!

Kindberg: Many of your poems are about people who have some kind of relationship to you—not necessarily an intimate relationship. Are people your main inspirations?

di Prima: I think that changes as your life goes on. When I was young, I think more. There was a period when I wrote a lot of what I call occasional verse, verse for people with birthdays, all kinds of personal stuff. Actually, it's like wearing out a shoe, you get tired of it. Or it goes away. It isn't like you're consciously tired of it, but you get to a place where the personal just doesn't get into the poem very much. It just doesn't. There are a lot of people now, a lot of young people, who are struggling with the idea that poetry shouldn't be personal. But I think it has to be personal until it stops being personal. You wear that vein out; you've mined that, you've got what you can from it. But where there's still an urgency to write a love lyric for example—and the whole of *Loba* is a love lyric—when it's urgent to still write a personal love lyric . . . it's ridiculous to say I should be writing impersonal poetry because that's what the poetic theory of the time is dictating.

Kindberg: There seems to be a disjunction between poetry in the US and the UK. I try reading off some well-known UK poets over here and no-body's heard of them. How about Simon Armitage, Christopher Reid, Carol Ann Duffy . . . ?

di Prima: I haven't read any of them. There was a period when there was a lot of contact, British poets were coming here. People such as H.D., yes, but even in the early period of my writing time people like Tom Roberts. There was a lot of contact. And with Canada, which we don't have now. I read in Toronto a lot, I read in Vancouver. A lot of poets came down here but that's all broken up now.

Kindberg: Do you think it might be not just that the books aren't getting over here but that there is an insularity in US poetry?

di Prima: There is an insularity, not only in America. It's been encouraged by the media. Have you seen the San Francisco newspapers? Maybe one page of international news, and the rest about what the mayor wore yesterday. And, for instance, within San Francisco each group of writers is pretty much unto itself. The slam poets, the Latino poets, the Asian American poets . . . It goes by the name of diversity and cultural identity but what it's doing is encouraging people not to get together and talk to one another.

Kindberg: Imagine that you sent a package of American poetry to Britain. What would be in it?

di Prima: Definitely the poetry of Robert Duncan. One poem that comes to mind is "Circulations of the Song"—or maybe *Ground Work* as a whole.

Some of the poetry of Frank O'Hara. I suppose I would put "Cottage" ["A Strange New Cottage in Berkeley"] of Allen's, rather than *Howl*. *Howl* was terribly useful at the time but "Cottage" seems to me more deeply human. I would put parts of *Maximus* by Charles Olson in there. And what about the women? You'd have to hear some Adrienne Rich, however that felt. She's from another world, she's more academic than me, but I love to read her. Then there's H.D. The things of H.D. I'd put in would be the last three long works. *Hermetic Definition*, and *Helen in Egypt* and *Trilogy*, especially *Trilogy*, the poem about being in the bombing in World War II in England. I'd put in Chuck Berry, and the blues. The blues is very important. I don't think you can make sense of poetry in America without someone like Miles, early Miles, and early-to-middle period Thelonious Monk. The line, the cadence, and the line and syncopation that they use, and the places where they would break up a phrase in the middle—that stuff is all part of the American poetic. Oh and I'd have to say that I'd put Philip Whalen in there, and also Michael McClure.

Kindberg: Is there anything else you would identify as being part of the American poetic spirit?

di Prima: For my generation, the abstract painters. The gestural. We were all pretty close in those days, we weren't all friends but we were aware of each other's work. We always wanted to hear jazz, and we would go to a painter's place and hang out. It was much more interlocking. I think the commodification of painting, of music, and the publishing scene is pathetic, it's horrible. You can work with small presses, which I've done all my life, or you can work with mainstream press. I'm working with Viking and Penguin now for the first time in my life. It's a complete disjuncture, two different worlds. And then there are the poets who just publish in the university presses. Regular bookstores won't carry them, because the market is too small. So if you go to a regular bookstore you can't find them. On every level there's that sense of commodification and how much it is worth. And does it look like everything else? Everybody's prose has been reduced to being the same as everybody else's prose.

Kindberg: You've mentioned *Loba*; what else are you working on now?

di Prima: I have just finished a long memoir called *Recollections of My Life as a Woman*.

Kindberg: When can we expect to see that?

di Prima: Well, probably '99, because the editor turned it into regular prose. Now I'm turning it back into my prose, and that's a long process. Everything that was a turn of phrase that came from Brooklyn/Italian/

American speech he would turn into regular English. So I'm reversing his changes.

I've pretty much completed a manuscript called *Death Poems for All Seasons*. I've been running a workshop around the country called the Poetics of Loss. I started it because of the AIDS epidemic. I'm doing it because I feel that people need to be able to talk about not only death but loss in general. This is a country of vast denial. You've probably noticed. And we're good out here compared to New York. In New York if you even talk about the past—not even about death, just the past—they'll say why are you being so morbid. And LA's like that too.

Kindberg: Does that extend to poetry as well? Richard Silberg said to me that it's almost a tradition not to have a tradition in poetry over here.

di Prima: I would say that the fashion is not to have a tradition. Just like the fashion is not to write personal stuff, not to be emotional. The kids at the institute I taught in two years ago gave me a list of what was taboo to write about. Politics, sex, emotion, family background.

Kindberg: Everything that counts!

di Prima: Right. I don't know why they were bothering, why they wanted to write.

Kindberg: Finally, alchemical processes feature prominently in your work. What does alchemy mean to you, and how does it link to your poetry?

di Prima: Some of the most gorgeous texts in the world. It's the science of transformation. There are laws of energy that pertain whether you are talking about metals or galaxies or human consciousness. There are energy laws of how things transmute from one thing to another. Those people who say that alchemy is all psychological, it's all laboratory work, it's all . . . are all right. But it's not all any of those things. Those are all special cases of general laws, and it's essentially those general laws to start with. I think they have been found, many times in the past, by adepts. I think they can be expressed but not necessarily in what we think of as the way words are normally used. In other words, I'm not interested in the purely descriptive, but in using words to evoke, or suggest things beyond that. So I think they can be expressed but not necessarily in what we think of as the way words are normally used. In other words, I'm not interested in the purely descriptive, but in using words to evoke, or suggest things beyond that. So I think they can be expressed. In the way they were expressed say in the *Hieroglyphic Monad* by John Dee—which reads as if he was doing a text of geometric theorems like Euclid, but when you start getting under the surface you start to realize . . . reading an alchemy text is for me like reading language within language within language. And it's also about what can't be said outright and has to be encoded, and how that's done—but not in any facile Language Poetry way. I guess I got caught because it's so utterly beautiful. What happened to me was some guy in New York named Felix Mann had a press called University Books and he did a reprint of two volumes of Paracelsus that had been translated in the nineteenth century, and he asked me to write the introduction. So he lent me these books which were beautiful big, fat, red-covered India-paper volumes. It was about '65. I was totally, utterly caught. I've been reading that stuff ever since. I haven't done any laboratory work, but you can't really do that stuff in the city!

The Tapestry of Possibility: Diane di Prima Speaks of Poetry, Rapture, and Invoking Co-Responding Magic

Peter Warshall / 1999

From *Whole Earth*, Fall 1999, 20–22.

Peter Warshall: Classic metaphor is presented as X is Y. "My love is a red rose." "My life is a journey."

Diane di Prima: Well, I think metaphor is exactly the opposite. All of those definitions make things less than they are. When you talk about metaphor, it's understanding that every single thing is multidimensional, and that behind every jade plant there are a million layers. There's Chinese poetry, there's jade itself, there's the way it flowers and tumbles. The way everything falls. Sort of floats downhill in it.

What I'm talking about is some apprehension of correspondences that makes everything richer, constantly richer. There's more than meets the eyes, as we like to say. There's more than actually meets the brain and the thinking part of the brain, too. So that in a good poem, you don't even know why you're taken. Why you're "rapt away"—like the rapture Jehovah's Witnesses are waiting for—into a much larger comprehension of how things speak to us, how things fit together, how there are all these levels beyond the material and yet with their roots right in the material.

When I was young, by reading alchemical texts I began to understand that everything meant more than I thought; that people used to think in a multilayered way. There was no simpleminded way to read, say, a text from the 1500s. You had to be able to let every thing and every statement in it go to places or depths that were more than its surface. For me, there's a feeling in them, of them resounding.

Having realized that all these people thought in a way that was so much more than one thing at a time, I was trying to listen to music that way, to look at a painting that way. I kept trying to open to these other possibilities, and that was kind of going to school, in a way, to the past. Now, I'm sure sometimes it happens other ways, like a sudden revelation, like when Jacob Boehme saw the light on the piece of pewter and the world opened up. I wouldn't know how everyone comes to multiple layers, but I think that coming to it completely changes you. Changes your life and changes your relation with the world as well as with other people. There are no equations in it: there's no "this equals that."

Against the studying of Western magical systems that we in the West, the Gentiles, based on Cabala, Agrippa, and so on, you get that sense of depth too. You can talk about Jupiter, or you could pick up this sapphire and put in on the shrine, or you can move toward the color blue. There's an interlocking of relations between all these different things. They are not intellectual. They become living. So that the color of something, or its basic energy, or something it exudes, or the number of its petals if it's a flower, all speak to you.

So if I think of metaphors like "life is a journey" as reducing metaphor to equation, all that stuff wants to make a very clear line between one thing and another, and is not willing to also see that things have these energies and live off of them forever—the actual force that anything has moving off of it into your heart, into your eye, into your soul, whatever. I don't even know if there are souls, but into your soul anyway. That energy is what corresponds, "co-responds"; and when it corresponds you co-respond to it in writing, you move toward something that seems like metaphor.

PW: There is a woman author who said that metaphor is a physical pictograph of a spiritual condition.

DdP: That's another one of those equations. It's sort of like saying that the only thing we're writing about is our spiritual states. I'm not sure that's true. Sometimes I'm really writing about the rock wall in the canyon. Maybe the rock wall in the Wind River Canyon isn't a metaphor for my spiritual state but it is just so beautiful and so moving and pours out such an energy that I need to write it. Or be a voice for it, just be a voice for it.

It may be that some metaphors are correlations for spiritual states, but there may be many, many metaphors, or whatever those things are, those images that arise that don't necessarily relate to the human. I think it's kind of a species-centric statement. When you're a poet, you spend a long time writing the "I" poem, and whether you hide the "I" or because you're being a language poet and don't use "I," it's still an "I" poem for a long, long time. And then when you reach the point where that's not so interesting, maybe you spend a long time, who knows—I'm not sure—writing poems that include your human family and the human landscape.

I'm not certain that there aren't entities that want voice. Robert Duncan used to talk about presence of a poem that arrived in the room and were just presences, having to be spoken. Sometimes the dead want voice. Sometimes the dead who have had a good voice want still more voice. "Shut up, Dante!" That kind of thing.

I'm not really sure exactly where metaphor begins, in the sense that you're starting with this world—which is where we all have to start all the time—and, starting with this world, you come up against the natural object. Where does it turn into a metaphor? Where is the mind? Where is the swift apprehension of relations in the mind? That bird leaving no trace in the sky is correspondence to one's thought. Thought leaves no trace.

For instance, in writing *Loba* [Diane's book-length poem], there wasn't any "Oh, I think I'll pick the wolf as a metaphor for a woman . . ." No. Wrong. First there was a dream that contained a world that I did not associate with a poem for over a year after I started the poem. The poem began as words in my head. Sometimes I get these broadcasts, and when I get them, I have to write them down or else they keep repeating like a broken record. And they won't go on to the next lines, but they won't stop.

So in the process of these first few broadcasts, around the third or fourth, it showed up that there was a wolf. At the beginning of Part 1, there was no wolf. But, by the end of Part 1, the wolf was like Shiva. She's dancing and bringing down the city around her ("she treads the salty earth, she does not raise breath cloud heavenward / her breath itself is carnage"). I really didn't know anything about where the thing was going or what it was. I still don't. At that point, I was conscious that it was a wolf; I wasn't conscious it was related to the dream. I had no idea for another year or two. I had almost forgotten the dream. But the door was opened for more of the poem.

Then the conscious part: that there was a wolf and some women— women and wolves here. I had the days to write; three days a week in the morning when a baby-sitter came. I would begin with collaging. I was making all these collages of wild animals, or animals and women, or women in improbable wild scenery. Eventually the poems would start. And would just go. So it was like making an invocation. Mostly, it was visual imagery. You suddenly find two things are adjacent to each other and you say, "Oh, that's what I want," or that somehow is satisfying.

PW: I love that moment when the wolf, Loba, looks down and you can see her fur over her socks and . . .

DdP: She's dancing in the bar, yeah. We have that always. Somebody's going to look and notice the fur. Last year at the Sonoma Mountain Zen practice, I actually experienced the true sense of my core feralness. And everything spoke to me constantly, every butterfly on the path when I would walk and do mantra and so on. It plugged into me with *Loba*, twenty-eight years earlier. So now when people say "What is *Loba* about?" I'm able to say it's about the feralness of the core of women, of the feminine in everything. In everyone. If you want an "about" . . . I didn't have an "about" for twenty-eight years.

Man in the Street

PW: How do all these variants of imagery move people?

DdP: Imagery is a tool. The closer you come to those primal images that are in us all, the more you do move people. I think we'd like to use the term "collective unconscious." But, it's too reductive, too squishy.

There's also the so-called "man in the street"—anyone, not consciously aware of metaphors or imagery, who responds to it, responds to correspondence. We all know it on some level.

I remember when politics was raging in the late sixties and early seventies, and I was writing all those revolutionary letters and reading them on the street and putting them in two hundred of those guerrilla-type newspapers around the country, through that Liberation News Service. I would go back east, where people are more inclined to be programmatic, to do poetry readings and things, and people would say to me, "What is your plan for the people of San Francisco?" or "the people of northern California," or "the people of the West," or whatever size they wanted to make it. As if because I wrote those poems, I had a clear-cut program in mind. And of course I didn't.

The Tapestry of Possibility

I chose poetry because I first read almost all the philosophers that were in the Carroll Street branch of the Brooklyn Public Library—and then I stumbled upon Keats. I realized how stupid it is to try to be consistent in a program or in a system of philosophy or of anything, when, through poetry, you hold all these different possibilities without having to resolve them.

There's a tapestry of possibility that we all live with, sort of a theater backdrop. There's a level of human life that's the outer scrim, the transparent fabric that creates special effects of light and atmosphere. And if you light the scrim up, this tapestry is infinite—or if not infinite, huge—possibility. You can write that scrim, which is transparent—it's like the material world is transparent—and look through it to the fully tapestry of possibility. The vastness . . . if you plug into some part of that, what comes alive and seeks you—"rapts" you away—grabs you as the artist. I wasn't looking for it. I think I would say I wasn't looking for it when that particular vast thing which now kind of informs all my work came to me.

If you plug into that place, people respond. You can do it for ill or for good. It's like one of those forces, like electricity. It's just there. Most people don't even talk about that tapestry, that cycle of birth, life, and death, and the blood at the beginning and at the end of it. The mess at the beginning and at the end of it, and how beautiful that is.

Diane di Prima's Brooklyn-born street wisdom never dismisses anything, be it the pattern of the stars, the destinies of children (she has five), dark timbers, fragile ankles, or the meanderings of the mind. Acumen and heart. She teaches privately and studies Buddhism and Western magic. She's known as an outstanding poet of the Beat period, constructs great collages, and has published thirty-two books, including the eight-part *Loba* (1998; 314 pp. $14.95, Penguin). Her memoir, *Recollections of My Life as a Woman* (Viking), is about to appear.—PW

Diane di Prima in Conversation with David Hadbawnik

David Hadbawnik / 2001

From *Jacket 2*, August 2001. Reprinted by permission of David Hadbawnik.

Early in August 2001, poet David Hadbawnik visited with Diane di Prima to interview her about her new book, *Recollections of My Life as a Woman.*

David Hadbawnik: First I wanted to ask you about what you write about your family, your early childhood. There have been some problems about that with your surviving relatives, but to me it seems that while there's a lot of hard stuff in the book, there's also a lot of insight and understanding and forgiveness. Could you talk about that, how specific things about your childhood and growing up shaped your attitude about men, how you say men are a luxury, and the whole attitude of being cool emotionally and masking your sexuality as a child.

Diane di Prima: I think to start with, there was that "men were a luxury" thing that I got at the grandparents' house, much as my grandfather was clearly the head of the family in terms of he was the most intellectual, he was looked up to, and so on. Yet at the same time, there were six daughters and one son that he had—the six daughters and my grandmother constantly were working around him and his ideals to keep things going. So that was the "men were a luxury" thing, and that was one thing, and maybe that's the deepest stratum for me. They were a luxury in the sense that you couldn't rely on them for basics, but they were there with brilliant ideas and often lots of excitement in terms of—I don't know, politically you could get in trouble.

But what I got at home, was that men were tyrannical, tended towards violence—so these were two completely different bundles of messages. And all women did was humor them and did what they wanted. So it was also working around them in a different way.

And the problems I'm having now are that both my brothers have put a lot of denial into the violence that resulted in that, and also it was different for them because I was born three years before either of them. [Three years] before my middle brother and seven years before my younger brother. And as my parents I think probably adapted to each other as well as their situation, it probably changed a lot, but as the oldest child anywhere you get all the flak. But my father as far as I can remember was always, when I was living at home still, was always considered an explosive person. He'd be very, very quiet and then he'd just blow up. So between that and the fact that the way my mother handled him was to be completely codependent and completely wanted to wait on him.

One time she was sick and she couldn't get out of bed, she had hurt her back, and she called me in. I was about eight, I don't know if I wrote about this or not—she called me in to her room and said "You let that man wash a dish." And here's this little eight-year-old I'm supposed to keep the guys from getting their own glasses of water, or washing, touching any housework at all, and I—I thought she was crazy. I stood there looking at her—"What do you mean I let him wash a dish?" You know, he's the grownup.

So given those two different sets of weird messages—they were different—neither set was such a kind of message that made you want to rush out and live with a man. With the grandfather and grandmother, they seemed quite happy, but if I was going to have all that excitement of a man that was a luxury, I might as well have the choice of when I wanted that around and when I didn't . . .

As when I was with LeRoi [Jones, a.k.a. Amiri Baraka], there was that excitement, but we didn't live together except very briefly, for a week or two, which I didn't even bother to write about. He moved out and got his own place, and he and I lived together briefly—he made a very beautiful house.

But anyway, the feeling was, you know, what's the pluses here, I know what the minuses are. What's the pluses when I can just be me, be who I was by the time I was eighteen—I can have my pick of these guys and I can have them when I tell them to come over.

The other stuff you asked me about, the family, the masking of sexuality . . . I think that stayed with me a lot. In one way I'm very present in my sex . . . much less now—but still, I always tend to hide my body in how I dress and like that. It was also the time, but it wasn't all the period. My favorite outfits were men's corduroy shirts and jeans, or white sweatshirts and black jeans, not tight jeans. And men's boots, from the navy surplus store.

And dressing up, I still don't know how to dress up. But I figured out a couple ways around it, and that's what I do. I don't know how to put on makeup. In fact, some friend is going to come over and we're going to give it another shot. That was partly because that was very threatening to my mother, who had some kind of breakdown that we have never figured out anything more about than what I wrote in the book.

DH: Well, for me it's interesting, the whole relationship that you had with your family, as someone who also feels a lot different from my family, and what ways did you reconcile with that or not reconcile with it, or just accept that you are different and let go of it, because in the book there are all these letters to your mother—"why did you let this happen to you" or "why did you do this," but most of them were unsent.

DdP: They were all unsent. They were letters I wrote all at one time, in a couple of days, after the last time she came to visit me on the West Coast, that trip I describe where we would keep going to the conservatory and then she said that remarkable thing about wanting to see everything there was to see in the world—that was her last trip out here. After she went home I wrote these letters. Because we had started to record a little family history, and this was all that stuff that had come up, questions: how come we don't know about this, how come no one in the family knows any of this—but I never sent them. She came to see me in one summer, and she died, I guess around a year after that. They were just scrawled on a yellow pad and put aside. More like notes, in case we got to talk again.

DH: So did you feel like you reached an understanding with your family?

DdP: In some ways yes, in some ways no. I think I reached an understanding with my mother. She used to come and stay in our house in Marshall on Tomales Bay, and she had a lot of positive things that she saw about my choices. About how the kids were and how they were raised, and she said a lot of positive stuff at that point.

My father died in 1969, and there was something going on for him in the way of understanding, but we never really talked. The problem has been with my own generation. Because when I left school and all that, certain wedges were set in place, between not only me and my brothers but me and my cousins and so on, by my parents, most particularly by my dad. He was terrified that anybody would find any of my books, find out how I was living, or any of that, and so the family has always thought of me—talking about cousins and people my own age—as this kind of like, they're supposed to be proud of me but they're not quite sure why, this kind of maverick.

And I have rarely if ever seen them since I left—fifty years, forty-eight years. I see cousins at my mother's wake, grandmother's wake a few years after I left, and occasionally at my brother's house like when he got married for the second time . . . And it never occurred to me to invite anyone from the family either of the times I got married. It was more like I walked on it, than tried to reach an understanding. The understanding worked for me more from the subconscious up, like that dream I described where I was praying to understand and forgive my father in that church, and I was being told that our background was really Arabic, that's how I had to understand Sicilian, if I understood that I would understand how he saw girls. . . . So it was working from the bottom up, from the subconscious up, and certainly didn't happen in his lifetime.

And at this point, I'm really dubious that there's much understanding to be gained, or achieved between me and my brothers. With each of my brothers at different times I felt I was pretty close, but when the book came out the fact of the matter was they were both so freaked out they wrote an article—I don't know if they published it—about what my parents were really like and how I was having false memory syndrome or something.

And so at that point I said "I give up"—because we're too old to keep going over the same ground. I thought I was pretty close to my brother Frank the last ten or twelve years, and I'm not mad, I was upset at first that they would refute the book without bothering to talk to me about it first, but they're just who they are. . . . So it's not really like a reconciliation.

I have a bigger family. I have a different family. I have a family that extends through generations of friends, people older than me all the way down to teenage people in the arts—so that's my family. And I have a certain understanding with my kids, I believe, with each one separately and differently. So that's the only family I really feel close to is my kids and grandkids. I feel like, really for me, you have to take your eyes off this blood-link thing, and put it on who's your real family. Who's really part of your tribe. I did when I was writing the book. I didn't let any of what they would think about it come up; I tried to keep a little book, or when I didn't have that I had it in my head, of pictures of people I'm really writing for.

Engravings of Keats at his window scribbling away, or photos of Jean Cocteau or H.D.—who am I really writing for, what is this for, you know? And it wasn't about them. I put in the family stuff because I thought it would be helpful to young artists or young people who wanted to be artists who were having a hard time or coming from a hard background. More than, because I wanted to say, "O woe is me, I suffered so much." At this point I don't think it's relevant, doesn't matter. None of that matters at this point.

DH: Well, another theme I found in the book is the notion of power, and your observation of the power struggles in your own family and the society you grew up in, and there's a quote when you're having a meeting with your uncle: "It is power I'm talking about, the use and abuse of power, power and secrecy and deals made in the dark. Coils of the unsaid winding through our lives, tangling and tripping us, holding the fabric together."

And that, for me, seems like a theme for the whole book, of how you discovered that and learned to use it for yourself, the power of words and your power as a woman.

DdP: That could be, I never really thought about that. I know that the slant I was given—the only handle I was given on reading history or reading society as a whole, was that hierarchical power, how it works. From the time I was little, men would meet in my house, to divvy up whatever the plums were, and so on, it was clear that that's how society works, but at what point I realized that was how a lot of one-on-one relationships work was much later, I think I was living with Alan [Marlowe] and we were hassling it out in Topanga Canyon, you know.

I wasn't really thinking about it as having power over anybody when I was having all those millions of affairs and all that, that was about peers sort of, but again, caught in the nuclear family situation it became power, a power game. Power of words—that's something else. I guess there was always the hope or the possibility that they would go on for a while. So in that sense, the sense of getting a book out is that you don't have to take care of those particular words out there anymore, they can take care of themselves.

DH: You talked a little bit earlier about how at an early age you chose to mask your sexuality and not have any relations with men, and then later, when you were living alone in New York for the first time after leaving school, you had a "parade of lovers," and was that a gradual or sudden change?

DdP: Oh, no, I think it was, once I got away from my mother who was so threatened by sex and sexuality, my father too, he thought he owned my body, my mother was threatened by female sexuality totally, once I was out of there, and once it wasn't a game, the social game of dating, and girls and boys and all that, and having status by who you were with, once it was just being with people, physically, that was not so hard for me.

So in that sense it was a sudden change. You walk out the door of that house, you get your own apartment, and you're a different person.

DH: It seemed like you went through a discovery that you had your own body, studying movement and dance.

DdP: Yeah, that started a little earlier when I was fifteen. Yeah, that was important. But then I think a lot of early sexuality, like I was eighteen when I got my own place, and you have to figure those early twenties too, a lot of discovering you have your own body is discovering how somebody else has their body, so for me I used to think of going to bed with someone as—I think I wrote that in the book as "embarking on a voyage of discovery," and adventure, each thing was different, each person was different, and I think what helped to find my physicality was to explore someone else's physicality, and all that mutual surprise that you have in the early years about what all that is.

DH: This book is called *Recollections of My Life as a Woman*, and I don't know to what extent you made it be consciously for women, but it seems to me there's just as much in there for artists and poets of any gender.

DdP: Yeah, I hope so. I call it that, because the title was there long before the book, and at that time in the mid-eighties I was thinking about writing a short book for my daughters about stuff that happened to me because I bought into certain myths of how women were supposed to be, like you're supposed to take care of everything, be all-powerful in terms of getting the work done, in terms of getting the kids, and all that, but then it turned into something else when I sat down to write it. But the title stayed because the title had been there.

And when I was writing the book I was writing it more for all artists, and all people too, but artists especially, and young people who thought they might want to do that. At this point in my life and at the turn of this particular millennium, I feel like we've got a bare spark left of creativity and joy and it's very threatened by a lot of darkness. So every chance I get as I run around my world I sort of blow on the embers, and hope that people can keep that joy of creativity going because there's not much else for us. Without it it's hardly worth being here.

DH: One thing that is perhaps a paradox, but encouraging to read about, was your decision not only to have children by yourself but to raise them by yourself. And despite that, defying the cliché of the lone artist as the male, or the female, deciding to have kids and that's it—you're going back into the conventional lifestyle.

DdP: Yeah, that's terrible because they're using their kids as an excuse. That's awful to do to their kids too, that's a real cop-out. Because if they want to go back to that lifestyle it's not their kids driving them.

DH: But it seems like there were some doubts that you had about that. For example, you had this vision of Keats warning you not to do it, and Kerouac saying . . .

DdP: Well, I had had that close relationship, séance relationship with Keats right along. And the life that Keats knew there wasn't any such thing. I mean it was quite personally a picture of the real Keats, and there was no such thing, it was just the work. So you could say I was dialoguing with that part of myself, but it was just the work. And people didn't do that. Women didn't do that, especially, but guys didn't do it either, if they had kids, they were doing art, they probably either abandoned the kids or whatever to go on with their work. And everybody said, "Oh, that's okay, they're guys, you know."

So my feeling was I wanted everything—very earnestly and totally—I wanted to have every experience I could have, I wanted everything that was possible to a person in a female body, and that meant I wanted to be mother. You know, and I wanted to go through the whole thing of seeing them grow up and what that would be and all that. So my feeling was, "Well"—as I had many times this feeling—"Well, nobody's done it quite this way before but fuck it, that's what I'm doing, I'm going to risk it. All I can do is lose."

And whatever that meant, the art would stop, or the kid would die of neglect, or I would just die of exhaustion, or something. That's what "All I could do was lose" was. But it's not really anything that we lose anyway. There's nothing that we won't lose, there's nothing we have to protect.

DH: There's kind of a funny passage where you try to find somebody who would have a baby with you but not raise it—

DdP: Yeah, so my lovers—"Would you like to be the father of a child?" I mean, hell, Isadora Duncan asked her lovers, they didn't say no. But [the men] were all scared.

DH: Why do you think that was?

DdP: Well, they thought I was crazy I guess. The last thing they wanted, men in that time, the main thing they were afraid of was being "caught," that was the phrase they would use, being caught by a woman. Maybe they were afraid if they had a child by a woman they would be caught; the last thing I wanted was them around when I had a child. But their conditioning of being free and not committing or being caught, was easily as strong as women's conditioning of getting married and having matching dishes. . . . So every-body was really, they were caught, they were all caught in the same box.

DH: Then there's that quote from Jack Kerouac that—

DdP: —unless you forget your babysitter you'll never be a writer.

DH: But that sort of turns into, because I didn't forget my babysitter that allows me to be the writer that I am. So that was another interesting thing.

DdP: Because to me it was, you can't give your word and not keep it, and the thing of it is, I knew I was already risking that I'd never be a writer. And another point, a very liberating point I don't think I wrote about, is, we'll never know in our lifetimes if we were "good writers" or not, because that stuff is decided way after we're gone, if the work survives. And it might or might not. But I constantly remember that [Robert] Southey was the great poet when Coleridge and Wordsworth and Keats and Shelley were writing. You could go through the periods after that—it goes on like that.

So you can never know, and the approbation of your fellows doesn't tell you, and you yourself if you're taking any risks can never know if they work or not, for sure, so I soon realized there was no way of knowing if I'd ever be a writer anyway. And then that working definition, if you write every day you're a writer. I mean if you get up every day and what you do is you go write, maybe that's all you need to know—not anything else.

DH: In that vein, you said you took it as a matter of course when Donald Allen left you out of the *New American Poetry* anthology, because of the affair with Roi, and even today it seems there's a question of recognition for the women of that era, compared with men, and—does that still bother you at all?

DdP: Well, I think I should have been in that anthology. It didn't bother me then because I was quite arrogant and self-assured enough to think it didn't matter whether I was in that one anthology or not. I got a letter from Don when this book came out denying that he told me that he was leaving me out for the reason that I say in the book, because Hettie [Jones, Baraka's wife] asked him to, and I don't distrust my memory on that one. I remember what doorway we were standing in in Roi and Hettie's apartment.

Of course Hettie also denies that that was the case—and Hettie might not have asked him, it might have been the way he dreamed up an excuse to get out of it, because he didn't want to be caught in this triangle. And no one would've thought twice about a white lie like that in those days. Especially Don who's very suave, and had a good position. So I'm not saying that he's deliberately lying about it now, maybe he doesn't even remember, but the thing is that at that point it was "Well, okay, so I'm not in it."

But I knew at that point, because some of the work I'd given him had been from the *New Handbook of Heaven*, it was "The Jungle" and pieces like that, and I knew it was as strong as anything in Roi's early work that was going in from that *Preface to a Twenty-Volume Suicide Note* [Baraka's first book], we were writing almost as if we were writing back and forth to each other at that point. And it seemed like, well, Fuck it, if not this anthology, another anthology, and not what you know in hindsight that this one anthology is going to define a period or movement, and I don't know if I would have worried even if I'd known that. Because I always felt the work finds its own places to go.

But there was the fact that, given the fact that me and Roi and Hettie, we were all basically in one position of misbehaving—how does it happen that the woman gets left out of the anthology? But I didn't even think about that. There was a European tradition that I was following a lot in my mind somewhere, you're the mistress, so you should stay invisible. And so I never even questioned that at one point.

DH: Did Donald ever give you a legitimate reason?

DdP: No, he didn't give any reason. I have the letter somewhere, but later when he did the second anthology and he put in people he had left out, and I guess he had left out some people he put in—he did a whole other *New American Poetry* from that same time and I was in that one, he said in the letter he wrote me then that it had been a severe oversight on his part. . . . It seems more likely that either Hettie asked him, or he just didn't want to get caught in our little psychodramas, which I can't blame him for in the least. And I was the one who was in the non-legit position, and that's always been my choice, that I would choose to have an affair with a married person and be in that position. Not that I had much choice about falling in love with Roi, but you situate yourself and I situated myself always outside the regular relationships and regular roles. Like I never worked a regular job after the first year [of leaving school at eighteen].

DH: Speaking of Roi, would you say that was the start of recognizing that men could be good for something more than what you had always thought?

DdP: Not really. No, Roi was more like me looking for my Grandpa, looking for the firebrand revolutionary, yeah, maybe a little bit nihilistic and so on at that point in his life. There's something about the way we came together that still feels like it had an element of kismet or fate in it, something that just had to happen, and it happened good. But Roi wasn't there for me, either for the abortion [of their first child] or after Dominique [Baraka and di Prima's daughter] was born. He was too bewildered, he was too hurting himself from too many points of view.

Not only about me and all his other ladies, his wife and everything else but that Black-white thing and did he or didn't he want to stay, and it was a beautiful, wonderful world he was welcomed in, the world of all of us artists, loved by folks like Frank [O'Hara] and so on, but then there was that other thing that he was called to, which was the Black Arts thing. So he's hurting on so many levels, but probably it was just as well there, for him and I to have talked all that out was ridiculous, we didn't have the tools, nobody had the tools at that time to figure anything out from somebody else's point of view, and we would've just gone in circles.

So what he did, he just used to come and sit and hold Dominique and go home and not say anything, I mean that's what he could do. But no, I didn't feel like, "Ah, now men are good for something"—no. What does he say to me when I come back from the abortion? He says, "You'll never forgive me." I mean, what kind of being there is that? I'm not blaming him. I'm just saying no, I didn't learn anything there. And I didn't learn anything with Alan [Marlowe, her first husband], I didn't learn anything with Grant [Fisher, second husband] of usefulness. Alan and I had a good working relationship, we made theaters and presses like nobody's business, so on that level he came a little closer to joining a family life; he was also the one who really cared about keeping a house together and all that stuff.

But in terms of really having a partner or equal peer I never experienced that with a man till I was with Sheppard [Powell—her current partner]. And it took the first ten years or so of being with him before I came to a real solid place of daily life-ness. Before that it was all insanity and art and stuff that I was probably too old for but he wasn't, a lot of staying up all night. But no. I found out with Roi that I could love a man, but my Grandma loved my Grandpa, it didn't make him reliable in terms of anything. Just made him a wondrous person.

I think what I had with Roi that my Grandma didn't was that exchange of the poem, back and forth, exchange of art back and forth. And doing the [*Floating*] *Bear* [magazine] together was a wonderful experience, difficult as it was. And again, he and I equally chose the work, but who typed, was me, and I didn't mind, I just took it for granted he wasn't going to do anything like that. And who did most of the physical work was a crowd of folks that either we both knew or that were friends of mine like Freddie [Herko], who would just come together and do it.

Sometimes Roi would show for those, because it was good crowds, he would run the press for a while, but I wasn't counting on him to be there for any of it, except when we chose.

And in the choosing again, that was a good example of where [being] cool worked, because we didn't discuss, "Well I think this piece is a"—"I think we should put in this Dorn piece"—"Well, Roi I don't like this Dorn piece." We didn't do that. Instead we just said, "Oh, okay, you like that, okay, that can go in. I think I'd like to put this in," and we just made space for each other's points of view without trying to mishmash them down into a common denominator. So cool sometimes worked very well for us.

DH: Speaking of that attitude in the Bay Area—when you had the Poets Theatre, you talked about the importance of having a surround of other artists, and it seems like you had that all along, but especially when the *Bear* was happening, and the Theatre—

DdP: That all started to take off around the same time, around '61.

DH: How important do you think that surround of artists was in terms of your own development as an artist, and how important do you think it is in general, and talk about how hard it is, and the difficulties of that today that you see.

DdP: Well I think I learned early on that, aside from what I learned early on, going through trying to read everything in *ABC of Reading* [by Ezra Pound], everything I learned through Pound, the place where I learned the most about poetics, was actually typing those poems for the *Floating Bear*, onto those green stencils.

By the time you start, since the *Bear* was the same size as a typewriter page, once you copy exactly the line breaks and that spacing that Olson had done, it gave you plenty of time to absorb it and to ponder why did he do it that way. You're typing a lot of poets, in my case I was typing a lot of poets that were further along, that were cutting edge in some other area than the area I was working in, like Dorn, so I don't think I ever learned more than I did typing. What are there, sixteen of those *Bears*, typing them, proofreading them, handling the material right onto the page.

That was big, and also the Poets Press books. *On Boar's Head* was completely prepped by me, for Poets Press, and including all the drawings that Philip [Whalen] had in it, had been cut out and photostated and pasted in, when he wrote me and said I couldn't do it because he'd just made a contract with Harcourt Brace. And each one of those you're typing with special ribbons on slick paper, so you're actually doing, you're repeating the process that the writer went through, and *On Boar's Head* was a monster, a huge book, and I finished at Millbrook in '67. So it was just about ready to go to press when Philip found a publisher who could give him money and he needed the money, but it never came out with all the pictures . . .

All of those were real important in terms of what I learned. In terms of the artists in general, there was so much happening, and one didn't realize that it wasn't happening like that always. There was no night when you weren't at a movie or seeing someone's new dance or going to a rehearsal of a dance you were in, rehearsing for Poets Theater, the amount of input was huge. Cecil [Taylor] would say "Do you want to come over, I want to practice all afternoon." And again, where cool worked, I wasn't going to come in and chat or anything. I was going to come over with my notebook and scribble.

So there was a constant input, to the point where it was subliminal. There was no time to analyze or say, "Well, what's Jimmy Waring doing that's new in this piece, or what's happening to form in that"—but you were just taking it in and taking it in to the point where it was bypassing, what is they call that, the left side of the brain, the way images do when you visualize. So you had this bank of stuff that was there for you when you wrote.

And you had all that human blessing energy of all these people. Some of them you didn't like but it didn't matter, you knew that it didn't matter. Because what was happening from them, this ectoplasm of creative energy that was in the air, it was thick. Maybe you dodged this one because he was always asking for dope, but they were all still part of it, it was like you couldn't have left out a single one of those without making a whole.

So I talked about this in writing classes, you know, in the day of Shakespeare everybody wrote sonnets, and songs, and everybody could write a least a passable whatever, or draw a passable whatever, all the ladies played piano. And that matters, in that you have a ground from which the people who have stature are going to grow, they don't have to start in a place where there's nothing at all and invent a platform and stand on that, there's like a real ground of fertile energy all the time. We had that then. And I'm not sure, I can't say "Oh, alas it died out this year or that year," because I don't know. I walked on the East Coast in my mind in '67 but permanently in '68, after Frank [O'Hara] died . . . I was out of there. I was out of there before it was over.

DH: I was really surprised to find that you were such good friends with Frank.

DdP: Oh, yeah, right down-the-street friends. Coming over for Sunday breakfast friends.

DH: Was he that way with other poets?

DdP: I don't know. He really adopted me in some ways. One poem I wrote after he died I said "you my big brother brought me up." And he's only a few years older than me, but sometimes in the arts a few years can make a big difference. He socialized me, brought out the part of me that was a social being, that could make witticisms at cocktail parties, and be at ease in all those crowds. Because he enjoyed watching it so much, it gave me confidence.

But I also knew him very much privately. I used to go over with Jeannie [her first daughter] for breakfast. I didn't meet a hundred poets there, it was me, sometimes his friend Joe LeSueur and people like that. And I remember when he said I want you to meet these younger people that have come on the scene—turns out now, they were two or three years younger than me, like Ted Berrigan, Ron Padgett, Tony Towle—these were three of his younger people the he was excited about, and Bill Berkson, although Bill knew him a little earlier than that. Bill was always—me and Bill and Frank would have lunch sometimes at the bar near the Museum of Modern Art, and to me Bill was this dear friend, young brother person, so I thought of them—three or four years made differences in how we were together, and how we were in the city.

But aside from Bill, I didn't see Frank with people a whole lot. I saw him at social events with millions of people, or sometimes I would go over with the bread and he'd make eggs in his own boiler, and do breakfast or something.

So I think Frank's death, although I was in the country when it happened, was one of those things that really tossed me out of that milieu, before that milieu was really winding down, the creative energy. I felt it still there when I would go read like in '72—I don't think I felt it there so much, say by '75 or '76, but around '76 I decided not to go back to the East Coast for a while, it was eight years before I read there again.

DH: You were feeling the pull of the West Coast . . .

DdP: I had been living here for four or five years. At first you go back a lot, and then you go back less, and then one day, I was there on a reading trip and I said, "I don't think I'm going to come back here for a while." And it was eight years. I came back with Sheppard and we stayed at Bob Wilson's house in Chelsea . . . but a lot happened in those eight years, it was '83—in the arts milieu, I mean. I don't know when it started to not feel like that in New York, but a lot of young people in New York, they still feel it like that. Although I don't know if there's that mixing up of all the different arts that we had.

DH: It seems that you were beginning to get an appreciation for the West Coast, that aesthetic, and different people like Mike McClure and George Herms and Wallace Berman, people like that, and that you perceived a real clash between those aesthetics, between the East and West Coast, and you hoped for some kind of cross-pollination. To what extent do you feel that that eventually happened?

DdP: I don't know if it ever happened. I don't see George's work at a million museums back east. I see it at a few out here. I think we were really hoping to bring it together, and one of the first places I was clear that it wasn't happening, I was talking to Bruce Conner last night, was how people hated *The Blossom* [by Michael McClure], with George's set, which was one of the most phenomenal things that I've ever experienced. It was like taking Artaud and assemblage by Michael, and putting it together and running with it. But, yeah we brought George out a few times, we tried to bring some of that together, but I don't know if it ever did happen. I wasn't at first seeing it as a clash, and the very first time I came out here I was interested in it, but before that, the very first, *Hymns to Saint Geryon & Dark Brown* by Michael McClure [1969] and that other big book that Philip put out, that first one, those both wended their way into my hands right after they were first out. That's why I was waiting for Michael to make his first trip, and put him up at my house his first time out, because that stuff was, to me, phenomenal, and of course we'd be printing it in the *Bear*. The *Bear* was real cross-pollination. I don't know that it got so far as being theater and visual arts-wise. What do you think how is it now?

DH: Well, I don't know.

DdP: There's a lot of New York aesthetic here, I don't know that there's much out there, I feel colonized more than cross-pollinated.

DH: Well, there was Margaret Kilgallen just died, and she had a show in New York, and there was a big piece about her in the *New York Times*, so that was surprising. . . . But my perception is that there's a huge schism.

DdP: You know, when that Beat show happened, I didn't see it in New York, but when it was coming out here I was talking to one of the guys who was curating it because we were setting up when I could perform and all that. And he asked me—I'm sure he asked everybody—"What do you think I can do to make it more cogent to right here?" I said put in more of the West Coast visual art, because that's who we are out here.

And people who saw the show in both places said it was a different show out here, East Coast and West Coast. So that's telling about how much we still haven't grokked each other, that it would even have to be a different show, that all that West Coast stuff wouldn't automatically be there, at the exhibit in New York, too.

DH: Speaking of the West Coast, when I read this quote of yours too, which is another thing that seemed really counterintuitive, or maybe just surprising the way you had this realization, that "One of the mistakes I made at that time, a mistake many artists make, to the end of their days, was thinking that surrendering control of the poem was and should be concomitant with surrendering control of my life." And how did that sort of affect your whole approach to life?

DdP: Just that I would sort of follow wherever my passion led in my life, and I think that's fine in the poem but you don't really have to, maybe you do, up to the time you're thirty-five or forty, maybe you do and maybe it wasn't a mistake, but just one thing you sort out over time. But just because whenever you're in the process of making a work whether it's a poem or painting or anything, you've completely put aside the self, doesn't mean you have to follow your nose, or follow your heart into all kinds of completely untenable situations because you've fallen in love, or this, that, and the other thing; that's what I meant by surrendering control of my life. Just going where my passion led. And it's not necessarily the smartest thing to do. You want to save that energy for the work, but it takes a long time to know that.

DH: Well, that struck me in terms of someone like Lew Welch, who seemed to feel like when he was open he had to be all the way open to whatever came and it was an either/or proposition. And maybe that destroyed him somehow.

DdP: It could. It's also that either/or proposition is something you find a lot discussed in books on addiction, that all of us who are somehow touched by those worlds tend to be black-and-white or either/or people. And it takes a long time to fill in all those modulations like, yes, I can totally surrender to *Loba*, that doesn't mean I have to pick up and pack and move to somewhere else every time some guy like Alan says "Oh, let's go live in, Ranchos de Taos. . . ." Not that it wasn't in some way very filling for me in terms of images for work and knowledge of landscape and so on, but I really did mix up the idea that you surrender with the idea that you also surrender on practical, daily-life terms. It gives you less energy to put into the work if you're constantly chasing after everything you want.

DH: One thing I wanted more of when I read this book was more gossipy stuff and details, like about meeting Ezra Pound, and people like that. Was that a conscious decision you made not to go that way, or was that just all you had to say?

DdP: No, I decided I didn't want to write a cute little book of anecdotes, and definitely didn't want to just drop names, you know. It wasn't all I had to say but it felt like it was enough, and there was so much I wanted to put in, too. Every little piece or every little section is pretty condensed, and I was still thinking "Oh, gee, I didn't write about . . ." So it was more, what were the things that were salient in terms of defining the time, and the time was part of it, too.

But also, how do you avoid that stupid thing that people are doing in their memoirs all the time of just constantly telling the story of this and the story of that? So hitting some mean there. So you would've liked more gossip, huh?

DH: I guess so, yeah.

DdP: People have complained that I didn't tell them enough about my affair with Roi and so on and so forth. But maybe that's still the same cool. I don't know.

DH: It seems like, I know one of your favorite ideas of Pound's is that "all times contemporaneous." And that seems to also be at work in the memoir where things progress not so much chronologically all the time but flashing back and forward in terms of insight and emotional moments and things like that.

DdP: I think that's true. Definitely there's a kind of chronology that I used as, what do they call that in sculpture? An armature. But then I didn't particularly, I wasn't particularly interested in telling a linear story. Do you even think time exists? I think it's just a construct of the mind that we make just to keep us from being overwhelmed. Everything might be happening all at once, and we've sorted it out this way. I don't know.

But I certainly wasn't interested in saying, "then, and then and then," and probably I even feel like I did that a little too much, but there was more jumping around than there is, and some of it, folks asked me to cut out, and I decided they were right. I'm not sure now they were right, but some of those pieces will go into book two. Maybe they fit better there. I trust where my mind goes, so that if I'm writing about 1937 and my grandparents, and then I remember my mother when she came out here in 1983 and what she said to me at the conservatory, that's where it goes, because there is a shape that the mind has already woven of all this material, and part of what I was trying to do in the book was lay out the actual process of remembering.

What is that process like? So sometimes I would repeat something, and add to it. And that would also drive my editors crazy, you know—"You said this on page 72!"—but I didn't say this plus that on 72, that on 72 became the key for me also remembering this on [page] 153, I mean it's no news, Proust did it and others, I'm not inventing something, but I was following more the shape of memory and also my consciousness rather than just the calendar years. So that was why that.

And as for why not more stories, the main story was what it took and how I did it to be able to stay with what I thought I wanted to do, which was to be a poet no matter what, and grow in the process, rather than just be a stuck poet that does the same thing for fifty years. And so that was the main story I wanted to stick to, and I wanted to stick to it hoping it would be useful as well as interesting. I mean, nice writing and interesting to read, but useful to other people.

So when I was doing the revisions I had two questions on the wall: 1) is it necessary to the integrity of the work? And 2) will it be helpful to others? And things came out sometimes just because they weren't necessary to the integrity of the work. I would guess that I have a small book of outtakes in the computer. They maybe were interesting stories in themselves but they didn't really add to the thrust of where the book was going.

DH: How do you feel about the reactions to the book so far? There was that terrible review in the *Times*.

DdP: Yeah, and I'm told the guy it was given to review in LA hated it, and since the main editors there liked it, they just killed the review rather than print a bad one. Well, you know there are all kinds of reactions, so I'm mixed about them.

DH: I guess the only ones I've read have been the *Times* and *Rain Taxi*.

DdP: The thing is that I read reviews that aren't particularly positive with an idea to, is there something here I can use, but what I'm finding a lot of the time, or maybe it's just my mind's little way out of the dilemmas, is that people just sound confused or really put off and upset and negative about my life, rather than the writing. I think I'm just threatening to some folks. And that would be true whether I was on the East Coast or the West Coast.

You know, about my work and the two coasts, I think my work is better received here than on the East Coast. For instance *Loba*. When *Loba* was being written, if I read it in New York, people had a million intellectual questions and they didn't understand. If I read it in Sonoma, all the young, single moms with their babies would come out of the woods, and they'd hear it and dig it. There was no problem. The work can be received more intuitively here than there. I'm talking about the real ground culture here.

My work is easier here for me, in that way. In terms of recognition and money and awards, that was way easier in New York, but it might have left me stuck in the same work forever. They liked what I was doing, they weren't going to want me to change it. But I think, I find this whole milieu much more compatible to work with than anywhere.

DH: One other thing you talk about a lot is weaving some other discipline into the dance, and for you that has been alchemy, magic, primarily, and to me that would be one of the reasons *Loba* would be better received on the West Coast than the East Coast. At what point did that particular strain start to be of such importance to you?

DdP: Well, I think I write in the end of the book how I had just gotten that gig to write the introduction to Paracelsus, in '65, and that's when I began to really read alchemy was then, 1965. The magic was around from the beginning, but got subsumed by the poetry after I left school, but came back around the same time, a year or two years later in '66, when I was living in Ranchos de Taos and started working with the cards every day. By '71 I had pretty much taught myself Kabbalah, and then the whole process wove itself into some coherence when I taught at the New College in 1980, and put together the Hidden Religions course there. But once I did the Paracelsus there was no stopping reading alchemy after that. It was all the time.

And I would read a passage and go to bed and dream about it, that kind of thing. That was also how I would work with the cards. I'd stare at the cards and take an afternoon nap and inevitably that card would be in the dream. So that stuff grew later, and the understanding of how it wove itself in to European consciousness, and which parts came at which point, that understanding came more around '80, when I started teaching [at New College in San Francisco].

DH: And that led to your whole friendship with Robert Duncan?

DdP: Being in that school did. Robert was really the soul of that whole program. In a lot of ways. And he said yes, with the idea that we'd do it for five years. We did it for seven.

DH: He also shared your interest.

DdP: They were very much his interests. He would never practice magic, though, and when in one summer course that we did there I brought in devices for visualization from the Golden Dawn, showed them to people and talked about actually practicing trance work with these symbols of the elements and sub-elements—he was quite upset. He would never practice it, and [said] that he needed neither religion nor magic, because poetry was a complete path in itself. And I think for him it was, but also he was a little afraid, because of his upbringing, of actually getting his feet wet. So we had lots of interesting tugs of war like that.

He came to one of my classes one time, and toward the end of the class there was a general discussion, and I don't know what came up, but he said "I don't want to see the whole picture, I just want to see my little piece that I have to work on, and just work on that little piece, I don't want to see the whole thing." And I said, "I want to know, I want to know it all, even if I never pick up a pen again." And the students were like, "Who's right here?" And it was, you know, all under the general aegis of friendship, but there was that definite line of difference, it was very strong.

But Robert had been, I can't say that's when the friendship began; Robert used to come and hang for days, he'd move into my house in Marshall in the seventies, and bring his French mysteries that he was teaching himself idiomatic French from, and his notebook, and he'd stay for days. And he always came to Christmases with the kids, because Jess doesn't like holidays, and so I'd have to say mid-seventies, through '75 on, he was there many weekends, many mornings . . . eating fried herring from the bay for breakfast. And he opened for one of Dominique's plays at Intersections, you know she had a theater till she was eleven or twelve, and he was the opening act one time . . .

Diane di Prima Interview

V. Vale / 2001

From *Modern Pagans: An Investigation of Modern Contemporary Pagan Practices*, 2001, 36–40. Reprinted by permission of V. Vale.

Diane di Prima has had a long career as a poet, writer, publisher, teacher, occultist, pagan, Zen practitioner, and Tibetan Buddhist. Her thirty-four books include *Memoirs of a Beatnik, Pieces of a Song: Selected Poems*, and most recently, *Recollections of My Life as a Woman*. She lives in San Francisco with Sheppard Powell, and studies with Lama Tharchin.

[*Re/Search* is edited by V. Vale and this interview originally appeared in that publication. Vale describes it as "Non-Stop Punk Rock, Black Humor, Anti-Authority, Provocative Publishing by V. Vale—A Cultural Remapping Project; Punk Is a Lifetime Philosophical Outlook!" See https://www.research pubs.com/about.]

Re/Search: You're well-known as a Beat poet, writer, and teacher. Are you comfortable appearing in the context of *Modern Pagans*?

Diane di Prima: I was thinking about that. Definitely there is the element in my belief system of paganism, but basically I'm a Tibetan Buddhist. But I've incorporated pagan practices in my life since around 1963—I wrote about this in my autobiography *Recollections of My Life as a Woman*. I invited twelve people over for my first Winter Solstice celebration at my house in New York, including Merce Cunningham and Cecil Taylor. I had done a lot of research on ritual in James Frazer's *Golden Bough*—in 1961 I had bought for myself the twelve-volume set of hardbacks which in those days didn't cost much—about forty-five dollars.

We did different kinds of ceremonies. I had an orange that was completely covered with cloves—like people hang in closets, I guess. It represented the sun, and I put it in the fire—we had a fireplace. The first year we didn't have birch, but each year thereafter we would burn white birch logs. Everybody got a little scroll on which they wrote the things they wanted to get rid of with the old year. Then they tied it up with a ribbon and put it in the fire. We did more things like that—all except Merce. We were describing it as "Write down your demons" and Merce said that he had no demons and immediately went home—very telling about that man, isn't it?!

We stayed up all night until the sun came up. We lit candles and stayed up to help the sun come back, because it is the longest night of the year. Every year since then the solstice has always been celebrated by me in one way or the other. Until maybe the late seventies I would stay up that night. As I got older I didn't do that, but I leave candles burning in the window sill on solstice night, and I do a ritual, although it has changed over the years.

So the solstices and equinoxes had an importance for me from early on, and I think that although it was buried under miles of agnosticism and philosophy in my parents' house, my mother would always say, "It's the longest night of the year" with great awe and amazement. So something had come down to her that she wasn't quite articulating.

I remember being shown how the sun illuminates the planets. Someone stuck a pencil through an orange, shined a flashlight beam in the dark on it, and rotated the orange, showing how the light would change as the planet revolved around the sun. It was like how Galileo or Giordano Bruno might have interpreted the universe. So I have a root in some kind of paganism like that, which was also very deep in my grandmother's Catholicism. There was a day when you ate no salt, a day when you ate no bread—St. Lucy or Santa Lucia's Day, which is celebrated in northern Europe, too, when Swedish women wear crowns of candles. The saint of light, Lucia, *lux*, Lucy—she was a very important figure in my grandmother's world. Although nobody said, "This is pagan," there was a basic interest and awe in the things of the turning of the seasons and being on the planet, that were handed to me from way back.

When I was in high school, eight women in our writing group did a lot of experimenting with the paranormal—telepathy, trance, and séance. That all went away when I became just a writer and dropped out of college, but it came back with a big bang when I was about thirty-one and started to fool around with Tarot cards, and would have lucid dreams. I was living in New Mexico. In the afternoons when it was hot I would stare at one card and go to sleep. When I awoke I would always have had a dream about that card. It didn't seem remarkable or strange—I didn't have to work at it—it just happened.

Tibetan Buddhism is concerned with, at the least, the thirty-one major star systems that have Dzogchen. It's not based in the material facts of life.

It's my main belief system, within which paganism fits quite comfortably as regards how you deal with Earth and being on it.

In Tibetan Buddhism, there is relative truth and absolute truth. Relative truth is about here, where we are, daily life, and the appearances of things. Absolute truth is about the emptiness (which isn't empty) and the constant creative principle in that, which they call the *dharmakaya*. They fit comfortably together. In the same way, Tibetan Buddhism fits together with my paganism and other kinds of ritual magic. (I'm not talking about Judaic Kabbalism; I'm talking about Kabbalistic magic which grew out of the Renaissance, transmitted by Cornelius Agrippa and others.) It's a seamless fit with no problems. So I have my Tibetan Buddhist practice, but if my daughter has a question, I will go to the Tarot cards.

R/S: Paganism is definitely Earth-based and grounded in very real practices in this world, but you overlay it with this other theory, if I can call it that, from Tibetan Buddhism, which is more concerned with causality, multiple dimensions of reality, and other cosmic theorizings. You can't necessarily prove it scientifically—

DdP: No, but you can prove it experientially. It's not easy—you don't just go off and prove it, like in a laboratory. You have to do the groundwork, then find a teacher, then get pointing-out instruction, and actual experience of indwelling, void, creative principle, that is also the same as vast, timeless, and spaceless creative principle. So you can't prove it scientifically, but you can prove it experientially. I'm reminded sometimes, when I am practicing, of that line in the *Book of the Law* by Crowley, "Certainty, not faith, while in life."

R/S: "Certainty, not faith, while in life"?

DdP: It's from the *Book of the Law*—another aspect of magic. So the pagan movement is wonderful and I am still continuing its practices, but I hardly think about them—they're just ingrained in my life. "Have you picked up the candles for the solstice?" Or, "Are you going to have time tomorrow for us to do something for the Eve of May?" You know? I have a meditation room in the house, which is wonderful because I can roll out of bed, sleepy or sick, and do my practice, then come back to my daily life, because that room is not used for anything else.

I also have a magical altar in the healing room where Sheppard does his healing work (that's his livelihood), and where I do occasional guided visualizations with my students, or a Tarot reading. And the magical altar is—how can I say—a landing place and a launching pad for spirits and energies and businesses of this world. It has an arrangement of things that represent the four elements, so I have, using the Tarot model, a cup, a disc, a sword, and a wand. And for the three principles from alchemy, I have a vial of mercury, a big chunk of sulfur from Sicily, and a big crystal of solidified salt.

So mercury, sulfur, and salt are the three principles of alchemy. I integrate this with the Zodiac, too. All this is part of what I used to teach when I taught "Structures of Magic" at our magic school, the San Francisco Institute of Magical and Healing Arts, which has been defunct since 1992.

For me, I started with just the simple notions I could get in Frazer's *Golden Bough* about the solstices and equinoxes and cross-quarter days and how they used to be celebrated. The whole set of volumes is indexed, so you can find information about the practices in the South Pacific in one volume, and information about Greece in another—with the index, you can find what you want. Then I would shamelessly make my own synthesis of what I wanted from all that, to use as a basic form, a ritual.

Solstices are easy. Equinoxes are more subtle, because you have that simple slight turning toward the light or toward the dark at that point. The cross-quarter days are wonderful—I was going to say divine in terms of earthly things—they're earthly deities. So something comes up every six weeks that you try to at least commemorate in some little way, even if you're very busy. I have this shrine downstairs that is the Earth magic shrine set up for that, having the elements and the principles of alchemy. Salt is that which remains after the transformation, the dross is that which remains after the mercury flies away (unless you catch it and use it), and sulfur is what is consumed from the burning. Those three principles work in the four elements—here I'm going by Paracelsus. Even if you only have half an hour, you can go down and commemorate the occasion in some way.

R/S: Do you actually believe you can cross over to the land of the spirits of the dead—

DdP: Well, have you ever met a ghost?

R/S: No.

DdP: Oh, I have. I'm not sure what part of a being does that. I believe in reincarnation. But I think there is a shell or some part of the persona that maybe hangs around, and it hangs around more if it's remembered more. I honor people who do a lot for ceremonies like the Day of the Dead, but I don't tend to do a lot of that. But after I do the winter solstice, I do a ceremony of cleansing the whole house, and then cleansing it again with sage and salt and so on and blessing each room, driving out any bad energy from the old year, and blessing it and calling in new energy, room by room.

You can do this systematically. As you go through each room you're lighting candles. You start around the time the sun goes down, so by the time you're done the whole house is lit only in candlelight. You sweep the bad energy towards the door or doors, depending how many entryways you have. When you get there you toss out a handful of dried beans or lentils to feed the dead, because that's what Pythagoras said fed the dead. You bless them. In the old days when I did it thoroughly, my kids would go out and paint a sign on the door—traditionally you would put an occult sign on the door to seal it against the bad energy from the past.

Every place in the world has the same rituals, really. After everything's done I've always added a casting of the I Ching for the New Year. What I do now in the last ten years as I got older and more people were going— especially since the AIDS epidemic in the last twenty years—I then go into the shrine room, in the candlelight, and one by one I say goodbye to all the people who died since the last winter solstice. I name them and I talk to them out loud, and I thank them for what they brought to my life. Sometimes I cry, or apologize for not having gotten back to them in time, or whatever, because we always have those feelings of something left undone when some- one dies.

R/S: Right.

DdP: I do all that, and try to put some closure on every person I lost that year, and look at everything full in the face. Sometimes it's short, and some- times it takes a long time. I'm not worrying about whether ghosts are there, or crossing barriers or anything, I'm just talking and blessing people, partly for my own closure, and to look at what the year has brought in the way of endings and loss. Then we can look forward to the next year.

I always consult the I Ching, some time between winter solstice and Epiphany (to go to another religion), but within the two weeks after solstice. Sometimes, right at solstice is a little too soon for the Ching to know what's up—it gives you a muddy transitional reading. So I wait a little longer.

R/S: Is Epiphany an observance from Catholicism?

DdP: Yes. Epiphany is the 6th of January. It's when the wise men found the child. It's an alchemical holiday, too, in that they brought basically mer- cury, sulfur, and salt—myrrh being the faculty of grieving for what's left behind; gold being the essence of sulfur, the finished transformational prod- uct; and frankincense being the principle of mercury, or the flying away— although it is solar; people juggle those around in different ways. The Three Wise Men are seen as the Three Principles in alchemy.

I've been collecting pictures and paintings of the Three Wise Men for years—all the different concepts of the wise men. And the child of course is the alchemical stone, or the principle of renewal or eternal life. In the old days, in the part of Italy that my family came from, Epiphany was when you gave gifts to the children. Not on Christmas, but on the day the wise men gave gifts to the child. And each child was seen as the renewing principle, Every child is the Christ child in that sense, and that was the kind of pagan Catholicism that my grandmother had. No one else in the family had that kind of religion. My grandfather on that side was an atheist and an anarchist; his wife was the one who had the pagan Catholicism. My parents were, as they sadly said, agnostics.

On the other side of the family, I didn't know the grandparents that well. My father's father was a wonderful storyteller of the Catholic stories, but I didn't get to know him well. So I had a mix in my life. The grandfather who was an atheist and an anarchist was also a great reader of Giordano Bruno, whom he saw as a political rebel. But Giordano Bruno is also a great magician. His books are hard to come by; I have a few. He taught a lot of inner work, transformational work through visualization—Frances Yates's *The Art of Memory* touches on this. He was a great magician. So now that we've confused all the different traditions—

R/S: No, you haven't. Earlier, were you making reference to *strega*, an Italian tradition?

DdP: No, the term *strega* is used in a more pejorative way to refer to a malevolent witch who is casting spells, the way most people think of witches. The Catholicism of my grandmother really didn't take sin seriously—that's why I say it was terribly pagan. She would say, "The Virgin Mary is a woman— she'll explain it to God!" about people screwing and that kind of stuff.

R/S: Earlier, you mentioned having seen a spirit or ghost—can you tell us a personal story? I realize you're describing your experiences; you're not saying this is real for everyone—

DdP: Well, I'm not a relativist. I think that what is real is real, but we all see different parts of it. We can only see what we see. I'm not saying I see everything or more than others; the parts I can see are the parts that I can see. But no, I don't think I think I want to do that. There are so many instances and they are so different from each other that I wouldn't even know how to start. You know what Blake said towards the end of his life, when they brought him news of one of his friends dying: "I can no longer think about death as anything other than walking from one room into another."

R/S: That's nice. So looking back, you've lived a life of paganism in practice, without being labeled a pagan. I think anyone who has been in a so-called "underground" always rejects the label applied to them. Like, my friend Philip Lamantia rejected the label "Beatnik" for himself—

DdP: Yeah, I don't like being called Beat. Not because I didn't have work that would definitely be called Beat, but because it's such a small percentage of all of my work. It's like being frozen in one moment—someone takes a photo of you in 1958 and that's how you're supposed to be for the rest of your life. That's silly. We didn't call ourselves Beats, *Life* magazine called us Beats! Then after a while, it stuck. There were some people who kept writing Beat writing—maybe Allen Ginsberg was one. But most of us wrote many different kinds of writing—and Allen, too. He wrote Sapphics [in Sappho's meter], he wrote blues—not all of it was Beat. Labels come from somewhere else—usually after the fact. That's why they don't work.

R/S: They're used to market products—

DdP: Yeah. I guess in Europe people like to have movements and label them. Didn't the Surrealists call themselves the Surrealists? They had a whole book of manifestos—very boring. I love Surrealism but I can't read those manifestos—

R/S: But don't you apply some of the Surrealist principles contained in Breton's *Manifestos of Surrealism* to your own inspiration process?

DdP: Of course. I consider some of them my foremothers and forefathers, especially the women painters like Remedios Varo.

R/S: It's great to hear of your Surrealist affinities, as well as your affinity for the so-called "occult." Surrealism and the occult are appraised in such a reductionist manner by most Americans—all they know are the labels—

DdP: It's just dopey. [*laughs*] We're in a kind of stupid society—forgive me for saying so—we're really in a very dumb age. Anybody who could take seriously the value of profit as a serious motivation for living—?! They act as if they have a moral imperative—God says, "Make money." It's so weird. And the whole world is following behind it at this point. It's so stupid because it makes this tunnel vision. People can't see—it's like they all have glaucoma, and they have no peripheral vision—they can't see anything that's right under their noses, or off to the side somewhere.

They kill their children really, in a way, by denying all forms of the supernatural and the non-material, because kids live with all that. They talk to nonexistent beings (maybe they're existent, who knows?) from the time they're little. When my oldest daughter Jeanne was about five, she loved Egypt. Together we would look at big art books checked out from the library. We'd be looking at painted sarcophagi or mummy cases and she would say, "On this part here they tell about the person's family, and over here they tell all the things he did that were important." She was five years old and she knew things I didn't know. We deny that about our kids—we destroy access to everything they have that we don't. That's part of the stupidity of the time.

The first time I took my daughter Dominique to the Metropolitan Museum of Art [NYC], we were in the Egyptian section and she spotted one of those necklace collars made out of blue faience glaze. She said, "That's my necklace! What is it doing there—I want my necklace!" She would scare me all the time. She would say things like, "I'm really glad I went to the zoo and saw the rhinoceros so I can tell my grandchildren it wasn't a myth." Under five years old and saying that . . .

R/S: That's scary—

DdP: It wasn't scary. It was sad-making too . . . it made me really sad.

R/S: Tell us why you're drawn to Tibetan Buddhism—

DdP: I started out as a Zen Buddhist. I met Shunryu Suzuki in 1962—that's described in *Recollections of My Life as a Woman*—my meeting him was quite fortuitous. And as soon as I met him, he was the first person I'd ever met that I trusted—I was a New Yorker . . .

R/S: Right, you don't trust anyone—

DdP: No, and I'd had a kind of very vicious upbringing. Whatever he did, I tried to understand what was in his mind that was so open—it didn't have little nooks and crannies of manipulation and fabrication in it. He was just there, he was just present. What he did was sit, so I got instruction and I started to sit. I used to write to his student Dick Baker and tell him how my meditation was going. He would tell Suzuki, and sometimes I would get instruction back and sometimes not. That went on until I moved to San Francisco in 1967. I came to SF for two reasons: to do political work with the Diggers (I started delivering their free food right away, that was my job), and to sit with Suzuki. Those were the two sides of the coin for me then.

I did Zen long before I had met Chögyam Trungpa, whom I met the year he came to this country. He went straight away to Tassajara, where I was for the summer, to meet Suzuki. That was in 1970. In 1974 Trungpa started Naropa Institute, and Allen invited me to come teach there—Allen was by that time a student of Trungpa's. I was like, "Ehh . . . I don't know." But Suzuki, before he died in December of '71, had said that Trungpa was like his son. He left one of his two Zen staffs (they have those teaching staffs that they carry) to Dick Baker and the other one to Trungpa. So I felt, "If he's my teacher's son, I should help him."

So in 1974 I went and taught classes and started going to all of Trungpa's lectures; he lectured twice a week. I taught at Naropa in '74, '75, '76—those were big teaching years for Trungpa. I continued to go to Naropa every other year until recently, when I stopped in 1997. So I put in my time there teaching summer writing school. Trungpa and I became quite close. Suzuki was dead, and the Zen Center—well, after one interview with Dick Baker I knew it was too bureaucratic for me, and started sitting on my own. For meditation instruction or guidance when something seemed a little off, I had Kitagiri Roshi in Minneapolis, if I was on the road, and sometimes Kobun Chino Roshi if he came around. They had both been at the Zen Center with Suzuki.

So I was catching instruction on the fly. When I started going to Naropa I would have a formal meditation interview with Trungpa every summer. He was helping me, but I was still practicing Zen—I was still committed to Suzuki's teaching. I practiced Zen until '83. Around '81 I started to do both healing work and trance visualization work for clients—people who felt they had a shadow in their life that was wrong, and so on. And in doing the visualization work, a few times I ran into forces (that's what I call them—I don't know what they were) that were way bigger than what I had been asked by my client to deal with. I would just put up a shield wall and call on larger forces to take care of them and go about my business. But I was aware that some of this work was kind of like Frodo in Tolkien's *Hobbit*: "If you shine a stronger flashlight, it's going to notice you!" So I started to wish I had a sangha, or other people I could sit with, just to ground myself after doing that kind of work.

I decided to ask Trungpa to be my teacher, because I knew that Tibetan Buddhism openly embraces the whole Western magical view. So I had an interview with Trungpa in '83. I wasn't teaching that year, but I flew out to Naropa in Boulder and stayed at Allen's house. Both Sheppard and I had interviews, and we asked Trungpa to be our teacher. I told him I was doing all this Western magic, and that sometimes I needed backup. I said, "I'm not prepared to give up Western practices and Western philosophy for the East." In my mind we're involved in a process that is going to take five hundred years to amalgamate all these things. We're bridge-makers, but we're barely at the beginning of the bridge!

I think I actually said, "I'm not prepared to give up Paracelsus for Padma-sambhava." And he laughed and said, "No problem." He told me he wanted me to have instruction in a practice which is pretty well known now, called "Taking and Sending," *Tonglen*, from one of his students. He told me to write him and stay in touch if anything came up—any questions or problems with my magical work or anything—so the switch was a quite natural one. I'd practiced Zen for twenty-one years, and I've practiced Tibetan Buddhism for eighteen years. I was receiving instruction in Tibetan View from 1974, so the switchover was quite natural. I love Tibetan practice.

In my last interview with Suzuki before he died, my last formal *dokusan*, he said, "Now is the time for you to find your own practice." Boy, that is scary when your teacher is dying. He said, "It is not Zen Center practice." He also said, "Now is the time for you to start living your own life"—which I had thought I had always been doing! He said, "Not your children's lives, not some man's life." It's taken me a long time to disentangle from my children's lives—I have five of them!

R/S: You overlay paganism, which deals with Earth reality and spirituality, with Tibetan theory, which concerns other planes of existence or reality—

DdP: You know, if we had only this plane, I would rather be dead. I mean—the material world is beautiful and wonderful, but if this was all there was (and I was at the despair that I reached in my teens)—well, you can see to the bottom of it all the time, and it was never enough. But with *dharma* there's always enough. There's always more you can see. It's deeper and it's fuller and it's faster. I love this Earth, but if this is all there was, it wouldn't be worth it.

Blake talked about us being in a golden cage, with the stars being our inspiration—like we're in a prison of materiality. Matter is great, but it's only the tip of the iceberg—literally! [*laughs*] It this was it, and it was only paganism, I would long ago have probably—not killed myself, but I probably wouldn't still be here, because my energy for it, my taste for it, would have gone long, long ago—probably in my forties.

R/S: So Tibetan Buddhism cosmology—

DdP: They use the word "View"; they don't always capitalize it, but that means their cosmology. I've always had this feeling since I was a little kid: it this was it, gawd—who would want it?! At the bottom of my saying that the culture is stupid, there's a real horror.

R/S: Apparently you put the two together and it's ultimately a deeper or more satisfying philosophy or view with which you can cope with living—

DdP: I put the two together. In Tibetan Buddhism, they have paganism— if you were Tibetan. But I don't know their paganism, and I don't need to learn another whole system of how to deal with the Earth. I have a good one, you see, which was in place long before I became a Tibetan Buddhist, but not long before I had the view that this place would not be enough.

R/S: Tibetan Buddhist cosmology involves other dimensions, planes, and worlds—

DdP: Yes—of course. That's so obvious; it's like the nose on someone's face that our world isn't all of it.

R/S: You're deeply interested in the big questions that are almost unanswerable—the whys: where did this universe come from, and why?

DdP: I think everyone starts like that. I remember as a little kid wondering about how amazing it was that anything existed. I think kids know that—that these questions are there. That's what I mean when I say we sell kids short in this culture. If classes for nine-year-olds had discussions of "Isn't it amazing that things exist!" I don't think you'd have any trouble teaching those kids anything. But they don't give them credit, or any context.

You know what keeps coming into my head, even though it's not exactly related: there's a great Zen story about Bodhidharma, the guy who went from India to bring Zen to China. He was summoned to teach the Emperor. The Emperor asked him, "What is the word of the Holy Truth?" And Bodhidharma said, "Vastness—no holiness." I think that's a key to how I see the Dharma taking root in America. We understand vastness, and it's a step from understanding vastness to understanding emptiness. You see what I'm saying? Emptiness is not empty, but full and creative. But to say "vastness— no holiness" takes this out of that pious place. Then there's only one more step to see what is really vast. Like that game kids play, "Well, if the universe ends there, what's outside it?" I think that children just naturally play mind-expanding games—a practice of psychedelia, in a way. All cultures probably do this.

R/S: There's a scientific explanation for emptiness: the theory that matter doesn't exist, only energy. On the level of the atom, with electrons spinning around a nucleus, there are no particles—

DdP: Of course. Hindus knew this forever and called it *maya*—illusion. *Lila*, the dance or play of *maya*, is what makes the world.

R/S: And the magic show uses DNA to accomplish its deed, in the incredible way that DNA works to create our world—

DdP: Yes. It's wondrous. And wonder is one of the vitamins that we seem to be real short of in America. We could use a lot of it, because it would fix us up good. We would have more respect for children, for madmen, for each other, for death, for birth—we would have a bigger capacity for everything; for pleasure and for joy! Wonder—we need bottles of wonder on the shelves of all the health food stores! [*laughs*]

Diane di Prima in Conversation: Not on the Road

Margarita Meklina and Andrew Meklin / 2002

From *Ars Interpres: An International Journal of Poetry, Translation and Art* no. 6/7 (2002). Reprinted by permission of Margarita Meklina.

The transcript of the meeting in the restaurant Amberjack Sushi, at Church and 16th Street in San Francisco, August 2002.

Q: We didn't write down any specific questions, just some notes for ourselves as a reminder . . . If you're not interested in one topic, then we move to the next one . . .

Diane di Prima: Next! Next! [*Diane di Prima laughs*]

Q: It's going to be very informal . . . and then we will assemble the pieces . . . and translate them to Russian and maybe Italian.

DdP: If you get a Russian article, I have a sister-in-law. She doesn't speak English, only Russian, she lives in New Jersey. You will make her so happy . . . my brother's third wife . . . they are very happy, very in love . . . [when they met] she was without a car, and working twelve hours a day for a very old man, taking care of him. In Ukraine she was an aeronautics engineer. She is a very intelligent woman but never learned English. And I would love the Italian version as well.

Q: Do you know Italian?

DdP: Very little. When I was four or five, war was going to start . . . my relatives were afraid to be in America, afraid to speak Italian . . . I was born in 1934, but by 1938 they knew it would be war. I spoke to my grandparents, when I was very small, then I had to stop. My parents transferred fear to me. . . . It was something forbidden.

In addition, my family didn't want me to connect with my relatives in Italy; they were very ambivalent about me because of my lifestyle; they thought that my relatives would be very upset, so, I went only two times to Sicily, both times to a poetry festival, and neither time my mother ever gave me any addresses.

All these family stories! My brother is very upset [about di Prima's published memoir *Recollections of My Life as a Woman*], and my mother's younger sister wrote me a very angry letter. They feel that I shouldn't tell family stories, family secrets. That's tough. I'm a writer, that's what I do. [*laughs*]

Q: I will read from here . . . [apologetically] I have some notes . . .

DdP: It's okay to have notes! [*Diane di Prima laughs*]

Q: I was thinking yesterday of the writers, of the poets of the Beat generation. Lawrence Ferlinghetti, Diane di Prima, Gregory Corso, Philip Lamantia . . . was it an Italian wave? Any specific reason for so many Italians?

DdP: I don't know . . . It's in the culture to be lyrical, they are drawn to poetry, they are drawn to some flowery prose, to music . . . everybody sings . . . it's in the culture, and I think it's very close in Sicily to Middle Eastern song. To melody lines in Middle Eastern music. It influenced me a lot.

Q: Could it be that the immigrant flavor gave a flavor for something different, for something new?

DdP: When I was four years old, my grandfather read me Dante, and poetry, and opera. He loved opera. He influenced my mind, together with political activism . . . Look at Corso, he had no [Italian] upbringing. [And he is] much more musical than Ginsberg. A different kind of sound.

Q: I met Ginsberg ten years ago in Turin.

DdP: Let's eat. We don't need to ruin our food for talking. Let's talk while eating.

Q: I met Ginsberg when he came to Turin. He was reading, and Philip Glass was playing the piano . . . Ginsberg gave a short lecture. And I asked him: do you have any regrets in your life? And his answer was a little bit aggressive. I was even taken aback. Yes, he said, I would like to seduce one more boy. Did I ask something wrong?

DdP: Not wrong, but it's a strange way to look at your life in terms of regret. . . . Maybe if you did something differently, your life would be different. You can't predict.

Q: What I meant was that maybe he wanted to study music or . . . spend one year in India . . . or become a Catholic priest . . .

DdP: That would be good for Ginsberg. He could've seduced one more boy! [*Diane di Prima laughs*]

Q: And how is Ferlinghetti?

DdP: He seems all right. At eighty-six he is allowed to be absent-minded.

Q: If he is absent-minded, is it still possible to interview him?

DdP: He is very reclusive, he is only interested in his paintings, but it's possible if you come to him and ask for a painting. He has a gallery there. He has shows in Rome every year. He is not interested in interviews as a poet.

Q: He doesn't go to his bookstore, the City Lights?

DdP: Sometimes. He might be in the office, but not by the counter.

Q: Is he still the owner of the City Lights?

DdP: They made a foundation. When he dies, there will be a foundation, so the store will continue and the building is a historical landmark, they wouldn't tear it down. He is supposed to do seminars, classes; they even asked me if I want to teach there.

Q: They have a wonderful website too.

DdP: There is another wonderful website. My daughter sent it to me. There was an artist, a man in Russia. And he had a specially equipped railroad car which was given to him by the last tsar. It had a dark room, and he went before the Revolution taking photographs in color. He invented color before the appearance of color photographs by doing different filters. On this website you can see the most beautiful color photography of those architectural places, which are not there anymore. And I look at the churches, landscape, different regions. I'm not interested in literature. I feed my mind with images. Why would I look at information? Information doesn't make a poem. Painting makes a poem happen, music, people, walking about the city. I don't need more head trips.

Q: Talking about music. You wrote about the Billie Holiday concert in Carnegie Hall which you attended. She is great, and so is Maria Callas.

DdP: Yes, she is wonderful. My partner, he is a great aficionado of all kinds of American music, gospel, blues, jazz, and so on, said that America has no visual imagination. Why television is so boring. We have genius for music, but not for eyes.

Last night we were at a concert where John Hammond Jr. was singing Tom Waits's song "Wicked Grin," and a group was so good! John Hammond . . .

Sheppard, my partner, worked for him in 1967. Then we saw him in the eighties, in the nineties. He is more grounded now as a musician.

I don't remember why this came up . . . the fact that American music is the one thing we have here, really. We also have poets but few people know us. We have great painters but very few.

Q: My favorite's Edward Hopper. Do you like him?

DdP: I like him okay, but I grew up with gestural work, with abstract expressionism. I like kinesthetic work, work with a lot of movement, body in it.

Q: Do you know in person some abstract expressionists?

DdP: I knew de Kooning a little. He was close to Amiri Baraka, when we were lovers. I'm a good friend of Mike Goldberg, who is the second-generation abstract expressionist. Frank O'Hara wrote a very important poem for Mike's birthday. He goes to Italy in summer, he has a home there. Alfred Leslie was an abstract expressionist, then later became a figure painter. A lot of his abstract work was lost when his loft burned in the late sixties; he lost all of his films. He made movies, too. Jamie Freilicher. In the last ten years she had a show in the Guggenheim. I knew Larry Rivers when I was still a New Yorker.

Q: You don't like New York anymore?

DdP: It's too difficult. I don't like the noise, it's rush-rush-rush. I don't like Paris—sorry! Even if you are there for a few days, it's too noisy. Drives me crazy. And everybody is running. Why are they running? My youngest daughter is having a baby. I couldn't get into a sleeper. Nobody flies. So, I have to fly. I'm going in October. And all the trains were full by July.

Q: In your memoir you talked a lot about your grandmother. Now that you are on the other side of the road, how do you see it? What about your role as a matriarch?

DdP: I don't see much of any of them; I gave them everything I could, and now they live their own life. I don't look over their shoulder; we get together once per year for a family reunion in one of their houses, and Michelangelo, my granddaughter, wants to be a poet. She is twenty-two. She is going to have a baby. Then we will be very close.

Q: Do you enjoy yourself in the grandmother's role?

DdP: Sure, I don't mind that I'm getting older; it's a natural way of the world. It's wonderful actually.

Q: As long as the brain works. The body is important, but the mind especially.

DdP: The body is important too, if you can keep it going, it's nice, since there are more options every day.

Q: You have a beautiful message on you answering machine, where you say: "Americans, my fellow Americans, we are pure and stupid."

DdP: That's what they are. American people in general have no intelligence; they are not in contact with world history at all. In a way they are pure, even right-wingers. On the other hand, they have no subtlety, no ability to see the whole tapestry of history, to see what stage we are in, how we fit in, what we are doing in it. And the very corrupt government, the most corrupt.

It was at the beginning of the Afghan war; I was stuck in the motel in New Jersey with my first watercolor show. We are sitting in this hotel, nothing to do, and we watch news. I'm seeing Afghan people getting out of their country with their backpacks. They are not so different from Western Americans in terms of how we approach essentials. Take an urban dweller in Sierra; there is a relation of how to survive between us and them. But no relation to human history, and that's why we are pure and stupid. They can't recognize that we are the same, very much like them, rather than like an educated Parisian or Roman. We are much closer to these people, whom we are bombing.

Q: Where were you on September 11?

DdP: My daughter called me up, at 6:30, when I was sleeping. She lives in Astoria, in New York; she bought that apartment with a view of Manhattan skyline. She was going to work and stopped by a shop run by an Egyptian; he was very excited. She couldn't understand why he was so excited. And the first tower was coming down. And she called me, "Mom, blah, blah, blah." And I asked her, "What are they doing it for?"

We finished talking, and I turned on the TV. And it was the second tower coming down. Between you and me, what did we expect? How can they be so stupid not to expect it if all this is happening everywhere else?

Q: Did these events change your way of seeing life?

DdP: Not the events, the way we respond to the events. I don't want to be in an airport: I'm not afraid of terrorism but I don't want to see the police state shoved under my nose every day. I'm not on the road anymore! And I used to go about four months a year. And then I stopped usual readings, lectures, panels. Now the only reason I'm going is because my daughter is having a baby.

Q: Isn't it somehow letting somebody else decide for you?

DdP: It's wonderful. The less I do the happier I am. I'm sixty-eight; I'd rather be at home, I'd rather paint. It was a part of my income. Now I do one third less. I've never made much money. Now I don't buy many books; I go to the library instead of the bookstore. I'm much happier now than on the road. I did it because I thought I had to. Because I thought somehow I could be of use to somebody who tries to become an artist or a writer. But I can't do it at the expense of my cheerfulness.

I don't want to pretend that the world is sane. They are going to put troops in airports, every kind of guns. The world is not sane. Here at the restaurant, there are beautiful flowers, a nice girl, not too much money. I would prefer where it's sane. Here is sane. My friend Michael McClure and I were here yesterday. He just came back from being on the road. He is seventy. He was grouchy. He said: "I'm not doing what I want; I'm doing things for my career." And I said to him: "Michael, you are seventy. Do what you want. You have a choice." I can see where I'm not going. A lot of choices that way. I can't be pushed by the material need.

I'm not teaching at universities, colleges; I teach privately. I rent a space from an artist on Cesar Chavez and Mission. She charges me very little. And I teach classes. I have no faculty meetings; I have no papers to grade; I don't have stupid people running my department; I'm lucky. Not so many people are registering, but it's okay. It's nice to have thirty students, but twenty to twenty-five is good. Once a year I have to get them, and then it's for nine months.

Q: You met Ezra Pound. He is controversial in Italy because of his connections with fascism. The American government put him into a mental institution to save him.

DdP: That's right; he was going to be killed for treason. And they declared him insane. Then it took ten–twelve years to take him out. And then he went back to Italy. I remember that time a little bit; I was so young, I was born in 1934, and it was in 1956. When I went to see him, he was there eight years or so.

Q: Do you have a special memory of him?

DdP: I wrote about it. I loved him and I still really do.

Q: He was pure and stupid?

DdP: Politically, in some ways, he was stupid but not economically; he talked a lot about manipulation of exchange rate, worldwide, how people were getting rich. He talked about money expiring every thirty days: you get it in the mail, it's for necessities. It goes in thirty days: you can't save it, can't use it for power. You can't spend them after thirty days have passed.

And Pound in terms of writing poetry techniques, nobody's caught up with *Cantos*. Charles Olson tried to emulate. He went farther in some ways, and in some ways he couldn't catch. Because in certain ways Pound had a lot of hermetic knowledge of Europe in those *Cantos*. Olson was innocent of this knowledge.

East, the Tantra, Hindu Tantra texts, so, he was trying to fill that in. Pound had nothing of the East, except that he accepted China. Olson didn't get any of it. Another person I was reading and was fascinated by her: Sheri Martinelli. She disappeared.

I was corresponding with her in the seventies; she became a recluse because, she said, she lost her beauty. She was a very beautiful woman. She lost all her beauty. So what? Big deal! She moved east, she was still with a man Pound told her to marry. He would arrange people to marry. They moved back to Carolina, I found out after she died. She died in the late eighties, early nineties, a wonderful painter. There is a book of her work or more than one produced in Italy with Pound's help.

Q: Was she really American Italian?

DdP: She was American, or American Italian, or that's her ex-husband's name. She was married and left her husband. And then moved to New York and became a fashion model, and got in touch with Ezra Pound. Anyway, visiting Pound was very inspiring to me. I was learning about poetry while reading his book.

Q: Are you more of a prose writer?

DdP: The memoirs are fun to do, but I'm a poet.

Q: *Floating Bear*, the legendary magazine you were publishing. In your memoir you write that you came up this name. LeRoi Jones, who would later become Amiri Baraka, didn't like your idea at first but then you explained that "Floating Bear" was the name of Winnie the Pooh's ship. At that time you were raising your little daughter, reading her children's books—that's why this reference to Milne's character. You said to LeRoi that the magazine would float or drown, because for Winnie the Pooh all his travels were successful adventure or a disaster. And then LeRoi agreed. You didn't sell *Floating Bear* in stores—you were sending it by mail to writers, painters, and musicians asking them for donations. The magazine—or let's say, a leaflet—was made on the mimeograph, before the God Xerox appeared. There you published Charles Olson, Gary Snyder, John Ashbery, Hubert Selby, Frank O'Hara, Allen Ginsberg, and other celebrities. Now *Floating Bear* is a bibliographic rarity, and one issue would cost you at least fifty bucks. And the whole collection of these "bears"—all issues published in the period from 1961 to 1971—costs around three thousand dollars. Would you like to place it on the Web?

DdP: I'm not interested in the Web. See, people write me and say: "do a little literary magazine on the Web." I'm not interested. I print my e-mails. I don't read off the screen.

Q: In your memoirs, you complained that you wasted a lot of time pasting and mailing.

DdP: Maybe you think I wasted my time, but I didn't waste it.

Q: Sorry, I mean that you had to do many manual things.

DdP: I love manual things. I'm doing it right now: we are making a little book, it's going to be a peace reading, me and David Meltzer, poet, and less known Clive Matson. He wrote a poem "Towers Down." Very ambiguous: "I'm crying. I'm celebrating. I'm crying for all the people. It isn't enough. I'm writing about towers, it's not enough." He expressed the ambivalence of being a radical-minded poet but at the same time being American. I wrote a poem called "Notes Toward a Poem of Revolution." It's thirteen short poems. I'm putting it together, it's a chapbook. I'm going to sell it at the peace reading.

Q: In Italy nobody is afraid of sex as here.

DdP: I remember my mother and her sisters sitting around and telling stories about their marriages and giggling about it . . . laugh, laugh, laugh . . .

Q: It's not changing.

DdP: No, it's not. Nothing is changing. Women's lib didn't happen. Repression of sex is as much as ever. They worry what would happen to kids. One of my husbands was worrying because we were living on the edge of the canyon, and he was worrying that they are going to fall, they are going to fall. And you have to figure that they have as much sense, kids, as kittens and puppies. Any animal has some sense. Relax! People are insane here.

Q: We have a lesbian friend who always says "womon" or "womyn" and has a real problem with men. Isn't it sexism the other way around?

DdP: Oh yeah. It takes a while to find a balance. It's just silly, but what can you do? It's like an ethnic group who gets a privilege and then gets arrogant for a while.

Q: Now everybody talks about PC [politically correct]. It's not another conformism?

DdP: It's so stupid, so what? [disinterested] So what?

Q: Freedom is also freedom to say things that people don't like. I don't mind if people say Italians are with the mafia. It's okay, part true, part not true. I don't care. As long as I am entitled to say what other ethnicities are. I believe in freedom.

DdP: Well, this freedom passed a certain point. There was so much racism in this country, against Blacks, Chinese. There should be a little bit more care that you would take. More Chinese people were lynched in California than Blacks in the South. Did you know that? American history just stinks. Stinks of blood. You should take this into account too. Sure, it's okay up to a point, but it's inappropriate to joke around and say to Chinese: "you are chink." You can't do it yet, it's too much history and it's too ugly. I hope that we are going to be more mixed up in terms of race . . . [*laughs*]

Q: Italians are mandolina, Mafia, pizza. I don't know how many times you were labeled like this.

DdP: No, not me. My friend, Rachel Guido, wrote a book *How to Sing to a Dago*. Dago is one of those slur words for Italians, like wop or guinea. I'm so tired of people saying, what is your ethnicity?

Q: Do you have a writer's block? What is writing block for Diane di Prima?

DdP: In 1968 I moved to California from New York and began sitting every morning at the Zen Center. It was a major change at that time. It takes a long time for my subconscious to catch up where I am. Never had to worry about the writing block. It starts again when it wants to. I don't sit down every morning and try to write. Poems come when they need to come. There is always overload. And if nothing comes at all, when I was younger, I would do translations, translate from Latin a lot; I learned it in high school, four years of Latin. I just bought Catullus again, I want some Ovid, *Metamorphoses*. Always journals, letters. It's not like I'm afraid of a pen or piece of paper. You can't get a block, when you have so many writing jobs, letters. It's usually when it's a big change. Then it takes time, sometimes it's half a year.

Q: What about your creative writing seminars? Any interesting people there?

DdP: Sometimes you get wonderful people and sometimes they are not so good. I do something that I call theory and study of poetics. We are going to study essays by Robert Creeley about line breaks, what he says about syncopation. We do Creeley for two months, and then look at Burroughs, then the book *The Third Mind* by Burroughs. About random techniques, he wrote it with Brion Gysin. In the beginning class there is a lot of random work. They also work with each other's images; they trade off vocabulary cards.

Q: Is it true that the editing part is more difficult than writing itself?

DdP: Very little editing. When I was a young poet, I did a lot of rewriting, that's how I learned my craft. Poems come clear, sometimes I just hear them and write them out, very little change. Sometimes when it gets stuck, I maybe take a few words out. My editor at Viking edited something by taking Italian syntax out of my English and he made a mess. I readjusted it again; he didn't know what he was doing. Pain in the neck!

Q: Did your Italian help you with English?

DdP: I wanted my Italian kind of rhythms to be seen through my English, especially in the early parts of the book. I started my phrases with "buts" or "ands"; I would leave extra words in and he wanted it to be school English. I think that's why so many books people should be interested in sound the same. Editors make them sound the same. I tried to read a memoir from a poet from Hawaii, Garrett Hongo—it sounds the same. Let's take Black English, there is really a rhythm. Or take Gary Thomas, Spanish writer from the East Bay. He is Puerto Rican, his English is from the streets, and now editors take it out. They make all the work like it went through a blender, like processed cheese.

Q: Why were Zen and Buddhism such an influence on Beat poets?

DdP: There is a book on that. *Beneath a Single Moon.* It's a beat anthology of mostly beat poets and poetry related to Buddhism. Gary Snyder wrote an introduction. I wrote an essay explaining some stuff.

Q: A sentence in your book really hit me. You were writing about the diseases of terror and an attempt to control, when you talked about physical diseases and how they were related to emotions.

DdP: Was it in my memoir? I don't remember. What was I talking about?

Q: About physical illnesses in your life, how they were related to your psyche, how they were related to your psychic involvement into various life situations.

DdP: I think my parents were afraid of everything, so, they lived in complete terror. It made me crazy, since it's not my nature. Now I feel that there is disease and terror everywhere, everything is crazy; everything is about destruction. It comes from an attempt to control. But how much insurance can you buy?

Q: And through Zen you could control better?

DdP: No, opposite, you shouldn't have any control. Think about painting, Japanese painting, no control, but enormous amounts of discipline went to the place that you had to control. That's what I'm saying of not doing poems, not to have to edit much. The Japanese painter Hokusai; when he was seventy, he finally knew how to make a dot. He said, if I can live for some ten more years, I can do a line.

Interview: Diane di Prima

Jackson Ellis / 2010

From *Verbicide*, February 2010. Reprinted by permission of Jackson Ellis.

In March of 2007, I pulled a copy of Diane di Prima's prose and poetry col-
lection *Dinners and Nightmares* off my bookshelf. At this time, I was in the
midst of compiling content for *Verbicide* magazine issue #20. I decided on a
whim to email the book's publishers [Last Gasp] in hopes to acquire rights
to reprint di Prima's flash fiction parable, "Untitled." While it was entirely
possible that my inquiry would be rebuked—or simply ignored—I received
a prompt response from the Bay Area publisher: they were passing my mes-
sage on to the author. Shortly thereafter, I received a polite personal response
from di Prima. Yes, we could reprint the story in *Verbicide*, and would I be
interested in some new short poems as well?

   Di Prima remains as fervently involved in the arts and education as ever.
From the onset of our correspondence, it was obvious that she is not about
to be regarded merely as a literary figurehead, but as an ongoing contribu-
tor to the arts—a presence whose voice continues to positively impact those
who listen, as it has for the last half-century.

   Though perhaps best known to the casual reader for her involvement in
the Beat movement of the fifties and sixties, poet Diane di Prima has, in fact,
authored more than forty books of poetry and prose and is the embodiment
of a modern-day Renaissance woman. A native of Brooklyn, di Prima spent
a number of years in Manhattan, where she founded Poets Press, cofounded
the New York Poets Theatre, and coedited the *Floating Bear* with LeRoi
Jones. She is among the founders of the poetry school at Naropa University
[with Allen Ginsberg and Anne Waldman], and since moving to San Fran-
cisco four decades ago has been a teacher and mentor to scores of aspiring
poets, writers, and artists. Di Prima is also a playwright, a painter, a social
activist, a mother, and a grandmother.

Adding to that list is di Prima's recent appointment as Poet Laureate of San Francisco. Following in the footsteps of Lawrence Ferlinghetti, Janice Mirikitani, Devorah Major, and Jack Hirschman, she was named the fifth laureate of San Francisco in May of 2009, and was inaugurated in February of 2010. "As poets, and artists in general," she states, "it's our job to create a community, to show others how to do it, to support each other, to get the work out—and also to keep some sense of possibility open, to keep some sense of celebration." In addition, over the course of the two-year appointment, di Prima aspires to work (through the neighborhood libraries) with kids after school, spreading her love of poetry and the arts.

It took quite a bit of wrangling to arrange a time and date that would work for the both of us to do this interview via phone, but in the time leading up to our two-plus hour talk I was fortunate to trade a decent amount of emails with Diane. Like any author, the words in her many books speak for themselves. But in our personal exchanges, I was pleased to learn that there is nothing at all put on in di Prima's work—the passion, intellect, and energy that comes across in the writing exists because it is a true reflection of the author. It was a pleasure to speak with di Prima; what follows is a lengthy excerpt of our conversation on February 23, 2010.

Jackson Ellis: As a youngster, you broke away from formal education early in your collegiate career. I found it interesting when I read *Recollections of My Life as a Woman* that, even though I went to college forty or so years after you, I identified with many of your reservations of the value of the college experience, and your descriptions of "the pretentious, awkward intellectual life, clipped speeches, stiff bodies, unimaginative clothes, poor food, frequent alcohol, and deadly mores," as well as the "cold intellect of campus." Now, however, it seems that you spend much of your time teaching writing via workshops and in collegiate settings. With your past—that is, having experiences in the classroom that fell short of your expectations—how do you approach teaching?

Diane di Prima: Well, for one thing, I teach very little in a classroom. I did a little more a few years ago, but I never was really hired by any college to do a whole lot—except for New College of California, and that was a completely off-the-wall kind of a program, in that it was run by me, Robert Duncan, David Meltzer, and Duncan McNaughton. It was a self-defined program in poetics, and not in creative writing. Robert was teaching things like "The King, The Sage, and The Fool in Shakespeare." I was teaching "The

Hidden Religions in the Literature of Europe"; it was a full-year course, and it was [about] all the heresies and all the remnants of prehistory that has stayed with us right through to now in our belief systems, and so on. [New College] was a place where you could define your courses: make them up and teach them. But that was awful enough because we still had faculty meetings, and of the five of us, I was the only woman—it still had its drawbacks, and after that first class I took my class out of that building and taught in my studio. It was making me sick being in the building! So that was it, everybody had to come to me for their classes.

So that was the only [collegiate] setting I ever worked for any period of time. Michael McClure got me a job for a couple of years; I was one of those "visiting faculty" members—not a very high-paying one either—at California College of Arts and Crafts. But in terms of "teaching within the system" it's been the minority of the amount of teaching I've done.

JE: What about Naropa University?

DdP: At Naropa, I was one of the people that started [the poetry program at the Jack Kerouac School] together with Anne Waldman and Allen Ginsberg, the three of us. It was for quite a while; but still, I would only come in the summers—the terms were too oppressive. So almost all the teaching I do right now I do in a loft in the Mission! People commit for nine months, and they come every month—and if they can't get there they send their money in for that month anyway, and if I can manage to make a recording then they get a recording of the class, and I'm available to answer questions for them. So that's my "base" class. I took three years off from that recently because I sold some archives.

But I haven't changed my opinions at all about academe. In fact, I think it's gotten a lot worse than it used to be, and all these MFA programs are just like mills for making money for the university; they're horrible—they get people because people think that they're going to get out with an MFA and be able to work, or get to be famous writers. The kids pay a lot—or at least, the grown-ups, most of them are adults who go to these things, these low-residency things—they pay a lot of money for them, and they don't pay the teachers who lead them very much.

JE: There's a bit of text by Nelson Algren—who was very critical of MFA programs such as University of Iowa—where he basically says that people, instead of going out and living and learning and gaining character, were instead being insulated from the world.

DdP: Most of the students of mine who've done one of those write much worse when they get out of it—much worse. They've gotten very stiff; they think they're supposed to hide what they have to say, and not be forthright in any way, and, you know . . . all this BS that's trendy right now.

JE: But it's like anything, you have to be open to the good ideas you're going to find, and you have to aggressively shut out the bad.

DdP: But most people don't. They don't shut it out, and they wind up writing worse than when they went in. So I teach, but I make up my own rules; sometimes I teach at home, sometimes I teach in a loft.

JE: Previously, you mentioned to me that aside from your work with students who are of college age and older, you'd be working with school-children at the libraries [as part of your poet laureate duties]. As a poet, a mother, and a grandmother, what are your best suggestions for fostering a love of the written word (and art in general) in young children?

DdP: I think the most important thing is that it doesn't matter if it's the written word or a drawn picture, you have to just give them a lot of space. Whatever they discover, and whatever they're doing, and whatever they're making is wonderful. Don't be prejudiced toward the word as opposed to the picture—that's important, because some people learn to read quite late and they're getting all kinds of blather for that—getting oppressed [because of] that! Every single one of them is different—kids, that is—I mean, I had five and not any of them were alike. You have to be alert to the signs of their own creativity and where they want to take it, and foster that.

I love to read to them. I made sure there were plenty of books around that they'd be interested in, and I'd read to them even when they were older, like twelve or so. From the five-year-old to the twelve-year-old, we'd all pile into one bed and I'd read! Especially in the rainy winters up here on the coast; I lived on the north coast for a while.

JE: My mom did the same for me; some of my best memoires are of my brother and me curling up on the couch with her while she'd read books like *Tarzan* and *The Hobbit*. She'd do voices for all the characters, and it really fed our imagination. I remember even as a kid, she'd read a book like *Charlotte's Web* and then I'd see the 1970s animated movie version and I'd think, Those aren't the right voices! The book was much better than the movie!

DdP: We had no television until they were all pretty much out of the house, except for my youngest. Until 1989, I never lived with a television. If we were at a friend's house and they were watching it, that was fine—I mean, I wasn't going to say, "Never watch TV!" But we didn't have one. They were writing plays; they were making up music; they were having very noisy, very bad bands. [*laughter*] You know, all the things that people naturally would do if you left them to their own devices instead of putting them in front of a screen.

JE: More on the topic of childhood—I noted in *Recollections* that you discuss your reaction to the bomb dropped on Hiroshima on August 6, 1945. It was your eleventh birthday, and it seems that as a child—living in Brooklyn and surrounded by so many people of so many different walks of life—that you were immediately confronted by the ugliest side of humanity, with all the anger and reactionism that came pouring out. It is interesting to note that when you read the poetry in Gary Snyder's *Danger on Peaks* that he—at the age of fifteen and in a completely different realm in Oregon than you in New York—was affected just as deeply. Even though you were both young at the time, do you believe that this event, perhaps, was the end of innocence for your generation?

DdP: I don't think there was any innocence in my world from the time I was four—the war was the end of innocence. But it was very much a defining thing [as to] how we thought.

JE: Do you think it was one of the catalysts behind the movements and subcultures that you grew into and became part of?

DdP: I think to a large extent it was; that was one part of it. The other part of it, for me, was the repression of McCarthyism. All of that put together. On the other side of that picture, though, I was growing up in Brooklyn, but by the time I was in high school I was spending a lot of time in Manhattan. As soldiers were repatriated I was meeting people from all over the country. So I was getting a sense of a lot more kinds of humans—Americans, anyway—that I wouldn't have gotten in a time where there hadn't been a war. What your normal New Yorker gets is just New York and New York–type people, but [there were] these kids from the Midwest, from the South, and from all over the country with all their points of view coming through.

In the time between 1945 and, say, the beginning of the real McCarthy crackdown—which, McCarthy's real crackdown had started by the late forties, but it didn't really come down on us as hard until we became aware of the Rosenberg [executions in 1953]—in that little period of time, there was a lot of openness. A lot of Black people were coming down from Harlem with the remnants of their renaissance, which had been plunked out by the Depression, and there was a lot of energy and a lot of different cultures you were exposed to because of the war that you wouldn't have seen or heard of otherwise.

So there were two things happening there [the war and the Red Scare]. There was repression and fear, and when I was first on my own, people were talking seriously about building cities under lead domes with artificial lights to protect them from their own nation—stuff that we now see in science fiction.

And it wasn't just a "Red" Scare. Wilhelm Reich died in prison, not for being a communist—he was just a heretic, that's all. People were heretics and they got killed.

JE: And they got blamed—

DdP: They didn't get blamed, they got killed. Getting blamed you can deal with; getting killed is final. Women I knew would get killed, like a say in *Recollections*, because they were promiscuous. They'd be sent somewhere and get shock treatment. There were a lot of things defining our generation, and the bomb was one of them—but that mentality that I'm trying to point to here is what made the bomb. It's the same mentality that kills somebody with shock treatment—up in [Boston,] forty shock treatments to John Wieners' head the first time his parents committed him.

The mentality was even bigger than the bomb, if you can imagine that. Without that mentality, nobody would've dreamed up making the bomb.

JE: Throughout your life you've been an advocate of peace and equality. I found it very interesting in *Recollections* to note all of your observances of the struggles, both politically and internally (and emotionally), of those who might be considered "minorities" due to race, sex, or sexual orientation— there was even a part that surprised me in *Recollections* where you mentioned a defrocked priest by the name of Charles Malley, who performed same-sex marriages in Manhattan in the 1950s. Even though the United States, as a whole, has—hopefully—evolved in the duration of your lifespan, how do you feel when you consider today's political and social climate?

DdP: I don't think we've evolved as much as we think we have, sadly. I don't think women have gotten anywhere near as much freedom as they think they have. I mean, if you have a couple and they're both artists and they have a child, you'll still find that it's the woman who figures out how to work and how to get some money, and the guy goes right on doing his art—but she maybe doesn't have the time to do hers anymore. I think that kind of thing still happens. I think that there's still an awful, obvious prejudice against homosexuality, and lord knows what the center of the country thinks about transgender [issues]—I haven't asked them in a while! [*laughter*] I'd thought by this time we wouldn't have any prejudice against people who were addicts, that it would just be "go to the doc, and get your prescription." I thought that we'd see the value of psychedelics, and [that] many, many other wonderful things would be going on.

I don't think we've made so much progress. In a way, the surveillance level—the ability to survey us all—makes the possibility of suppression and repression huge! Huge compared to what they could have done—and did do—in the fifties, what I've written about, with friends getting chased by the FBI, and so on. I think it's way worse.

JE: These problems are beneath the surface, rather than "in your face" as they might've been—but they still exist.

DdP: I think that's true. I mean, people don't like to think of themselves as "backward"; in those days they didn't care.

JE: You live in San Francisco, easily the most progressive city in America, and I live in Vermont, one of the two or three most liberal states in the country. Do you think people who live in such places might have to work harder to avoid having a skewed vision of social progress, or do you think the things we're speaking of are more intensified by such a vantage point?

DdP: All you have to do is look, and you don't have to work very hard. All you have to do is read the paper—you still have papers where you live, don't you? [*laughter*] All you have to do is look, and I don't think we have to look harder than anybody else to see how bad it is, because people are blatant about it—they're proud of it! It's right there in our face. It's a different type of [flagrance] than "Women should stay at home and cook," but it's the same thing. It's in all the fields, everywhere—academe, for one, is notoriously backward.

During the eight years of Bush you could see how bad it was, but clearly, one man being elected doesn't have the chance of a snowball in hell. He and his family are moving into the house of the enemy. What do you do in that situation?

JE: Do your best in the at least four years you're allotted—but so too [will political opportunists] to make him the "fall guy."

DdP: Right, he'll be the fall guy, and I think he knew that ahead of time and didn't care. Also, there are certain things you're going to have to cut back on because you don't want to come out of there missing a family member. I think the so-called "secret government" is stronger than it has ever been; it was made so under Bush, Rumsfeld, Cheney, and those nice guys who I still think should be brought to justice. Many [people do]; we've been signing petitions all over the web! [*laughter*]

JE: It's going to be interesting to see what the power of the internet and/or the petitions really is.

DdP: Well, they've managed to ignore [the demand for] single payer, and I think hundreds of thousands of people have signed for that! The one thing we have different today—and they're fighting like crazy to figure out how to control it, but it got too big before they manage to get to it—is the web. It [allows] communication between people all over the place. [We're] able to see what's happening in Iran, or in Haiti, and so on, rather than just relying on word.

In the sixties we made our own syndicated news service called Liberation News Service. [We got] a room with a phone under a made-up name—rented under an anonymous name too, the room—and people would man it around the clock to get the news from our friends who were on the road, who were travelling anywhere in the world, who could call us and say, "They just raided the American Indian Headquarters in Vancouver." Or such and such has just happened in Iran, or in Nepal, or wherever. News was person-to-person at that point. Now we've got the web, and even if we can't trust a lot of it, with a good "truth filter" we still can filter out a lot of good information, and stay in touch with more people and more places. Of course, it gives "them" an easy way to infiltrate—you don't have to look for "the man," he's right there everywhere! [*laughter*]

JE: And for all the different, reliable news sources that [are available], there's so much bad information masked as good that it can be misleading, and it can bring a lot of zealots together. While you've got the *Guardian* at your fingertips, anytime you want, you've also got Drudge and Breitbart.

DdP: I know. My junk filter every day has to take away messages from a group called "Patriot" who would like me go to a teabag thing somewhere. [*laughter*]

JE: Exactly, there are so many of those things—websites that try to suck the reader in with talk of "patriotism," and "duty," and just doing the right thing; they get you so fucked up with a sense of purpose that you can have a hard time deciphering the crux of their position.

DdP: I don't have a hard time. I was taught very, very early to filter any information in any newspaper and read it in terms of, "Okay, most of this is propaganda. Is there any truth here?" People always ask me, "How did you manage to stay so independent?" and so on and so forth. But I never thought of that [point] until right now—it's possibly one of the biggest things I was taught early on: to look for what they were trying to make me do. My father's paranoid belief was that they had mandated universal education because they could control everybody by reading if everybody read! And if he was alive now, he'd say now that they've got television, no wonder they're not putting any money into teaching people how to read. I'm not saying he wasn't, in a lot of ways, a crazy person—he was. But in a lot of ways . . . I was handed Machiavelli's *The Prince* when I was seven and I was told, "Unless you read this, you'll never understand history."

JE: I understand what you mean about filtering [information]—but there are a lot of people who can't, and those are the people who are the enablers of those in power who would suppress gay marriage, universal health care, things like this. The healthcare issue is the most mind-boggling of all.

DdP: It is, isn't it? People are saying, "Yes, yes, kill us. Please refuse us medicine; please refuse us what we need. We'll just sit around and be scared." [*laughter*]

That's another thing to consider when you're teaching your kids and getting them to learn how to read. One of the things I taught at New College—where I had people that I could really teach and teach them on my terms in my way—was when you start a book you have to first [consider], "What is this person's point of view; what is he trying to convince me of?" Then you can read between the lines, and [figure] out what's information, and what's him trying to convince me of something. That's part of what you would teach your kids with anything besides *Narnia* or *Charlotte's Web*; if you start reading a little history together or anything else.

What I remember my father did was he would have us read a part of a Shakespeare play, like Mark Antony's famous speech, and say, "Look at how he's manipulating the crowd! Look at how he's getting them to weep for Caesar!" Now, Caesar never did anything for these people. He's saying, "When the poor have cried, Caesar hath wept." Is it any different now, I ask you? No, they still say that. "Oh, my heart bleeds for the Haitians." Yeah, now why don't we cut it out and go feed them?

JE: So you're talking about lip-service—

DdP: I'm talking about teaching people to read between the lines of what's being told to them. I think everybody should learn that in first grade—maybe second grade. In first grade you're a little too innocent, but by second grade you're not. When you're seven years old you're ready to look with some suspicion at the grown-ups. [*laughter*]

JE: You and I have both dedicated a lot of our lives to independent publishing. I've been running Scissor Press and *Verbicide* and doing other various media projects since around the age of nineteen; you've had decades of publishing experience copublishing the *Floating Bear*, running Poets Press, and Eidolon Editions. I loved to read in your autobiography that as a child you would make newsletters for fun, because it reminded me of how I used to write little baseball magazines in my bedroom when I was a kid.

DdP: Right! They made this thing [a hectograph] where you could pull off about ten copies using gelatin; I think it was the forerunner of the Ditto machine. You just wrote with certain kinds of pens, put it on this gelatin tray, and then you could put pieces of paper down and offprint from it. It was great!

JE: I used my dad's Xerox machine.

DdP: See, we had no Xerox machine! Xerox [machines] came in the mid-sixties. That's very interesting to remember—before that we were typing ten carbons when we wanted to get a lot of copies of something. [*laughter*] That's kind of mind-boggling to me!

JE: That's a lot of work for what would now seem like a very minimal end product! So at what age did you seriously consider undertaking publishing as a lifelong endeavor?

DdP: I don't know that I've ever [not been] involved in either making a magazine or [publishing]. When I was in high school we had our school magazine, and I was the editor of it for most of the years I was in high school. I never really thought of it as a primary thing I was doing; the primary thing I was doing was writing. But I always wanted to get my hands on a press. I was able to get a hold of a mimeograph machine somewhere; that was a big way to get copies out.

JE: You've seen a lot of extreme changes in how people produce and receive the written word, and I'd first like to ask you to compare and contrast traditional mimeograph publishing vs. computer desktop publishing. What are the benefits and drawbacks of each, as compared to one another?

DdP: Well, I think that people are relying a little too much right now on the idea that the cyber-network is going to be here forever. When they don't make a hard copy of something, they really think that nobody's ever going to pull the plug and that there could ever be a day when the country is in chaos—a million little nations [with] no electric grid. If there's no electric grid, how can there be a cyber-grid? I think that's a big drawback.

We've talked about some of the big advantages of [the present], that you can reach so many people. But I've never written a blog or done any of those things because I don't think that I could reach people more than superficially. When I first read something, maybe I don't even like it, but I throw it back on the shelf. And six months or six years later I go, "Whoa, what was I thinking?" You don't have that chance [with online publications] unless you print things out, and since I can't read much on the screen I always print out everything.

JE: It's funny that you mention reaching people only on a superficial level—when you consider where independent publishing is going these days and how everyone is shifting to the web, I really felt that with *Verbicide* we were one of the last holdouts [printing our magazine] because I couldn't stand that thought of being online-only. We did three to four issues a year, printing between 5,000 and 25,000 copies per issue—

DdP: That's a lot of work.

JE: It was a lot of work, but even if we moved only half of those copies, I guarantee you that the people who picked them up . . . they put them in their backpacks, they read them on train rides, they read them on buses, they read them on subways or while they were out hiking, in their bedrooms at night with a reading lamp on—

DdP: I'm an example! How long after I was mailed a bunch of *Verbicide* [copies] did I write you back about loving a guy's story? It was in a pile of stuff I was going to read, and then one day, whoa—you don't get that chance that much. I mean, you can go back to the archives, but how many people do that?

JE: We've talked a lot about being on the receiving end of a published product—having a book or an album as a consumer or end-user, if you will. As a publisher, now, do you think that mimeograph publishing intensifies the "intimacy" you feel with the work you are publishing, since it is so much more labor intensive? I'm specifically referring to the fact that traditional publishing required you to have office space in Manhattan to run Poets Press back in the sixties, whereas desktop publishing really only requires you to have space for a desk and a computer—like me, in my basement.

DdP: Yeah, but do you actually make the product there?

JE: No, we put it together, but then we ship it off [for production].

DdP: I had the press, the copy camera . . . I had the stuff to make the copy that went into the camera to get photographed and made into a negative. Then the metal plate [was made] and the metal plate then went onto the offset press. I don't think I published a book by just typing it and running off copies, say, either on a computer or on a copying machine. I have published a couple pamphlets where I just typed them and brought them to somebody else to print, but then I don't feel like I'm involved in that at all. So yes, I like the craftsman [aspect] of it; I like the hands-on feeling of it. I like standing around and watching a press spit out a thousand copies of an image by an artist friend.

JE: I can imagine that's nice—I was never actually involved in the printing of *Verbicide* [other than the first two photocopied issues]. During the last year or two of publishing it in a physical form, I'd supply a mailing list and the printer would ship it out, and it would save a lot of time and a ton of money. But for a long time, I was mailing out physical copies, and I would have stacks of envelopes—and I remember what a satisfying thing that was, dumping those in the mail.

DdP: How many people did you mail to?

JE: Most copies were going off to our distributors. But I think my [direct] mailing list was at its peak around 1,200 people.

DdP: That's how big the *Floating Bear* got at its high point, 1,200 people. We started with 117 names out of my address book and LeRoi Jones's address book—but those 117 names caused a lot of change in the world. And I'm not sure that numbers of people reached are as important as how you reach them.

What you're doing is trying to change the world. You have to have the people that it's getting to be people who are then going to then get up and do something about it—even if what they do about it is write a story because [they've been] inspired so much—which they might then send to you, or you might never hear about.

But I [wonder about] the many, many people who are at their computer for hours surfing the web, whether they are people who also have any inclination to get up and do anything. I don't know how many do or not; I'm not criticizing those folks, but I just don't know. It seems to me the more creative ideas could've evolved by this time—about Haiti, about how to get the goods where they had to go—if everybody who was reading about it got up and did something. That's just a current example—I think we could've figured a lot more out about New Orleans much faster than we did. One place where [the internet] worked creatively and well was in Seattle at that first WTO thing, but since . . . they figured out how we did that, and we haven't figured out how to go around what they figured out! [*laughter*] Yet! But we will figure that out.

I think there are some—but not that many—people who, when they read something or see something, seriously conceive of themselves as creators or makers or changers of the world. It can be any of those—you might just stay home and play your flute, but that's making something, and all of that goes into the changing of a world. But just going, "Oh wow, look at this," doesn't do anything.

JE: And as a publisher, or writer or artist—any kind of creator you want to consider yourself—if you're putting something out there, you can only hope for the best. You can't force anything on people; you just have to hope you inspire them.

DdP: No, you can't force them. I guess what I'm saying is that there has to be a place for the seed to drop—that sounds almost biblical—where you're dropping the words [that will] result in something happening. Of course, we don't know that, and we can't measure it.

Two hundred people is what I'm estimating were in all the cities that Ginsy reached in '56—Allen Ginsberg, when he first did *Howl.* But in each city he put all those people together with each other. I think two hundred of us were at first in communication, but a lot of change happened; I'm not saying any one of us did it, but a lot of change happened in people's heads, really, it had to happen. But right now, a lot of change has to happen again.

How many issues of [*Verbicide*] have you put online? New ones I mean, not the archive?

JE: Well, the way we go about it with the website is that we update it five days a week, Monday through Friday. We put something new up every day.

DdP: Ah, so it doesn't just come out once in a while as a "chunk."

JE: It's a little bit every day, and whereas those "chunks" [putting out a quarterly magazine] used to require a lot more intensive work leading up to the release date, we always had a month or so of downtime between them. Now there's not a ton to do, but it's every single day, and we get a lot more emails to respond to.

DdP: I get about a hundred a day, and I don't even have much of [an online] presence! Somebody else invented a Myspace page for me; a woman in Australia who I don't know made it up. She's a painter, and she felt like I needed a presence. She keeps offering to turn it over to me, and tell me what to do, but I don't want to be bothered with it. I think I'm going to get off all social networking sites at the end of my laureateship. Off all of them.

JE: I saw you had a Facebook profile, but it doesn't really look like something you were interested in maintaining.

DdP: Once in a while I'll put a political thing up on it if it means one click after I've signed a petition . . . otherwise, I don't bother with it. People who I know and already have an email address for want to be my Facebook friend . . . they can be my friend, but I'm going to write them person-to-person, not through a Facebook. I'm too paranoid for that! Am I writing to you, or do you want 90,000 people to see what I have to say? It's all exhibitionist; it's ridiculous. [*laughter*]

JE: It's basically more for product promotion and attention-seeking than real communication. I identify that, but [since I have] a website, I sort of have to embrace the fact that it's a good place to promote and reach new people.

DdP: Facebook?

JE: Facebook, or Myspace, or whatever the flavor-of-the-month social networking is. I've seen it go from Friendster, to Orkut, to Myspace, to Facebook and Twitter—there's going to be something new after that, it's not the end-all be-all. Within just a couple years there has to be a sea change of social networking, and you have to keep up with it.

DdP: Well, I think that a lot of people are keeping up with it who don't particularly like us—and I'd just as soon have them work a little harder to find out what I'm up to! [*laughter*]

JE: So, an interesting, completely unverified anecdote I've heard is that more business partnerships fail than marriages, and given that marriages often fail about 50 percent of the time, that's a pretty discouraging number. You had an interesting relationship with LeRoi Jones [now known as Amiri Baraka] when publishing the *Floating Bear* in the sixties, because you were both business partners and lovers.

DdP: We weren't business partners, because there wasn't any money to be made. Nobody paid for it; you couldn't buy it if you wanted to.

JE: "Partners-in-crime" might be a better way to put it.

DdP: We were collaborators on an artistic project, is what you'd have to say—which is different than business partners.

JE: I would think there's that dynamic, though—the fact that you were creative partners, publishing together, it would seem that a bit of the business dynamic would exist.

DdP: I would disagree with you on that. The aim is completely different. If you know you want to make money, if there's something in it for you, that's one thing—there was nothing particularly in it for either of us. It was, "Let's get these guys' work out." I'm sure you've experienced that; you do that a lot.

Sometimes you disagree about what you think is good work—what we would do is we would trust the other one's judgment. So if I liked something and Roi didn't, it went in. If he liked something and I didn't, it went in. It was usually quid pro quo. Most of it was an aesthetic that we both agreed on . . . sometimes, you know, I'd think, Oh, this is a little too dry and macho for my tastes. But I wouldn't even say that: I'd say, "Oh, okay." I would trust that his aesthetic was sound, because I'd known it long enough, and vice versa. Since we had nothing to lose—

JE: And nothing really to gain, either.

DdP:—and nothing to gain, so that I don't know that it was that kind of dynamic.

JE: Well, my main question is what do you find more difficult: maintaining a civil partnership in love, or in creative collaborations?

DdP: Creative collaborations are never a problem. Neither are—for me—relationships, because when they don't work, you stop—unless you have a very clear reason why it's important to keep going.

JE: You have a very pragmatic, cut-and-dry approach to both.

DdP: Yeah. I've been with Sheppard Powell for thirty-one years. Again, it works by trusting each other. If one of us only wants to eat yogurt for two months and the other misses hot meals, the other either cooks or goes out and has a hot meal! It's the same with everything else—one of us is very messy, and the other one is very neat. You know, it spills over—one of us gets a little messier, the other gets a little neater. If the relationship at its core is working, why would these things be a problem? They're just things. It's just the superficialities of daily life. Nobody that I've ever been with, [never] have we ever been concerned about money—not that we have any—but I've never been unable to find shelter and a meal. So I don't worry! I think of lot of the relationship "stuff" that doesn't work comes around the issues of money and time, because these become power issues for the other one.

If you're doing an artistic collaboration, you're doing it for the joy of it. If there's not joy, stop! If you're in a relationship, you're doing it for the love and for the joy of it—and, sometimes there is a practical [element] there, like if you have a kid together. You stay as long as it seems necessary—which is really never as long as most people seem to think it is . . .

JE: What sparked me to ask that question in the first place is twofold—one, pulling from my own experiences in publishing *Verbicide*, where some collaborations just don't seem to work out—there can be power struggles—

DdP: Power struggles in the sense of what gets published?

JE: In the sense of what gets published, artwork, overall vision and direction—there can be jealousy over who gets credit for certain things—

DdP: See, I've never crossed paths with that stuff—I don't know where I would've run into it . . . in the theater, when I had a theater, no. That just didn't happen.

JE: Well, you stated in *Recollections*, for instance, that it was "uncool" in your youth to feel romantic jealousy, but there seemed to be a hint of jealousy in terms of LeRoi getting more credit for the *Floating Bear* than you.

DdP: No, there wasn't; that was years and years later that it even occurred to me that I did all the work! [*laughter*] I'm putting that out there for good reason; I'm putting it out there so young women who are thinking they're liberated take a good look at their situation. I didn't really mind doing all the work; I was home. He was out. I had a kid—not his, but I had a kid and I was home. I had time and I love to type. Unfortunately, it has made me have incredible arthritis at the age of seventy-five in my thumbs, but what can I do? I might've gotten that even if I didn't type!

But there was none of that then at all, and when there was jealousy it was kind of a "communal jealousy." I'll give you an example: when I was married to my youngest kid's dad, he was having an affair with a woman who became, consequently, one of my very best friends. And we would go to the baths together, she and I, every Sunday morning, leaving him with the kids. We would giggle for hours about the faux pas he made, in and out of bed. Like, one time he stopped by her door and rang the bell on the way home from my house, and he made this stupid remark: "Did you know that your house is exactly halfway between the bar and Diane's?"

Well, that gave us hours of giggles! [*laughter*] I mean, guys are just— excuse me, I know you're a guy, but we'll just say, "guys in those days"—guys in those days were just stupid! [*laughter*] Like, when LeRoi's male lover— which we all knew who he was, George Stanley—was going back to the West Coast, all of us mistresses of Roi's got together and gave him a farewell party. One made the salad, one made the soup, and we giggled over it a lot.

JE: Switching gears, what are some of your experiences working with a major publishing house as opposed to working with independent publishers, or self-publishing?

DdP: [When you work with a large publisher] you can reach a lot of people, and that is the only good thing because you lose a lot of control.

JE: I've heard that when you work with a big publisher they will pretty much take control of [certain artistic aspects], like the cover—for instance, the cover of *Recollections* is a photo of you reading. Did you have any input on that?

DdP: Oh, that photo on *Recollections*, I didn't mind that. That's a photo that was taken at Gaslight in '58, because I had just put out *This Kind of Bird Flies Backward*; it was made by an old friend, there was no problem. The one I really fought them about was the cover of *Loba* . . . which I think sucks.

JE: Did they ever relent and consider your viewpoint?

DdP: The first cover they sent me was even worse. I said no, and they said, "Oh, we'll just keep going until we find something you like," but then when I said no again they said, "Look, we're out of time, you have to make up your mind." I said, "I can make a wonderful cover out here." I knew they didn't want a handmade collage in this day and age—I thought I'd go over to Michael McClure's wife's house, she designs books for a living, she's a sculptor. And I knew what I wanted, and we would just do it on the computer and send it to them. They said, "No, we have to use our own stable of artists." Stable. So then they sent me these god-awful looking wolves, and I said, "Um . . . you guys don't know how to draw a wolf!" And they said, "Oh no, we only use clipart." [*laughter*] This is a stable of artists?

I suggested to put in the blue rose behind [the wolf head]—at least the cover is blue; at least it made it jump out at you. But now everybody thinks it's a horror book! There's this clipart wolf with staring eyes in front of a blue, abstracted rose! [*laughter*]

JE: That's pretty funny. Well, it's sad and funny.

DdP: Yeah, that's why one avoids New York. [*laughter*]

JE: So you've had experiences with major publishers, you've had experiences with small publishers, and you've been a publisher. If you had to choose only one, what is the most rewarding: seeing a book of your own writing professionally published, or being the publisher of and vessel through which other authors who you deem to be important become seen?

DdP: Those are two different things; I can't say one is better than the other. I really can't.

You have an obligation to your work to get it out. It's like you have to kick your kids out the door; it's the same thing. It doesn't want to be your work, it doesn't want to sit in your house. It's very rewarding to get it out, but I would always try now—if I could—to get it out through friends. There are very big business advantages to getting it out through Penguin, which is that more people get to see it. But unless I had more control I would never do that [again], and I would definitely never take an advance, because then you have a deadline—and deadlines just don't work for me! [*laughter*] I have to finish things when I finish them.

JE: You don't want to impose that kind of [pressure] on creative output.

DdP: Right. But on the other hand, doing a press is a very big pleasure, not only for the people [whose work] you're getting out, but it also creates a community—and that in itself is very important.

JE: Back in 2002, I interviewed a man named Henry Rollins who is best known as a punk and hard rock musician and television host on IFC. However, he is also a publisher, avid reader and writer, and is very well-known for frequent public speaking engagements. Anyway, in 2002 he and I were discussing literature, and he told me how he had published spoken word albums and gone on a reading tour with Hubert Selby Jr., who he described as an incredibly sweet, gentle person, whose actual character completely belied the brutal nature of his writing. I found it interesting that you , too, described Selby in such flattering terms.

DdP: Oh, it wasn't flattering—he was a really good friend. He was a really, really staunch, good, loyal, gentle, quiet friend.

JE: It was interesting to read this in your book, especially as your recollections take place decades before Rollins knew him.

DdP: Yeah, it was right around the time that I think he'd just finished *Last Exit to Brooklyn*. There was some uproar about some story, maybe it was in the *Chicago Review* or something—some place had been censored for a story of his. So yes, it was early on, very early on. I was hanging with him around '58, '59.

JE: Who else in your life, in terms of authors and artists, have you known who've created works—or public personas—that would lead readers or observers to perhaps inaccurate, misleading assumptions of the creator?

DdP: William Burroughs. Oh, Burroughs was the sweetest man. And [he also had] a great interest in magic, and a lot of other things he stopped talking about when others came into the room, but he would talk about with me. His love of animals was so amazing, and tender. He told me he wanted to drive to Duke University to adopt a lemur; they had lemurs that were extra to their work. But he said he was so old and it would outlive him, and it was such a great responsibility—he didn't feel like he could do that to a lemur. And he really wanted to! He was a very tender man. Very, very giving. But you had to not be looking . . . It was because I didn't want anything from him. All I wanted was to be his friend—and I could see how lonely he was.

We had such lovely times, and then other people would walk in the room and that drawl and that "tough" look would come out, and he'd start clowning around and putting on different hats—you know, it was the same person, but he was just protecting himself. So that's one who comes quickly to mind. I'm sure there are tons.

The feelings I have for Charles Olson are immense and very loving. I don't see at all the person that most people see—men, I think, are a little afraid of him because they either have to relate to him as a father, or they don't know how. He was a very dear friend, as well as a man full of so much information—I tripped with him in Gloucester in '66 or '67. He was wonderful, I just love him!

If you're a woman, you have the disadvantage [that] you're a woman and nobody pays attention to you. But the ones who do, who see through that . . . In those days, women thought they were going to find or nab an artist or a writer who was going to get famous later, and then they would have everything: they'd have the artistic life and they'd have the bourgeois life. I didn't want either of those things; I could give myself an artistic life and I wasn't interested in the bourgeois life—in fact, it would send me screaming out the door! When they realized that there's nothing going on there that they need to protect themselves from . . . I've had incredibly wonderful relationships with some guys. The ones I name are just some of them—Ezra Pound in St. Elizabeth's [Hospital] handing us the food he stole off the lunch table so that he, I, and the woman I came down with (who was also a writer) and the people we were staying with in DC could eat. He'd say, "Line those stomachs! Artists have to eat!" And he handed us all this canned fruit salad and cold sausages and things from the madhouse lunch.

JE: Regardless of gender, I think anytime anyone lets down their mask—however thick it may be—if you can find something rewarding inside of them and connect, you're lucky.

DdP: I think it starts with you not putting them on a pedestal—one, not wanting anything; two, not putting them on a pedestal, but just seeing who they are. I mean, they're just people, and often the most famous people in our kind of world are the loneliest. Everybody's made up an idea before they meet them.

JE: At the age of seventy-five, you've seen and accomplished so much. I've often heard that a key to a long, happy life is to continue to dream and set goals throughout. The question that I'm trying to frame is, What wishes and dreams do you have in your life? I'm not asking about regrets or things that are done or undone, but rather things you realistically could do, or want to do. What do you want to accomplish? What do you look forward to?

DdP: "Accomplish" and "look forward to" are not always the same! [*laughter*] I would like to get my work in some kind of order; I have more books unpublished that I have out in the world, by far. I'd like to get my work in some kind of order, my papers in some kind of order, so that people can make some sense of things. I tend to have a habit of writing a poem wherever I am on whatever I've got, like in the back of whatever book I'm reading. I'd like to be able to help people find those later. I'd like to get my work in order, and aside from that, make sure that whatever—if anything—arrives from it in the way of [money] goes to my sweetie and my kids. I love to paint—but I have no ambitions for it. If I had my druthers in this world right now, I would be doing nothing except writing, typing up the writing I've got, painting, and meditating.

Index

About the Editor

Credit: Eastern Michigan University/
Division of Communications

David Stephen Calonne is the author of *William Saroyan: My Real Work Is Being*; *The Colossus of Armenia: G. I. Gurdjieff and Henry Miller*; *Bebop Buddhist Ecstasy: Saroyan's Influence on Kerouac and the Beats*, with an introduction by Lawrence Ferlinghetti; and biographies of Henry Miller and Charles Bukowski (in the Critical Lives series of Reaktion Books, London). Most recently he has published *Conversations with Gary Snyder* (Jackson: University Press of Mississippi, 2017), *The Spiritual Imagination of the Beats* (New York: Cambridge University Press, 2017) *Diane di Prima: Visionary Poetics and the Hidden Religions* (New York: Bloomsbury, 2019), *Conversations with Allen Ginsberg* (Jackson: University Press of Mississippi, 2019) and *R. Crumb: Literature, Autobiography, and the Quest for Self* (Jackson: University Press of Mississippi, 2021). He has edited several volumes of the fiction and prose of Charles Bukowski for City Lights and has lectured in Paris and many universities, including the University of Chicago, Columbia University, University of California at Berkeley, the European University Institute in Florence, the University of London, Harvard University, and Oxford University. He has taught at the University of Texas at Austin, the University of Michigan, and the University of Chicago, and presently teaches at Eastern Michigan University.

Printed in the United States
by Baker & Taylor Publisher Services